Ready, Set, Go—With the Experts for a Winning Start as a *Beginning Office Worker* in the Civil Service!

Demand for the 160,000 entry-level clerical positions at the federal, state and local levels of government is at an all-time high. If you're among the many thousands seeking a job as a Clerk, File Clerk, Statistical Clerk, Payroll Clerk, Receptionist, an Audit Clerk or Account Clerk—this comprehensive, up-to-date self-study guide will give you the preparation you need for top scores. All the essential material is here to help you sail through the required exams—and claim the job you've earned.

Start now! Discover the proven source to success—the one test-prep book that generously gives you a high-scoring edge.
Here are:

- Important facts on the most recent developments in office work procedures
- In-depth discussions on all topics—from Filing, Alphabetizing and Coding, to Arithmetic Computations and Office Practice
- Ways to build your confidence
- Test-taking strategies to use—to put you ahead
- Over 50 sample tests—including answers—for invaluable test practice

Plus much, much more!

OUTSMART YOUR COMPETITION! GO WITH THE EXPERTS—AND GET THE RESULTS YOU WANT!

BEGINNING CLERICAL WORKER

BEGINNING CLERICAL WORKER

John C. Czukor

Prentice Hall
New York • London • Toronto • Sydney • Tokyo • Singapore

Previously published as *Beginning Office Worker*

Eleventh Edition

Prentice Hall General Reference
15 Columbus Circle
New York, NY 10023

An Arco Book

Library of Congress Cataloging-in-Publication Data

Czukor, John C.
   [Beginning office worker]
   Beginning clerical worker / John C. Czukor.
     p. cm.
   Reprint. Originally published as: Beginning office worker.
  11th ed. 1988
   ISBN 0-13-068206-3
   1. Office practice—Examinations, questions, etc. 2. Civil
service—United States—examinations. I. Title.
HF5547.5.C98   1989
651.3'7'076—dc20   89-29039
                             CIP

Manufactured in the United States of America

6 7 8 9 10

CONTENTS

Part One

INTRODUCTION

Part Two

REVIEW OF SUBJECTS AND PRACTICE TESTS

Part Three

PRACTICE TESTS FOR CLERICAL ABILITY

BEGINNING CLERICAL WORKER

HOW TO TAKE A CIVIL SERVICE EXAM

The first step in taking a civil service exam is getting an official announcement from the relevant government agency. You will find the address and telephone number of the nearest Federal Government Personnel Office, the local office of your state civil service commission, and offices of county, municipal, town, and village governments in your telephone book. Call to find out how to get an announcement and application form. Then write or go in person, as instructed. Read the announcement carefully and follow the directions exactly. Fill out the application form carefully and send it along with the required fee.

The government agency to which you have applied will send you an admission blank and instructions for taking the exam. The instructions will include the location, date, time of the exam, and a list of things to bring with you, such as sharpened number-two pencils with erasers, positive identification that includes your picture and/or signature, a watch, and, of course, the admission blank.

Before the exam day find out how to get to the test location. Be sure you know where it is, how to get there, and how long it takes to get there. You might want to make a "dry run" to check out the transportation and time involved. You do not want to be late on test day, and you do not want to be nervous about being late.

The day before the exam, review any subject areas in which you are weak. Then reread this chapter. Sharpen your pencils and put them with your admission blank, identification papers, watch, and whatever other materials you will need to take with you to the test. Get a good night's sleep. Set your alarm for a time that will allow you to eat a good breakfast (if you are scheduled for a morning exam) and to get to the test site on time.

On test day allow ample time for getting to the examination center. Upon entering the exam room, choose a seat with good lighting, good ventilation, and a view of the clock, if possible. If you cannot see the clock, you can always rely on your watch.

A test monitor will hand out papers and will give instructions. Listen closely and follow all of the instructions. If you have any questions, *ask*. There is no penalty for asking questions, even questions that might appear to be foolish. The penalty for misunderstanding instructions might be a low score.

The monitor will give you a test booklet and will tell you the time limits. The booklet may look large, but do not panic. There is plenty of time. Most civil service exams allow thirty minutes for every fifteen questions. You will be able to answer many of the questions in only a few seconds, which will leave you enough time to answer such questions as reading comprehension or arithmetic questions that, by their nature, take longer to read and understand. If you are having trouble answering a particular question, mark that question, go on, and come back to it later.

Once the signal is given to begin the exam, you should:
- READ all the directions carefully. Skipping over the directions or misunderstanding them can lead to your marking a whole series of questions incorrectly.
- READ every word of every question. Be alert for exclusionary words that might affect your answer—words like "not," "most," "all," "every," "least," "except."
- READ all of the choices before you mark your answer. The greatest number of errors are made when the correct answer is the last choice given. Too many people mark the first answer that seems correct without reading through all the choices to find out which answer is *best*.

The following list consists of important suggestions for taking a civil service exam.

Read these suggestions before you go on to the exercises in this book. Read them again before you take the exam. You will find them all useful.

1. Mark your answers by completely blackening the space for the answer you selected.
2. Mark only ONE answer for each question, even if you think that more than one answer is correct. You must choose the best answer. If you mark more than one answer, the scoring machine will give you no credit for that question.
3. If you change your mind, erase completely. Leave no doubt as to which answer you mean.
4. If you do any figuring calculations in your test booklet or on scrap paper, remember to mark your answer on the answer sheet as well. Only the answer sheet is scored.
5. You must mark your answer to every question in the right place. Check often to be sure that the answer number corresponds to the question number. If you find that you have slipped "out of line," you must take the time to find where you went awry and change your answers accordingly.
6. Do not dwell too long on any question. Although you have plenty of time, your time is not unlimited. If you are unsure of your answer, make a mark next to the question in the test booklet so that you may return to the question when you have completed the rest of the exam; but mark your best guess for each question in order.
7. Answer EVERY question. Most civil service exams do not penalize you for wrong answers, and so there is no harm in guessing. If you do not know the answer, eliminate any choices you know are wrong and guess from among the remaining choices. Even a wild guess gives you a chance to get credit for a correct answer. If you have skipped a difficult question to save time during the test, make sure you go back and fill in the answer space, even if you are still not sure of the answer. Do not leave any answers blank on your answer sheet. Even wild guesses are better than no answers at all.
8. Stay alert. Be careful not to mark a wrong answer because you were not concentrating. An example of this type of error might be: The correct answer to a question is choice B, *Dallas,* and you mark choice D instead of B.
9. Check and recheck. There is no bonus for leaving early, and if you finish before the time is up, stay until the end of the exam. Check your answer sheet to be certain that every question has been answered and that every answer has been marked in the right place. Check to be certain that only one answer is marked for each question. Then look back into the question booklet for the questions that you marked as guesses only. This is your opportunity to give any difficult questions more thought and to improve your chances by changing a wild guess into a calculated guess.

GOOD LUCK!

Part One

INTRODUCTION

HOW MUCH STUDY AND PRACTICE DO YOU REQUIRE?

Start your preparation for the exam by doing the Diagnostic Test. The results of the Test will show how much study and practice you will require in the various subjects that are usually covered by questions on actual examinations. The test consists of 100 questions relating to these areas.

After completing the Diagnostic Test and checking your answers against the Answer Key, enter your score for each subject on the Diagnostic Table. The entries on the Table will pinpoint the subject areas in which you are strong, average, or weak. This will serve as your guide in preparing for the exam. Concentrate your preparation on the areas in which you are weak, but do not neglect the areas in which you are average or strong. Since your score on the actual exam is based on your answers to *all* of the questions, a high score in one area offsets lower scores in other areas.

Following the Answer Key, you will find Explanatory Answers for each question, which explain why the Key Answer is the correct choice. Review all of the Explanatory Answers carefully. The explanations will help you to understand the process of selecting correct answer choices.

Answer Sheet For Diagnostic Test

1 Ⓐ Ⓑ Ⓒ Ⓓ	26 Ⓐ Ⓑ Ⓒ Ⓓ	51 Ⓐ Ⓑ Ⓒ Ⓓ	76 Ⓐ Ⓑ Ⓒ Ⓓ
2 Ⓐ Ⓑ Ⓒ Ⓓ	27 Ⓐ Ⓑ Ⓒ Ⓓ	52 Ⓐ Ⓑ Ⓒ Ⓓ	77 Ⓐ Ⓑ Ⓒ Ⓓ
3 Ⓐ Ⓑ Ⓒ Ⓓ	28 Ⓐ Ⓑ Ⓒ Ⓓ	53 Ⓐ Ⓑ Ⓒ Ⓓ	78 Ⓐ Ⓑ Ⓒ Ⓓ
4 Ⓐ Ⓑ Ⓒ Ⓓ	29 Ⓐ Ⓑ Ⓒ Ⓓ Ⓔ	54 Ⓐ Ⓑ Ⓒ Ⓓ	79 Ⓐ Ⓑ Ⓒ Ⓓ
5 Ⓐ Ⓑ Ⓒ Ⓓ	30 Ⓐ Ⓑ Ⓒ Ⓓ Ⓔ	55 Ⓐ Ⓑ Ⓒ Ⓓ	80 Ⓐ Ⓑ Ⓒ Ⓓ
6 Ⓐ Ⓑ Ⓒ Ⓓ	31 Ⓐ Ⓑ Ⓒ Ⓓ Ⓔ	56 Ⓐ Ⓑ Ⓒ Ⓓ	81 Ⓐ Ⓑ Ⓒ Ⓓ
7 Ⓐ Ⓑ Ⓒ Ⓓ	32 Ⓐ Ⓑ Ⓒ Ⓓ Ⓔ	57 Ⓐ Ⓑ Ⓒ Ⓓ	82 Ⓐ Ⓑ Ⓒ Ⓓ
8 Ⓐ Ⓑ Ⓒ Ⓓ	33 Ⓐ Ⓑ Ⓒ Ⓓ Ⓔ	58 Ⓐ Ⓑ Ⓒ Ⓓ	83 Ⓐ Ⓑ Ⓒ Ⓓ
9 Ⓐ Ⓑ Ⓒ Ⓓ	34 Ⓐ Ⓑ Ⓒ Ⓓ Ⓔ	59 Ⓐ Ⓑ Ⓒ Ⓓ	84 Ⓐ Ⓑ Ⓒ Ⓓ
10 Ⓐ Ⓑ Ⓒ Ⓓ	35 Ⓐ Ⓑ Ⓒ Ⓓ Ⓔ	60 Ⓐ Ⓑ Ⓒ Ⓓ	85 Ⓐ Ⓑ Ⓒ Ⓓ
11 Ⓐ Ⓑ Ⓒ Ⓓ	36 Ⓐ Ⓑ Ⓒ Ⓓ Ⓔ	61 Ⓐ Ⓑ Ⓒ Ⓓ	86 Ⓐ Ⓑ Ⓒ Ⓓ
12 Ⓐ Ⓑ Ⓒ Ⓓ	37 Ⓐ Ⓑ Ⓒ Ⓓ Ⓔ	62 Ⓐ Ⓑ Ⓒ Ⓓ	87 Ⓐ Ⓑ Ⓒ Ⓓ
13 Ⓐ Ⓑ Ⓒ Ⓓ	38 Ⓐ Ⓑ Ⓒ Ⓓ Ⓔ	63 Ⓐ Ⓑ Ⓒ Ⓓ	88 Ⓐ Ⓑ Ⓒ Ⓓ
14 Ⓐ Ⓑ Ⓒ Ⓓ	39 Ⓐ Ⓑ Ⓒ Ⓓ Ⓔ	64 Ⓐ Ⓑ Ⓒ Ⓓ	89 Ⓐ Ⓑ Ⓒ Ⓓ
15 Ⓐ Ⓑ Ⓒ Ⓓ	40 Ⓐ Ⓑ Ⓒ Ⓓ Ⓔ	65 Ⓐ Ⓑ Ⓒ Ⓓ	90 Ⓐ Ⓑ Ⓒ Ⓓ
16 Ⓐ Ⓑ Ⓒ Ⓓ	41 Ⓐ Ⓑ Ⓒ Ⓓ Ⓔ	66 Ⓐ Ⓑ Ⓒ Ⓓ	91 Ⓐ Ⓑ Ⓒ Ⓓ
17 Ⓐ Ⓑ Ⓒ Ⓓ	42 Ⓐ Ⓑ Ⓒ Ⓓ Ⓔ	67 Ⓐ Ⓑ Ⓒ Ⓓ	92 Ⓐ Ⓑ Ⓒ Ⓓ
18 Ⓐ Ⓑ Ⓒ Ⓓ	43 Ⓐ Ⓑ Ⓒ Ⓓ	68 Ⓐ Ⓑ Ⓒ Ⓓ	93 Ⓐ Ⓑ Ⓒ Ⓓ
19 Ⓐ Ⓑ Ⓒ Ⓓ	44 Ⓐ Ⓑ Ⓒ Ⓓ	69 Ⓐ Ⓑ Ⓒ Ⓓ	94 Ⓐ Ⓑ Ⓒ Ⓓ
20 Ⓐ Ⓑ Ⓒ Ⓓ	45 Ⓐ Ⓑ Ⓒ Ⓓ	70 Ⓐ Ⓑ Ⓒ Ⓓ	95 Ⓐ Ⓑ Ⓒ Ⓓ
21 Ⓐ Ⓑ Ⓒ Ⓓ	46 Ⓐ Ⓑ Ⓒ Ⓓ	71 Ⓐ Ⓑ Ⓒ Ⓓ	96 Ⓐ Ⓑ Ⓒ Ⓓ
22 Ⓐ Ⓑ Ⓒ Ⓓ	47 Ⓐ Ⓑ Ⓒ Ⓓ	72 Ⓐ Ⓑ Ⓒ Ⓓ	97 Ⓐ Ⓑ Ⓒ Ⓓ
23 Ⓐ Ⓑ Ⓒ Ⓓ	48 Ⓐ Ⓑ Ⓒ Ⓓ	73 Ⓐ Ⓑ Ⓒ Ⓓ	98 Ⓐ Ⓑ Ⓒ Ⓓ
24 Ⓐ Ⓑ Ⓒ Ⓓ	49 Ⓐ Ⓑ Ⓒ Ⓓ	74 Ⓐ Ⓑ Ⓒ Ⓓ	99 Ⓐ Ⓑ Ⓒ Ⓓ
25 Ⓐ Ⓑ Ⓒ Ⓓ	50 Ⓐ Ⓑ Ⓒ Ⓓ	75 Ⓐ Ⓑ Ⓒ Ⓓ	100 Ⓐ Ⓑ Ⓒ Ⓓ

DIAGNOSTIC TEST

Use this test to pinpoint your strengths & weaknesses.

Time allowed for the entire examination: 4 Hours

1. As a clerk in an office in a city agency, you have just been given a new assignment by your supervisor. The assignment was previously done by another clerk. Before beginning work it is most important that you

   (A) find out who did the assignment previously
   (B) understand your supervisor's instructions for doing the assignment
   (C) notify the other clerks in the office that you have just received a new assignment
   (D) understand how the assignment is related to the work of other clerks in the office

2. Assume that you are a clerk in a city department. Your supervisor has given you an important job that must be completed as quickly as possible. You will be unable to complete the job by the end of the day, and you will be absent from the office for the next few days. Of the following, the most appropriate action for you to take before leaving the office at the end of the day is to

   (A) lock your work in your desk so that the work will not be disturbed in your absence
   (B) ask another clerk in the office to finish the job while you are away
   (C) tell your supervisor how much of the job has been done and how much remains to be done
   (D) leave a note on your supervisor's desk, advising him that you will continue to work on the job as soon as you return to the office

3. Assume that, as a newly appointed clerk in a city department, you are doing an assignment according to a method that your supervisor has told you to use. You believe that you would be less likely to make errors if you were to do the assignment by a different method, although the method your supervisor has told you to use is faster. For you to discuss your method with your supervisor would be

   (A) desirable because he may not know the value of your method
   (B) undesirable because he may know of your method and may prefer the faster one
   (C) desirable because your method may show your supervisor that you are able to do accurate work
   (D) undesirable because your method may not be as helpful to you as you believe it to be

4. Assume that you are responsible for receiving members of the public who visit your department for information. At a time when there are several persons seeking information, a man asks you for information in a rude and arrogant manner. Of the following, the best action for you to take in handling this man is to

   (A) give him the information in the same manner in which he spoke to you

(B) ignore his request until he asks for the information in a more polite manner
(C) give him the information politely, without commenting on his manner
(D) ask him to request the information in a polite manner so as not to annoy other people seeking information

5. As a clerk in a city agency, you are assigned to issue applications to members of the public who request the applications in person. Your supervisor has told you that under no circumstances are you to issue more than one application to each person. A person enters the office and asks for two applications, explaining that he wants the second one in case he makes an error in filling out the application. Of the following, the most appropriate action for you to take in this situation is to

(A) give the person two applications since he may not know how to fill one out
(B) ask your supervisor for permission to give the person two applications
(C) give one application to the person and advise him to come back later for another one
(D) issue one application to the person and inform him that only one application may be issued to an individual

6. Miss Smith is a clerk in the information section of a city department. Of the following, the most desirable way for Miss Smith to answer a telephone call to the section is to say,

(A) "Hello. Miss Smith speaking."
(B) "Miss Smith speaking. May I ask who is calling?"
(C) "Hello. May I be of service to you?"
(D) "Information Section, Miss Smith."

7. It is not good filing practice to

(A) smooth papers that are wrinkled
(B) use paper clips to keep related papers together in the files
(C) arrange the papers in the order in which they will be filed
(D) mend torn papers with cellophane tape

8. Suppose that as a clerk in an office of a city department, you have been assigned by your supervisor to assist Mr. Jones, another clerk in the office, and to do his work in his absence. Part of Mr. Jones's duties is to give routine information to visitors who request it. Several months later, shortly after Mr. Jones has begun a three-week vacation, a visitor enters the office and asks for some routine information that is available to the public. He explains that he had previously received similar information from Mr. Jones. Of the following, the most advisable action for you to take is to

(A) inform the visitor that Mr. Jones is on vacation but that you will attempt to obtain the information
(B) advise the visitor to return to the office after Mr. Jones has returned from vacation
(C) tell the visitor that you will have Mr. Jones mail him the information as soon as he returns from vacation
(D) attempt to contact Mr. Jones to ask him whether the information should be given to the visitor

Answer questions 9 through 18 by referring to the Code Table and directions below.

CODE TABLE

S	N	W	C	T	Q	I	A	J	X
1	2	3	4	5	6	7	8	9	0

DIRECTIONS: The table above provides a corresponding number for each of the ten letters used as codes in the questions. On the first line there are ten selected letters. On the second line there are the ten numerals, including zero. Directly under each letter on the first line there is a corresponding number on the second line. Every question consists of three pairs of letter and number codes. Each pair of codes is on a separate line. Referring to the Code Table above, determine whether each pair of letter and number codes is made up of corresponding letters and numbers. In answering each question, compare all three pairs of letter and number codes. Then mark your answers, as follows:

A. *if in* none *of the three pairs of codes do* all *letters and numbers correspond*
B. *if in only* one *pair of codes do* all *letters and numbers correspond*
C. *if in only* two *pairs of codes do* all *letters and numbers correspond*
D. *if in* all *three pairs of codes do* all *letters and numbers correspond*

Example:

TQIAJX	567890
TQICCW	567433
JCWQTA	943658

In the Example above, only in two pairs of codes do all of the letters and numbers correspond (on the first and third line). On the second line the number corresponding to the letter C should be 4, not 3. Since in only two of the pairs of codes do all of the letters and numbers correspond, the answer to the Example is C.

9.	JWNAST	932815
	CIJNSW	497213
	QAXTCJ	680549
10.	WIQWTS	376351
	AJIXSN	897012
	TAXISQ	580716
11.	SJSWCT	101245
	XCTWNI	041327
	IJAXCW	728043
12.	XCNIAN	042786
	TAJNIX	587290
	SCJSCX	149140
13.	WACISJ	284719
	IQANXW	768203
	WQXJIN	360792
14.	SWTCQA	135468
	NJAAWS	298831
	XIQTJA	076598
15.	NQTJQI	263067
	AXASIC	808174
	WCIQTX	347650

16.	XQNWCT	062345
	IWCXJA	734098
	CQNSWT	246135

17.	IAIXNA	797028
	ATNISN	853712
	QIQXNJ	676028

18.	SWTJIQ	130967
	NQJTSW	268513
	CIWAXJ	473809

19. Under a subject filing system, letters are filed in folders labeled according to subject matter. Assume that you have been asked to file a large number of letters under such a filing system. Of the following, the *first* step that you should take in filing these letters is to

(A) arrange the letters alphabetically under each subject
(B) determine under which subject each letter is to be filed
(C) arrange the letters by date under each subject
(D) prepare cross references for each letter that should be filed under more than one subject

20. Suppose that your supervisor gives you a folder containing a large number of letters arranged in the order of the dates they were received and a list of names of persons in alphabetical order. He asks you to determine, without disturbing the order of the letters, if there is a letter in the folder from each person on the list. Of the following, the best method to use in doing this assignment is

(A) determine whether the number of letters in the folder is the same as the number of names on the list
(B) look at each letter to see who wrote it, and then place a light check mark on each letter that has been written by a person on the list
(C) prepare a list of the names of the writers of the letters that are in the folder, and then place a light check mark next to each of the names on this list if the name appears on the list of persons your supervisor gave you
(D) look at each letter to see who wrote it, and then place a light check mark next to the name of the person on the list who wrote the letter

Each of the questions 21 through 28 consists of four names. For each question, select the one of the four names that should be third *if the four names were arranged in alphabetical order in accordance with the Rules for Alphabetical Filing given below. Read these rules carefully. Then, for each question, indicate in the correspondingly numbered row on the answer sheet the letter preceding the name that should be* third *in alphabetical order.*

Rules for Alphabetical Filing

Names of Individuals

1. The names of individuals are filed in strict alphabetical order, first according to the last name, then according to first name or initial, and finally according to

middle name or initial. For example: William Jones precedes George Kirk, and Arthur S. Blake precedes Charles M. Blake.

2. When the last names are identical, the one with an initial instead of a first name precedes the one with a first name beginning with the same initial. For example: J. Green precedes Joseph Green.

3. When identical last names also have identical first names, the one without a middle name or initial precedes the one with a middle name or initial. For example: Robert Jackson precedes both Robert C. Jackson and Robert Chester Jackson.

4. When last names are identical and the first names are also identical, the one with a middle initial precedes the one with a middle name beginning with the same initial. For example: Peter A. Brown precedes Peter Alvin Brown.

5. Prefixes such as De, El, La, and Van are considered parts of the names they precede. For example: Wilfred De Wald precedes Alexander Duval.

6. Last names beginning with "Mac" or "Mc" are filed as spelled.

7. Abbreviated names are treated as if they were spelled out. For example: Jos. is filed as Joseph and Robt. is filed as Robert.

8. Titles and designations such as Dr., Mrs., Prof. are disregarded in filing:

Names of Business Organizations

1. The names of business organizations are filed exactly as written, except that an organization bearing the name of an individual is filed alphabetically according to the name of the individual in accordance with the rules for filing names of individuals given above. For example: Thomas Allison Machine Company precedes Northern Baking Company.

2. When numerals occur in a name, they are treated as if they were spelled out. For example: 6 stands for six and 4th stands for fourth.

3. When the following words occur in names, they are disregarded: the, of, and.

Example

(A) Fred Town   (2) (C) D. Town   (1)
(B) Jack Towne   (3) (D) Jack S. Towne   (4)

The numbers in parentheses indicate the proper alphabetical order in which these names should be filed. Since the name that should be filed *third* is Jack Towne, the answer is (*B*).

21. (A) Herbert Restman
    (B) H. Restman
    (C) Harry Restmore
    (D) H. Restmore

22. (A) Martha Eastwood
    (B) Martha E. Eastwood
    (C) Martha Edna Eastwood
    (D) M. Eastwood

23. (A) Timothy Macalan
    (B) Fred McAlden
    (C) Thomas MacAllister
    (D) Mrs. Frank McAllen

24. (A) Elm Trading Co.
    (B) El Dorado Trucking Corp.
    (C) James Eldred Jewelry Store
    (D) Eldridge Printing, Inc.

25. (A) Edward La Gabriel
    (B) Marie Doris Gabriel
    (C) Marjorie N. Gabriel
    (D) Mrs. Marian Gabriel

26. (A) Peter La Vance
    (B) George Van Meer
    (C) Wallace De Vance
    (D) Leonard Vance

27. (A) Fifth Avenue Book Shop
    (B) Mr. Wm. A. Fifner
    (C) 52nd Street Association
    (D) Robert B. Fiffner

28. (A) Dr. Chas. D. Peterson
    (B) Miss Irene F. Petersen
    (C) Lawrence E. Peterson
    (D) Prof. N.A. Petersen

DIRECTIONS for questions 29 through 42:
Each of the questions in this test consists of three names or numbers. For each question, compare the three names or numbers and decide which ones, if any, are exactly the same. Mark your Answer Sheet as follows:

> *Blacken "A" if all three are exactly the same*
> *Blacken "B" if only the first and second are exactly the same*
> *Blacken "C" if only the first and third are exactly the same*
> *Blacken "D" if only the second and third are exactly the same*
> *Blacken "E" if all three are different*

29. 5261383	5261383	5261338
30. 8125690	8126690	8125609
31. W. E. Johnston	W. E. Johnson	W. E. Johnson
32. Vergil L. Muller	Vergil L. Muller	Vergil L Muller
33. Atherton R. Warde	Asheton R. Warde	Atherton P. Warde
34. 2395890	2395890	2395890
35. 1926341	1926347	1926314
36. E. Owens McVey	E. Owen McVey	E. Owen McVay
37. Emily Neal Rouse	Emily Neal Rowse	Emily Neal Rowse
38. H. Merritt Audubon	H. Merriott Audubon	H. Merritt Audubon
39. 6219354	6219354	6219354
40. 2312793	2312793	2312793
41. 1065407	1065407	1065047
42. Francis Ransdell	Frances Ramsdell	Francis Ramsdell

43. The sum of 284.5, 3016.24, 8.9736, and 94.15 is, most nearly,

    (A) 3402.9   (B) 3403.0   (C) 3403.9   (D) 4036.1

44. If 8394.6 is divided by 29.17, the result is most nearly

    (A) 288   (B) 347   (C) 2880   (D) 3470

45. If two numbers are multiplied together, the result is 3752. If one of the two numbers is 56, the other number is

    (A) 41   (B) 15   (C) 109   (D) 67

46. The sum of the fractions 1/4, 2/3, 3/8, 5/6, and 3/4 is

    (A) 20/33   (B) 1 19/24   (C) 2 1/4   (D) 2 7/8

47. The fraction 7/16 expressed as a decimal is

    (A) .1120   (B) .2286   (C) .4375   (D) .4850

48. If .10 is divided by 50, the result is

    (A) .002   (B) .02   (C) .2   (D) 2

49. The number 60 is 40% of

    (A) 24   (B) 84   (C) 96   (D) 150

50. If 3/8 of a number is 96, the number is

    (A) 132   (B) 36   (C) 256   (D) 156

51. An office uses an average of 25 fourteen-cent, 35 seventeen-cent, and 350 twenty-two-cent postage stamps each day. The total cost of stamps used by the office in a five-day period is

    (A) $312.25   (B) $155.55   (C) $430.75   (D) $432.25

52. A city department issued 12,000 applications in 1979. The number of applications that the department issued in 1977 was 25% greater than the number it issued in 1979. If the department issued 10% fewer applications in 1975 than it did in 1977, the number it issued in 1975 was

    (A) 16,500   (B) 13,500   (C) 9,900   (D) 8,100

53. A clerk can add 40 columns of figures an hour by using an adding machine and 20 columns of figures an hour without using an adding machine. The total number of hours it would take him to add 200 columns if he does 3/5 of the work by machine and the rest without the machine is

    (A) 6   (B) 7   (C) 8   (D) 9

54. In 1975, a city department bought 500 dozen pencils at 40 cents per dozen. In 1978, only 75% as many pencils were bought as were bought in 1975, but the price was 20% higher than the 1975 price. The total cost of the pencils bought in 1978 was

    (A) $180   (B) $187.50   (C) $240   (D) $250

55. A clerk is assigned to check the accuracy of the entries on 490 forms. He checks 40 forms an hour. After working one hour on this task, he is joined by another clerk, who checks these forms at the rate of 35 an hour. The total number of hours required to do the entire assignment is

(A) 5   (B) 6   (C) 7   (D) 8

56. Assume that there is a total of 420 employees in a city agency. Thirty percent of the employees are clerks and 1/7 are typists. The difference between the number of clerks and the number of typists is

(A) 126   (B) 66   (C) 186   (D) 80

57. Assume that a duplicating machine produces copies of a bulletin at a cost of 2 cents per copy. The machine produces 120 copies of the bulletin per minute. If the cost of producing a certain number of copies was $12, how many minutes of operation did it take the machine to produce this number of copies?

(A) 5   (B) 2   (C) 10   (D) 6

DIRECTIONS: Questions 58 to 72 each contain a word in capitals followed by four choices of meaning. Choose the definition that most closely corresponds with the word in capitals. On the answer sheet indicate the letter preceding your choice.

58. CAPACITY

(A) need   (B) willingness   (C) ability   (D) curiosity

59. EXEMPT

(A) defend   (B) excuse   (C) refuse   (D) expect

60. CONFORM

(A) conceal from view   (B) remember   (C) be in agreement   (D) complain

61. DEVIATE

(A) turn aside   (B) deny   (C) come to a halt   (D) disturb

62. COMPILE

(A) confuse   (B) support   (C) compare   (D) gather

63. MANIPULATE

(A) attempt   (B) add incorrectly   (C) handle   (D) investigate closely

64. POTENTIAL

(A) useful   (B) possible   (C) welcome   (D) rare

65. AUTHORIZE

(A) write   (B) permit   (C) request   (D) recommend

66. ASSESS

(A) set a value   (B) belong   (C) think highly of   (D) increase

67. CONVENTIONAL

    (A) democratic (B) convenient (C) modern (D) customary

68. DEPLETE

    (A) replace (B) exhaust (C) review (D) withhold

69. INTERVENE

    (A) sympathize with (B) differ (C) ask for an opinion (D) interfere

70. HAZARDOUS

    (A) dangerous (B) unusual (C) slow (D) difficult

71. SUBSTANTIATE

    (A) replace (B) suggest (C) verify (D) suffer

72. IMMINENT

    (A) anxious (B) well-known (C) important (D) about to happen

Each of the questions 73 through 82 consists of a sentence that may or may not be correct. Examine each sentence carefully and determine whether it is

(A) incorrect because of faulty grammar or sentence structure
(B) incorrect because of faulty punctuation
(C) incorrect because of faulty capitalization
(D) correct

For each question, mark in the correspondingly numbered row on your answer sheet the letter preceding the answer you have selected. The incorrect sentences contain only one error.

73. The office manager asked each employee to work one saturday a month.

74. Neither Mr. Smith nor Mr. Jones was able to finish his assignment on time.

75. The task of filing these cards is to be divided equally between you and he.

76. He is an employee whom we consider to be efficient.

77. I believe that the new employees are not as punctual as us.

78. The employees, working in this office, are to be congratulated for their work.

79. The supervisor entered the room and said, "The work must be completed today."

80. The letter will be sent to the United States senate this week.

81. When the supervisor entered the room, he noticed that the book was laying on the desk.

82. The price of the pens were higher than the price of the pencils.

DIRECTIONS: Each of the questions 83 through 90 consists of a group of four words. One word in each group is incorrectly spelled. For each question, indicate in the correspondingly numbered row on the answer sheet the letter preceding the word that is incorrectly spelled.

83. (A) installment   (B) retrieve   (C) concede   (D) dissappear

84. (A) accidentaly   (B) dismissal   (C) conscientious   (D) indelible

85. (A) perceive   (B) carreer   (C) anticipate   (D) acquire

86. (A) plentiful   (B) across   (C) advantagous   (D) similar

87. (A) omission   (B) pamphlet   (C) guarrantee   (D) repel

88. (A) maintenance   (B) always   (C) liable   (D) anouncement

89. (A) exaggerate   (B) sieze   (C) condemn   (D) commit

90. (A) pospone   (B) altogether   (C) grievance   (D) excessive

Answer questions 91 through 100 on the basis of the information in the passage below.

Microfilm is a method of copying records in miniature. Because of increasing need for information, many organizations are using microfilm as a solution to some of their information problems. Since microfilm cannot be viewed by the naked eye, the micro images are magnified by a reader or reader printer.

Microfilm was first used as a method of saving space or protecting vital records. Today, however, there are additional reasons why an organization would want to preserve records on microfilm rather than in some other way. Microfilm can be used, for example, as an information storage and retrieval tool, as part of an active organizational procedure or system, and to move records from one location to another.

The use of microfilm saves storage space, since one to two cabinets of microfilm hold the equivalent of a hundred cabinets of original records. In fact, microfilmed records will usually occupy only 2 percent of the space taken by records in their original form.

In protecting vital records against loss through disaster, theft, or negligence, microfilm is used by many organizations as a means of ensuring the security of essential information.

As part of an active organizational system or procedure, microfilm is used frequently. Banks use it to microfilm their customers' checks prior to returning them with the bank statement. Most large department stores return original sales slips charged by customers against their accounts with a copy of the customer's monthly statement. Before doing so, however, the stores will microfilm the charge slips to obtain a copy for future reference. Similarly, governmental organizations have found wide application for the use of microfilm.

Finally, microfilm is used to move records from one location to another; the documents are microfilmed and then transmitted by a high-speed electrostatic printer.

91. According to the information in the previous passage, one of the original reasons for using microfilm was to

    (A) save time
    (B) save money
    (C) save space
    (D) eliminate telephone work

92. According to the information in the passage above, microfilming can be basically described as a method in which records are

    (A) filed
    (B) moved
    (C) looked at
    (D) reduced in size

93. Which of the following is *not* mentioned in the passage above as a use for microfilm?

    (A) Destroying outdated records
    (B) Protecting vital records
    (C) Retrieving information
    (D) Moving records

94. According to the information in the passage above, department stores use microfilm to

    (A) film shoplifters
    (B) keep copies of charge slips
    (C) film canceled checks
    (D) keep copies of personnel applications

95. According to the information in the passage above, a reader printer is used

    (A) as a high-speed duplicator
    (B) to view microfilm
    (C) to reduce images
    (D) as a substitute for the typewriter

96. According to the passage above, an organization will use microfilm to send records from one place to another by

    (A) electrostatic printer
    (B) mail
    (C) messenger
    (D) air freight

DIRECTIONS: Answer questions 97 through 100 solely on the basis of the information given in the passage below.

Each year there are more and more time-saving machines designed and manufactured to lighten the work load. Some are simply improved versions of standard equipment such as the typewriter; others are more recent additions to the modern office, such as miniature electronic calculators. Before selecting a new piece of equipment, careful consideration should be given to various important factors: nature of the work, economy, speed, quality of output, operator training time, and service maintenance cost.

For example, assembling and preparing letters, reports, brochures, etc., for mass mailing can be a slow and tiresome process if done by hand. Machines for collating, folding and inserting, addressing, and mailing can save considerable time and cost and reduce fatigue.

Collators gather papers together into sets. Some collators will count, line up, and staple pages, in addition to arranging them in order. Collators come in all sizes and some are high-speed, fully automated models.

If an office staff sends out large amounts of mail to the same people, an addressing machine will eliminate the need to type labels on envelopes. Folding machines fold paper for mailing. They are used for bulk mailings.

Inserting machines carry the mailing operation further by gathering the folded letters or papers and inserting them into envelopes. Some machines will even collect letters, fold and insert them, seal the envelopes, and stamp and address them.

If there is a need to get a lot of correspondence out, it is possible to rent a postage meter. A postage meter automatically seals envelopes and stamps them. It can get the mail out in about a quarter of the time it would otherwise take. The postage meter is taken to the post office periodically and set for the amount of postage purchased.

97. According to the information in the passage above, one recent addition to the office that is used to save time is the

   (A) microprocessor
   (B) word processor
   (C) miniature calculator
   (D) computer terminal

98. According to the information in the passage above, which one of the following is *not* indicated as an advantage of using a postage meter?

   (A) Time can be saved in getting out correspondence
   (B) Letters will be inserted in mailing envelopes
   (C) Mailing envelopes will be sealed
   (D) Mailing envelopes will be stamped

99. According to the information in the passage above, one function of a collator is to

   (A) fold envelopes
   (B) multiply and divide
   (C) insert letters
   (D) staple pages together

100. In the preceding passage, which one of the following is *not* indicated as an important consideration in selecting new office equipment?

   (A) Cost savings
   (B) Time savings
   (C) Training difficulty
   (D) Office morale

Answer Key For Diagnostic Test

Judgment in Office Work

1. B	3. A	5. D	7. B
2. C	4. C	6. D	8. A

Table Coding

9. C	11. A	13. B	15. C	17. A
10. D	12. B	14. D	16. C	18. B

Filing

19. B	21. D	23. B	25. C	27. A
20. D	22. B	24. D	26. D	28. A

Name and Number Comparison

29. B	33. E	37. D	40. A
30. E	34. A	38. C	41. B
31. D	35. E	39. A	42. E
32. A	36. E		

Arithmetic

43. C	48. A	53. B
44. A	49. D	54. A
45. D	50. C	55. C
46. D	51. D	56. B
47. C	52. B	57. A

Vocabulary

58. C	63. C	68. B
59. B	64. B	69. D
60. C	65. B	70. A
61. A	66. A	71. C
62. D	67. D	72. D

Correct Usage—Grammar, Punctuation Capitalization

73. C	75. A	77. A	79. D	81. A
74. D	76. D	78. B	80. C	82. A

Spelling

83. D	85. B	87. C	89. B
84. A	86. C	88. D	90. A

Reading Comprehension

91. C	93. A	95. B	97. C	99. D
92. D	94. B	96. A	98. B	100. D

Explanatory Answers

Elucidation, clarification, explication, and a little help with the fundamental facts covered in the previous test. These are the points and principles likely to crop up in the form of questions on future tests.

1. **(B)** This question requires the selection of the most important of the choices given. It is of primary importance that the recipient of work instructions clearly understand them. Finding out who performed the work previously may be of some importance on occasion because the present performer of the work may refer to the person who performed the work previously for clarification if needed. However this reason is subordinate to understanding work instructions given by the supervisor.

2. **(C)** There is only one course of action to be taken in this situation. Your supervisor is expecting you to complete the job by a certain time. If you find that you cannot fulfill his expectations, he should be notified so that he may take appropriate action.

3. **(A)** Suggestions that are offered for work improvement are usually appreciated by a supervisor. There is no harm in presenting your point of view to your supervisor. If you present a better method of work performance, it will be appreciated.

4. **(C)** A receptionist must continue to act in a courteous manner no mater how rude visitors may get. The use of courtesy is infectious; it is likely to influence rude visitors to alter their manner.

5. **(D)** Your orders have been specific. There has been no room left for you to alter them. The visitor's reason for requesting an additional application is that he may make a mistake while filling out the original. This is not reason enough for you to disobey your instructions; he should be careful while completing his application.

6. **(D)** When answering a telephone it is proper to identify the section of an agency and the person answering the telephone to the caller at once.

7. **(B)** The use of paper clips to keep related papers together in a file is unsatisfactory. They are likely to become dislodged. Other types of more permanent paper fasteners should be used. The other three choices are satisfactory procedures for preparing papers for filing.

8. **(A)** The key phrases in this question are "to do his work" and "which is available to the public." Your assignment is to act in the absence of Mr. Jones and do his work, and since the information is available to the public, it should be dispensed to the visitor.

9. **(C)** In the pairs of codes on the first and third lines all letters and numbers correspond. On the second line the number corresponding to the letter I should be 7, not 9.

10. **(D)** In the pairs of codes on all three lines all of the letters and numbers correspond.

11. **(A)** In none of the pairs of codes on any of the three lines do all of the letters and numbers correspond. On the first line the number corresponding to J should be 9, not 0. On the second line the number corresponding to T should be 5, not 1. On the third line the number corresponding to J should be 9, not 2.

12. **(B)** In the pairs of codes the letters and numbers correspond only on the third line. On the first line the number corresponding to the letter N should be 2, not 6. On the second line the number corresponding to the letter J should be 9, not 7, and on the same line the number corresponding to I should be 7, not 9.

13. **(B)** In the pairs of codes the letters and numbers correspond only on the second line. On the first line the number corresponding to W should be 3, not 2. On the third line the number corresponding to J should be 9, not 7, and on the same line the number corresponding to I should be 7, not 9.

14. **(D)** In the pairs of codes on all three lines all of the letters and numbers correspond.

15. **(C)** In the pairs of codes on the second and third lines all of the letters and numbers correspond. On the first line the number corresponding to T should be 5, not 3.

16. **(C)** In the pairs of codes on the first and second lines all of the letters and numbers correspond. On the third line the number corresponding to C should be 4, not 2, and on the same line the number corresponding to Q should be 6, not 4. Also on the same line the number corresponding to N should be 2, not 6.

17. **(A)** In none of the pairs of codes on any of the three lines do all of the letters and numbers correspond. On the first line the number corresponding to A should be 8, not 9. On the second line the number corresponding to N should be 2, not 3. On the third line the number corresponding to J should be 9, not 8.

18. **(B)** In the pairs of codes all of the letters and numbers correspond only on the third line. On the first line the number corresponding to T should be 5, not 0. On the second line the number corresponding to J should be 9, not 8.

19. **(B)** This process is frequently referred to as coding. The first step in this process would be the determination of the subject each piece of material is to be filed under.

20. **(D)** The simplest way to find out if there is a letter from each person on the list is to look at each letter in the sequence they are arranged and check off the writers' names on the list. If, after having looked at all the letters, there is a check mark next to each name on the list, there must be a letter in the folder from each person listed.

21. **(D)**
    (A) Herbert Restman (2)
    (B) H. Restman (1)
    (C) Harry Restmore (4)
    (D) H. Restmore (3)

22. **(B)**
    (A) Martha Eastwood (2)
    (B) Martha E. Eastwood (3)

    (C) Martha Edna Eastwood (4)
    (D) M. Eastwood (1)

23. **(B)**
    (A) Timothy Macalan (1)
    (B) Fred McAlden (3)
    (C) Thomas MacAllister (2)
    (D) Mrs. Frank McAllen (4)

24. **(D)**
    (A) Elm Trading Co. (4)
    (B) El Dorado Trucking Corp. (2)
    (C) James Eldred Jewelery Store (1)
    (D) Eldridge Printing, Inc. (3)

25. **(C)**
    (A) Edward La Gabriel (4)
    (B) Marie Doris Gabriel (2)
    (C) Marjorie N. Gabriel (3)
    (D) Mrs. Marian Gabriel (1)

26. **(D)**
    (A) Peter La Vance (2)
    (B) George Van Meer (4)
    (C) Wallace De Vance (1)
    (D) Leonard Vance (3)

27. **(A)**
    (A) Fifth Avenue Book Shop (3)
    (B) Mr. Wm. A. Fifner (2)
    (C) 52nd Street Association (4)
    (D) Robert B. Fifner (1)

28. **(A)**
    (A) Dr. Chas D. Peterson (3)
    (B) Miss Irene F. Peterson (1)
    (C) Lawrence E. Peterson (4)
    (D) Prof. N. A. Petersen (2)

Questions 29 through 42:

After a careful review of these questions, the correct answers are self-explanatory. These questions test your powers of observation and your ability to pay attention to details. Although accuracy is the obvious key to answering these questions, it is also important that they should be completed at a reasonable speed. With practice, speed in answering these types of questions can be improved significantly.

43. **(C)**
      284.5
    3016.24
        8.9736
       94.15
    ―――――――――
3403.8636 or 3403.9 (answer)

44. **(A)**

$$
\begin{array}{r}
287 + \quad \text{(answer)} \\
29.17\overline{)8394.60} \\
5834 \\
\overline{2560\ 6} \\
2333\ 6 \\
\overline{227\ 00} \\
204\ 19 \\
\overline{2\ 81}
\end{array}
$$

45. **(D)**

To find the missing number in this multiplication problem, simply divide the given multiplied number into the product.

$$
\begin{array}{r}
67 \text{ (answer)} \\
56\overline{)3752} \\
336 \\
\overline{392} \\
392
\end{array}
$$

46. **(D)**

$$\frac{1}{4} = \frac{6}{24}$$

$$\frac{2}{3} = \frac{16}{24}$$

$$\frac{3}{8} = \frac{9}{24}$$

$$\frac{5}{6} = \frac{20}{24}$$

$$\frac{3}{4} = \frac{18}{24}$$

$$\frac{69}{24} = 2\frac{7}{8}$$
(answer)

$$2\frac{21}{24} \text{ reduced to } 2\frac{7}{8}$$

$$
\begin{array}{r}
24\overline{)69} \\
48 \\
\overline{21}
\end{array}
$$

47. **(C)**

$$\frac{7}{\underset{4}{\cancel{16}}} \times \frac{\overset{25}{\cancel{100}}}{1} = \frac{175}{4} = .4375 \text{ (answer)}$$

48. **(A)**

$$50\overline{).100} = .002 \text{ (answer)}$$

100

49. **(D)**

40% is equal to ⅖, therefore ⅕ of 60 here is equal to 30, and 5/5, or the whole number, is 5 × 30 or 150.

50. **(C)**

$\frac{3}{8} = 96$

$\frac{1}{8} = 32$

$\frac{8}{8} = 8 \times 32 = 256$ (answer)

51. **(D)**

DAILY STAMP USE

25 × 14¢	=	$ 3.50
35 × 17¢	=	5.95
350 × 22¢	=	77.00
		$86.45 Daily

$86.45 × 5 days = $432.25 (answer)

52. **(B)**

1979 —	12,000	(given information)
1977 —	15,000	increase of 25%, or 3,000 (¼ × 1200) from 1979 figure
	− 1,500	10% (1,500) fewer than 1977
1975 —	13,500	(answer)

53. **(B)**

$\frac{3}{\cancel{5}_1} \times \cancel{200}^{40} = 120$ by machine

120 ÷ 40 = 3 hours

$\frac{2}{\cancel{5}_1} \times \cancel{200}^{40} = 80$ by hand

80 ÷ 20 = 4 hours

4 + 3 = 7 hours (answer)

54. **(A)**

$$(1975) \quad \begin{array}{r} 500 \\ .40 \\ \hline \$200.00 \end{array}$$

(1978) 25% of 500 = 125

500 − 125 = 375

$$\$.40 \times 120\% = \quad \begin{array}{r} \$ \ .48 \\ 375 \\ \hline \$ \ .48 \\ 30 \ 00 \\ 15 \ 00 \\ \hline \$180.00 \ \text{(answer)} \end{array}$$

55. **(C)**

$$\begin{array}{rl} 490 & \text{total} \\ - \ \ 40 & \text{first hour} \\ \hline 450 & \text{balance to be done} \end{array}$$

$$\begin{array}{rl} 40 & \text{first clerk} \\ 35 & \text{second clerk} \\ \hline 75 & \text{together one hour} \end{array}$$

$$\begin{array}{ll} \overset{\displaystyle 6 \text{ hours}}{75)\overline{450}} & \quad 6 \text{ hours} \\ \quad\ \ \underline{450} & \underline{+ \ 1 \text{ hour}} \\ & \quad 7 \text{ (answer)} \end{array}$$

56. **(B)**

30% is equal to $\dfrac{3}{10}$

$$\dfrac{3}{\cancel{10}} \times \overset{42}{\cancel{420}} \times 126 \text{ clerks}$$

$$\dfrac{1}{\underset{1}{\cancel{7}}} \times \overset{60}{\cancel{420}} = 60 \text{ typists}$$

$$\begin{array}{r} 126 \\ - \ \ 60 \\ \hline 66 \text{ (answer)} \end{array}$$

57. **(A)**

$$\$12 \div 2\cancel{c} = 600 \text{ copies} \quad \overset{6\ 00}{.02)\overline{12.00}}$$

600 ÷ 120 = 5 minutes (answer)

Questions 58 through 72:

The use of the dictionary is recommended in reviewing these questions. It is advisable that you look up the meaning of all words of which you are unfamiliar —both correct and incorrect. When you encounter new or not quite familiar words, the use of the dictionary is the only sure way to increase your vocabulary.

73. **(C)** *Saturday* should be capitalized, as are all of the days of the week.

74. **(D)** Correct. *Neither* or *nor* calls for a singular verb.

75. **(A)** you and *him*. Following a preposition (*between*) both pronouns in the sentence must be in the objective case.

76. **(D)** Correct. The object of the verb *consider* is *whom;* therefore, the personal pronoun is correctly in the objective case.

77. **(A)** "... punctual as *we.*" The personal pronoun should be in the nominative case, since it is the subject of the verb *are.*

78. **(B)** The commas are unnecessary. If we eliminated the phrase the commas set up, it would change the meaning of the sentence.

79. **(D)** Correct. Since the sentence gives the exact words of the supervisor, his statement is correctly enclosed between quotation marks.

80. **(C)** *Senate* is part of a proper noun and should be capitalized.

81. **(A)** *Lying* is correct. When an object is resting on a surface or a person is in the act of reclining, use *lie, lay* (past tense), *lying.*

82. **(A)** *Price,* the subject of the sentence is singular. Therefore, it takes a singular verb, *was.* It is a common error to make the verb agree with the noun next to it in the sentence, in this case with *pens* instead of the subject.

83. **(D)** di*s*appear

84. **(A)** accidental*l*y

85. **(B)** ca*r*eer

86. **(C)** advantag*e*ous

87. **(C)** gua*r*antee

88. **(D)** an*n*ouncement

89. **(B)** s*ei*ze (one of the exceptions to the *i*-before-*e* rule)

90. **(A)** pos*t*pone

91. **(C)** First sentence of the second paragraph.

92. **(D)** First sentence of the first paragraph.

93. **(A)** The destruction of original records is not mentioned, although it is often done.

94. **(B)** Fifth paragraph, third sentence.

95. **(B)** Last sentence of the first paragraph.

96. **(A)** Final paragraph.

97. **(C)** First paragraph, second sentence.

98. **(B)** Read the last paragraph. The postage meter does not insert letters into envelopes.

99. **(D)** Third paragraph, second sentence.

100. **(D)** Office morale is not mentioned at all in this passage.

Use of the Diagnostic Table

In the Diagnostic Table below, there are three lines for every subject area listed in the Answer Key. Each line shows the number of correct answers, indicating whether your knowledge in that area is strong, average, or weak.

Count the number of your correct answers in each subject area and enter your scores on the appropriate lines of the Diagnostic Table. Your scores of correct answers on the table will pinpoint the areas in which you need more study and practice to improve your test performance.

Diagnostic Table

Subject Area	Correct Answers		Your correct answer score
Judgment in Office Work	8 7 0–6	←Strong→ ←Average→ ←Weak→	
Table Coding	9–10 7–8 0–6	←Strong→ ←Average→ ←Weak→	
Filing	9–10 7–8 0–6	←Strong→ ←Average→ ←Weak→	
Name and Number Comparisons	13–14 10–12 0–9	←Strong→ ←Average→ ←Weak→	
Arithmetic	13–15 11–12 0–10	←Strong→ ←Average→ ←Weak→	
Vocabulary	13–15 11–12 0–10	←Strong→ ←Average→ ←Weak→	
Correct Usage	9–10 7–8 0–6	←Strong→ ←Average→ ←Weak→	
Spelling	8 7 0–6	←Strong→ ←Average→ ←Weak→	
Reading Comprehension	9–10 7–8 0–6	←Strong→ ←Average→ ←Weak→	

Part Two

REVIEW OF SUBJECTS AND PRACTICE TESTS

Study Materials and Practice Tests

Study materials and practice tests are provided for the various subjects covered by questions on actual exams. Before starting on the practice tests for a subject area, review the study material for that subject. This will give you the necessary background knowledge to answer those questions. The study material will refresh your knowledge of what you have learned in school and will also cover additional information directly related to office work.

For test questions that measure the ability to perform clerical office work, no study materials are provided because answering these questions requires no prior special knowledge. They test powers of observation and attention to detail. Accuracy and speed are crucial to achieve a high score on these tests. Although you cannot study for questions relating to clerical abilities, you can improve your score significantly by extensive practice. This book provides numerous clerical-ability tests of various kinds, which will enable you to increase your score through practice.

JUDGMENT IN OFFICE WORK

No specific prior knowledge is required to answer these questions. They should be approached using common sense and careful judgment. In choosing your answers the following considerations should be helpful.

Employers expect accurate work and a high rate of production. To maintain a high production rate, the best possible use of time must be made. Consider what is the most efficient way to achieve the purpose of the assignment. From among the choices offered, select the one that will result in the best quality and greatest quantity of work, requiring the shortest time and the least cost. The relative importance of these considerations will depend on the conditions stated in the question. Be careful not to overlook any terms, conditions, or qualifications stated in the question, as they may be keys to the correct answer. For instance, if the question states that a close deadline must be met or complete accuracy is of great importance, such factors must be given careful consideration before deciding on your answer.

If the question refers to an office procedure or to a specific instruction given by the supervisor, the correct answer will probably depend on the observation of such rule or instruction.

You should also keep in mind that in the course of daily work certain hazards may be encountered in the office. A desk drawer or shelf that extends into an aisle can cause a bruised shin or even a broken leg. A wastebasket left in the aisle also may cause mild to severe injury. A file drawer left open can bruise a shoulder, a hip, or a knee. Too many file drawers open at the same time can cause the cabinet to tip over, dumping its contents on anyone who happens to be in the way. Exam questions may involve safety aspects of office work. Common sense and your personal experiences should be your guide for answering questions on avoiding hazards in the office.

In answering questions involving dealings with the public, it must be kept in mind that one must be courteous, tactful, and patient at all times, even if unreasonable attitudes or outright rudeness is encountered.

Receiving Visitors in the Office

Almost everyone in an office has to receive visitors, at least occasionally. Tact, courtesy, and efficiency in receiving visitors are always important. You should treat every visitor as if you were his host or hostess—that's what you really are, even in an office. Find out whom the visitor wants to see. If he is a stranger and does not have an appointment, find out the purpose of his visit—someone other than the person he asks for may be the person he should see. If the visitor seems hesitant about asking for someone, ask if you can help him.

If it is not possible for the visitor to see the person he asks for—because of previous appointments or conferences, or because the person is out—ask him if he will call later for an appointment or offer to call him. This overcomes much disappointment in being turned away.

If a visitor must wait, see that he has a chair, even if you have to get one from another room. Don't try to entertain him—many visitors prefer to sit and think.

If the visitor makes conversation, talk only about things in general. If he asks anything about the business of your office, be courteous in answering, but give only such information as you know he is entitled to. If the visitor regularly does business with your office, discussions do not have to be quite so general, but be sure that any information you give is what your supervisor would want him to have. Have an understanding with your supervisor—don't guess—about the way he wants his visitors received. As a general rule, if the person a visitor wants to see is engaged:

A visitor without an appointment should wait until the person he has come to see is free, or he should see someone else.

A visitor with an appointment should be announced immediately. If the person he has come to see is only temporarily busy, he is expected to wait a few minutes before being admitted.

An important visitor should be announced immediately—whether he has an appointment or not—unless the person he has come to see is busy with someone equally important. In that case, ask him to wait a few minutes until the conference is over.

Telephone Use and Courtesy

Tact, courtesy, and efficiency in handling telephone contacts are of vital importance to public relations, as well as to efficient work. Rules cannot be made to cover every situation, but you will not need a set of rules if you

1. Handle every call with tact and courtesy, regardless of its importance.
2. Do everything you can to tell the caller what he wants to know or to find the person he wants.
3. Handle the instrument itself correctly.

The office telephone should be used as little as possible for personal calls. When you must use an office phone for a personal call, make the call brief. Discourage your friends from calling you at the office. Personal calls take time from your work and tie up the phone when it may be needed for business calls. Too many personal calls make an unfavorable impression.

The way you handle the instrument is important. Your lips should be held an inch from the mouthpiece for best results. Talk in your normal voice. Remember that your phone is "tuned" for the normal voice—if you whisper, shout, or mumble, your voice is unnatural and hard to understand. Speak clearly.

Business Definitions

The list of business definitions on page 39 consists of terms frequently encountered in the course of daily work in both government and commercial business. Familiarity with the meanings of these terms will be helpful in raising your exam score.

Accounts receivable—The various amounts of money that a business is due to receive.

Affidavit—A declaration in writing sworn to before a person legally competent to take oaths.

Amortization—The process of gradually repaying a debt or obligation before the time on which it falls due.

Annuity—A sum of money paid yearly for the period of a life.

Asset—Property that may be used in the payment of debts.

Assignee—An individual who receives property or power by transfer from another.

Attorney-in-fact—One who is appointed by another to make contracts for him.

Bank draft—An order from one bank to another to pay a specified amount, made payable to a third party. Bank drafts are purchased by the remitter from the originating bank and are endorsed to the remitter's creditor.

Bankrupt—One who has been unable to meet his bills as they fall due and has been declared bankrupt by a court.

Barter—A contract to exchange goods for goods instead of for money.

Beneficiary—One who has the profit, benefit, or advantage arising form a contract or an estate.

Bibliography—A list of books relating to a particular subject.

Bilateral contract—A contract in which both parties are bound to fulfill obligations toward each other.

Bill of exchange—An unconditional order in writing by one person to another signed by the giver, charging the person to whom it was given, to pay on demand or at some future time a certain sum to a specified person.

Bill of lading—A receipt, usually in duplicate or triplicate, of goods received, given by the carrier to the shipper.

Bona fide—In good faith, honestly.

Bond—A specially sealed instrument in writing to secure the payment of money or the performance of an obligation.

Budget—A statement of probable revenue and expenditure and of financial proposals for the ensuing year.

Capital—The money or the principal invested in a business.

Cashier's check—A check drawn by a bank upon itself and signed by the cashier or other authorized officer.

Chattels—Personal and real property.

Certified check—A personal check that has been presented to the bank cashier, who has marked it "certified," signed his name, and charged the amount against the drawer's account just as if it had already been paid out. A certified check is guaranteed by the bank. When a person to whose order a check is made out signs his name on the back of the check—i.e., endorses it—the check is payable at the bank to whoever presents it. Checks dated on Sundays or holidays are acceptable at banks.

Chronological—Pertaining to time and the arrangement of events in the order of time.

Close the books—To calculate the income and expenditures of an organization for some specified period.

Codicil—A supplement, adding to, revoking, or explaining something in the body of a will.

Collateral security—Property transferred by the owner to another individual to secure the carrying out of an obligation.

Commercial draft—A form of letter, sent through a bank, from one person to another, requesting that a certain sum of money be paid to the person presenting the letter.

Consign—To send goods to a buyer or to an agent to sell. Payment is made if the goods are sold. If the goods are not sold, the consignee returns the consignments to the consignor.

Contract—A formal agreement between two or more parties. In law a contract is recognized as an obligation to do or not to do a particular thing.

Debenture—A sealed instrument given by a company as security for a loan.

Demurrage—The allowance made by a shipper of goods to the owners of a ship for detaining the ship in port longer than the period agreed on. The term is also applied to railroads and other forms of transportation.

Discount—To buy or accept for less than face value, the difference going to the purchaser. The amount deducted is called a discount.

Dividend—A portion of the earnings of a corporation distributed on a percentage basis to holders of stock in proportion to number or par value of shares held.

Endorse—To write one's name on the back of negotiable paper for the purpose of transferring title and guaranteeing payment.

Escrow—A sealed instrument given by one party to another to deliver to a third person when that third person performs a certain act or acts. It is in force until delivered to that third party.

Estimate—A statement of the probable cost of work to be done or goods to be purchased.

Executor—One appointed by the terms of a will to carry out the provisions of that will.

Facsimile—An exact copy.

Factor—An agent employed to sell merchandise for a compensation called a "factorage" or "commission."

Foreclosure—A court action by which a mortgagor is banned from the redemption of his property and thereby loses it.

Franchise—A privilege or liberty given by a government to certain individuals.

Indemnity—That which is given in payment for a loss or damage.

Inventory—A detailed account, catalog, or schedule of possessions. An organization will take an inventory in order to know what merchandise it has on hand.

Invoice—A list sent to the purchaser containing the items, together with the prices and charges, of merchandise sent or to be sent to him.

Jurat—The phrase at the end of an affidavit to which the officer taking the oath subscribes his name.

Legacy—Property, especially personal property, bequeathed by a will.

Letter of credit—A letter sent by one bank to another stating that an individual has established a certain amount of credit and that he may write drafts against that credit.

Liabilities—Everything that is owed by a business or an individual.

Monopoly—Exclusive control by some individual or company of the sale of some particular product.

Notary public—A public official authorized to take oaths.

Note—A written promise to pay a stated sum of money, generally at a specified time. The one who signs or promises to pay the note is called the maker, and the one to whom the note is payable is called the payee. A note made payable to the bearer or to the order of the payee is a negotiable note. A note made payable to the payee only is a nonnegotiable note. A time note is one in which the time of payment is specified. If no time is indicated, the note is payable on demand and is called a demand note. When two or more persons jointly sign a note, it is called a joint note. A note is said to mature on the date it becomes due.

Personal check—A check drawn by an individual on his own bank account. It is guaranteed only by the individual. The essential difference between a personal check and a commercial draft is this: a personal check is used for making payment to a creditor, whereas a commercial draft is used as a means of collecting from a debtor.

Postal money order—An order of one post office to another to pay the amount named in the order to the person to whom it is made payable.

Proxy—The authority whereby one person represents another at a meeting.

Receipt—A written acknowledgment by an individual, stating that he has received money or other value and what the money was received for.

Remit—To send in return, as money in payment of goods.

Requisition—Any formal request. In an office a requisition is usually for supplies.

Stencil—A thin sheet of paper or metal in which a pattern is cut through with interrupted lines or dots. It is used by placing it on a surface and laying on a color through the spaces with a brush or sponge. A special type of stencil is used on mimeograph machines.

Stipulation—One of the terms of an agreement. A stipulation is usually laid down as a requirement or condition.

Surname—The second or family name which is added to the Christian or given name to make it more specific.

Tariff—A duty levied according to a list of articles of merchandise that are imported or exported.

Underwriter—One who issues a policy of insurance.

Business Abbreviations

Acct. or a/c—account

A.D.—in the year of our Lord (After the death of Christ)

ad. inf.—without end

ad. lib.—at pleasure

ad. loc.—to or at the place

ad. val.—according to value

adv't or ad—advertisement

ac., aet., aetat.—aged (of age)

A.F.L.—American Federation of Labor

ag't.—agent

A.M.—(ante meridian) forenoon

am't—amount

anon.—anonymous

a/o—account of

app.—appendix

apt.—apartment

a/s—account sales

ass't, assist.—assistant

att.—attention

avg.—average

avdp.—avoirdupois

B.A.—Bachelor of Arts

bal.—balance

bbl.—barrel

B.C.—Before (birth of) Christ

b.e. or b/e—bill of exchange

bibliog.—bibliography

bkt.—basket

B/L or b/l—bill of lading

bls.—bales or barrels

blvd.—boulevard

b. pay.—bills payable

b. rec.—bills receivable

b. s.—bill of sale

B.S.—Bachelor of Science

bu.—bushel

bx.—box

c. or cts.—cent or cents

c.a.d.—cash against documents

can.—cancelled

cap.—capital

cat.—catalog

c.c.—cubic centimeter

cet. par.—conditions remaining the same

cf.—compare

chgd.—charged

chron.—chronological

c.i.f.—cost, insurance, freight

cir.—about

c.l.—carload lots

c.l.d.—cost laid down

co.—company

c/o or C/O—care of

c.o.d.—cash on delivery

C.P.A.—Certified Public Accountant also Civil Practice Act

cr.—creditor

cu.—cubic

cum. int.—with interest

cwt.—hundred weight

d.—day

D.A.R.—Daughters of the American Revolution

dbl.—double

D.D.—Doctor of Divinity

dec.—deceased

dft.—draft

disct.—discount

Dist. Atty.—District Attorney

do.—ditto (the same)

doz. or dz.—dozen

dr.—debtor

d.t.—delirium tremens

dwt.—pennyweight

ea.—each

ed.—editor

e.e.—errors excepted

e.g.—for example

est.—established

et. al.—and others

etc.—and so forth

et. seq.—and following

F.—Fahrenheit

ff.—following, folio

F.O.B.—free on board

ft.—foot or feet

f.v.—on the back of the page

gal.—gallon

G.H.Q.—General Headquarters

gi.—gill, gills

H.I.M.—His (Her) Imperial Majesty

h.p.—horsepower

ib or ibid—the same

id.—the same

i.e.—that is
in.—inches
in loc.—in place
in loc. cit.—in the place cited
inst.—instant (the present month)
inv.—invoice
invt.—inventory
I.O.U.—I Owe You
I.Q.—intelligence quotient
I.R.A—Independent Retirement Account
i.t.—in transit

J.P.—Justice of the Peace
jt.—joint

kc.—kilocycle
kg.—keg, kilogram

l/c—letter of credit
ll.—lines
l.s.—place of the seal

M—thousand
M.A.—Master of Arts
Messrs.—gentlemen
mfg.—manufacturing
mfr.—manufacturer
m or **min.**—minute
misc.—miscellaneous
mm—millimeter
m.o.—money order
mos.—months
MS.—manuscript
MSs.—manuscripts
mtg.—mortgage

n.b.—(nota bene) note carefully
neg.—negative
n.g.—no good
n.p.—notary public
n/p—net proceeds

o/a—on account
o/d—on demand
o/e—omissions excepted
op. cit.—the work cited
o.t.—overtime
oz.—ounce or ounces

par.—paragraph
Pat. Off.—Patent Office
p.c.—percent
pd.—paid
per. an.—each year

pfd.—preferred
Ph. D.—Doctor of Philosophy
phr.—phrase
pkg.—package
P.L. & R.—Postal Laws and Regulations
P.M. or **p.m.**—afternoon
pp.—pages
propr.—proprietor
pro tem—for the time being
prox.—next month
pseud.—pseudonym

q.e.d.—it has been proven
qt.—quart
q.v.—see this

re—regarding
recd.—received
regd.—registered
ret.—retired
r.f.d.—rural free delivery
R.S.V.P.—please reply
R.P.O.—Railway Post Office
RR—railroad
rt.—right

sic.—exactly so
soc.—society
sq.—square
seq.—the following
S.R.O.—Standing Room Only
s.s.—namely
stet.—let it remain as it is (printing)

tr.—transpose
t.—ton

ult.—last month

vid.—see
viz.—namely
vox pop.—voice of the people
vs. or **v.**—versus
V.S.—see the foregoing
v.v.—vice versa

wk.—week
wt.—weight

X—experimental

yd.—yard
yr.—year

Answer Sheet For Judgment In Office Work Practice Test

1 Ⓐ Ⓑ Ⓒ Ⓓ
2 Ⓐ Ⓑ Ⓒ Ⓓ
3 Ⓐ Ⓑ Ⓒ Ⓓ
4 Ⓐ Ⓑ Ⓒ Ⓓ
5 Ⓐ Ⓑ Ⓒ Ⓓ
6 Ⓐ Ⓑ Ⓒ Ⓓ
7 Ⓐ Ⓑ Ⓒ Ⓓ
8 Ⓐ Ⓑ Ⓒ Ⓓ
9 Ⓐ Ⓑ Ⓒ Ⓓ
10 Ⓐ Ⓑ Ⓒ Ⓓ
11 Ⓐ Ⓑ Ⓒ Ⓓ
12 Ⓐ Ⓑ Ⓒ Ⓓ
13 Ⓐ Ⓑ Ⓒ Ⓓ
14 Ⓐ Ⓑ Ⓒ Ⓓ
15 Ⓐ Ⓑ Ⓒ Ⓓ
16 Ⓐ Ⓑ Ⓒ Ⓓ
17 Ⓐ Ⓑ Ⓒ Ⓓ

18 Ⓐ Ⓑ Ⓒ Ⓓ
19 Ⓐ Ⓑ Ⓒ Ⓓ
20 Ⓐ Ⓑ Ⓒ Ⓓ
21 Ⓐ Ⓑ Ⓒ Ⓓ
22 Ⓐ Ⓑ Ⓒ Ⓓ
23 Ⓐ Ⓑ Ⓒ Ⓓ
24 Ⓐ Ⓑ Ⓒ Ⓓ
25 Ⓐ Ⓑ Ⓒ Ⓓ
26 Ⓐ Ⓑ Ⓒ Ⓓ
27 Ⓐ Ⓑ Ⓒ Ⓓ
28 Ⓐ Ⓑ Ⓒ Ⓓ
29 Ⓐ Ⓑ Ⓒ Ⓓ
30 Ⓐ Ⓑ Ⓒ Ⓓ
31 Ⓐ Ⓑ Ⓒ Ⓓ
32 Ⓐ Ⓑ Ⓒ Ⓓ
33 Ⓐ Ⓑ Ⓒ Ⓓ
34 Ⓐ Ⓑ Ⓒ Ⓓ Ⓔ

35 Ⓐ Ⓑ Ⓒ Ⓓ Ⓔ
36 Ⓐ Ⓑ Ⓒ Ⓓ Ⓔ
37 Ⓐ Ⓑ Ⓒ Ⓓ Ⓔ
38 Ⓐ Ⓑ Ⓒ Ⓓ Ⓔ
39 Ⓐ Ⓑ Ⓒ Ⓓ Ⓔ
40 Ⓐ Ⓑ Ⓒ Ⓓ Ⓔ
41 Ⓐ Ⓑ Ⓒ Ⓓ Ⓔ
42 Ⓐ Ⓑ Ⓒ Ⓓ Ⓔ
43 Ⓐ Ⓑ Ⓒ Ⓓ Ⓔ
44 Ⓐ Ⓑ Ⓒ Ⓓ Ⓔ
45 Ⓐ Ⓑ Ⓒ Ⓓ Ⓔ
46 Ⓐ Ⓑ Ⓒ Ⓓ Ⓔ
47 Ⓐ Ⓑ Ⓒ Ⓓ
48 Ⓐ Ⓑ Ⓒ Ⓓ Ⓔ
49 Ⓐ Ⓑ Ⓒ Ⓓ Ⓔ
50 Ⓐ Ⓑ Ⓒ Ⓓ Ⓔ

JUDGMENT IN OFFICE
WORK PRACTICE TEST

Time: 60 minutes. 50 questions.

DIRECTIONS: Select from the choices offered in each of the following the one that is correct or most nearly correct.

1. An invoice is usually a

   (A) check   (B) bond   (C) bill   (D) inventory

2. A letter that contains payment of a bill is called

   (A) a collection letter
   (B) a letter of remittance
   (C) an adjustment letter
   (D) an order letter

3. An enforceable business agreement is called

   (A) a contract   (B) a bill of lading   (C) an invoice   (D) a statement

4. An assignee is

   (A) a series of payments made periodically
   (B) a legal seizure of valuables
   (C) a state of insolvency
   (D) one to whom property is turned over

5. "A clerk in a city agency should realize that each letter he sends out in response to a letter of inquiry from the public represents an expenditure of time and money by his agency." Of the following, the most valid implication of this quotation is that such a clerk should

   (A) use the telephone to answer letters of inquiry directly and promptly
   (B) answer mail inquiries with lengthy letters to eliminate the need for further correspondence
   (C) prevent the accumulation of a large number of similar inquiries by answering each of these letters promptly
   (D) use simple, concise language in answer to letters of inquiry

6. Assume you are the receptionist for Mr. Brown, an official in your department. It is your duty to permit only persons having important business to see this official; otherwise, you are to refer them to other members of the staff. A man tells you that he must see Mr. Brown on a very urgent and confidential matter. He gives you his name and says that Mr. Brown knows him, but he does not wish to tell you the nature of the matter. Of the following, the best action for you to take under these circumstances is to

   (A) permit this man to see Mr. Brown without further question, since the matter seems to be urgent

47

(B) refer this man to another member of the staff, since Mr. Brown may not wish to see him

(C) call Mr. Brown and explain the situation to him, and ask him whether he wishes to see this man

(D) tell this man that you will permit him to see Mr. Brown only if he informs you of the nature of his business

7. Suppose that you are assigned to the information window of a city department where you come into daily contact with many people. On one occasion a man asks you for some information in a very arrogant and rude manner. Of the following, the best reason for you to give this man the requested information politely is

(A) he may not mean to be rude; it may just be his manner of speech
(B) it is the duty of city employees to teach members of the public to be polite
(C) he will probably apologize for his manner when he sees that you are polite
(D) city employees are expected to be courteous to the public

8. A city agency whose employees come into frequent contact with the public can gain public approval of its work most effectively by

(A) distributing pamphlets describing its objectives and work to the people who come into contact with the agency
(B) encouraging its employees to behave properly when off duty so as to impress the public favorably
(C) making certain that its employees perform their daily services efficiently and courteously
(D) having its officials give lectures to civic groups, describing the agency's efficiency and accomplishments

9. A visitor to an office in a city agency tells one of the clerks that he has an appointment with the supervisor of the office, who is expected shortly. The visitor asks for permission to wait in the supervisor's private office, which is unoccupied at the moment. For the clerk to allow the visitor to do so would be

(A) desirable; the visitor would be less likely to disturb the other employees or to be disturbed by them
(B) undesirable; it is not courteous to permit a visitor to be left alone in an office
(C) desirable; the supervisor may wish to speak to the visitor in private
(D) undesirable; the supervisor may have left confidential papers on his desk

10. Assume that you are a newly appointed clerk in a city agency. While your superior is at a conference that may last for several hours, a visitor enters the office and asks you for information on certain of your agency's procedures with which you are not familiar. Of the following, the best action for you to take is to

(A) ask the visitor to return to the office later in the day when your superior will have returned
(B) ask the visitor to wait in the office until your superior returns
(C) ask a more experienced clerk in your office to answer the visitor's questions.
(D) advise the visitor that the information that he is seeking will be given to him if he writes to your superior

11. Assume that you are one of several clerks employed in the office of a city department. Members of the public occasionally visit the office to obtain

information. Because your desk is nearest the entrance to the office, most of these visitors direct their inquiries to you. One morning when everyone, including yourself, is busy, a visitor enters the office and asks you for some readily available information. Of the following, the best action for you to take is to

(A) disregard his question in the hope that he will direct his inquiry to another clerk
(B) inform him politely that you are busy now and ask him to return in the afternoon
(C) give him the requested information concisely but courteously and then continue with your work
(D) advise him to write a letter to your department so that the information can be sent to him

12. A clerk notices that a visitor has just entered the office. The other clerks are not aware of the visitor's presence. The most appropriate of the following actions for the clerk to take is to

(A) attend to the visitor immediately
(B) continue with his/her own work and leave the visitor to one of the other clerks
(C) cough loudly to direct the attention of the other clerks to the presence of the visitor
(D) continue with his/her work unless the visitor addresses him directly

13. Of the following, the most appropriate greeting for a receptionist to use in addressing visitors is

(A) "Please state your business."
(B) "May I help you?"
(C) "Hello. What is your problem?"
(D) "Do you wish to see someone?"

14. A clerk in a city agency informs Mr. Brown, an applicant for a license issued by the city agency, that the application filed by him was denied because he lacks eighteen months of the required experience. Shortly after the applicant leaves the agency's office, the clerk realizes that Mr. Brown lacks only six months of the required experience. Of the following, the most desirable procedure to be followed in connection with this matter is that

(A) a printed copy of the requirements should be sent to Mr. Brown
(B) a letter explaining and correcting the error should be sent to Mr. Brown
(C) no action should be taken because Mr. Brown is not qualified at the present time for the license
(D) a report of this matter should be prepared and attached to Mr. Brown's application for reference if Mr. Brown should file another application

15. Suppose that you are the secretary to Mr. Smith, the administrative official who is responsible for securing special equipment, supplies, and services for your department. In carrying out his duties, Mr. Smith interviews agents of companies interested in having your department utilize their products and services. You have been informed by Mr. Smith that he does not wish to see certain agents. The best one of the following methods that you may use in denying an interview to one of these unwelcome representatives is to

(A) inform him frankly and bluntly that Mr. Smith has left specific instructions that certain agents are not to be granted interviews
(B) tell him that Mr. Smith has left the office and will not return that day

(C) take his calling card, note the reason for his call, and then tell him that he will be notified by mail or telephone when Mr. Smith wishes to see him

(D) make a note of the nature of his business; then inform him that Mr. Smith will be busy for the remainder of that day and request him to return to the office at a later date

16. As a secretary to a division chief, you may receive requests for information that you know should not be divulged. Of the following replies you may give to such a request received over the telephone, the best one is

(A) "I regret to advise you that it is the policy of the department not to give out this information over the telephone."

(B) "If you hold on a moment, I'll have you connected with the chief of the division."

(C) "I am sorry that I cannot help you, as we are not permitted to give out any information regarding such matters."

(D) "I am sorry, but I know nothing regarding this matter."

17. You overhear two of your fellow workers, a typist and a file clerk, quarreling during working hours. The best of the following procedures for you to follow immediately is

(A) reprimand both workers for creating a disturbance

(B) pay no attention to the quarrel

(C) report the matter to your superior

(D) defend the abused person

18. Accuracy is of greater importance than speed in filing chiefly because

(A) city offices have a tremendous amount of filing to do

(B) fast workers are usually inferior workers

(C) there is considerable difficulty in locating materials that have been filed incorrectly

(D) there are many varieties of filing systems that may be used

19. "Many persons dictate so rapidly that they pay little attention to matters of punctuation and English, but they expect their stenographers to correct errors." This statement implies most clearly that stenographers should be

(A) able to write acceptable original reports when required

(B) good citizens as well as good stenographers

(C) efficient clerks as well as good stenographers

(D) knowledgable in correct English usage

20. "A typed letter should resemble a picture properly framed." This emphasizes

(A) accuracy   (B) speed   (C) convenience   (D) neatness

21. Of the following, the chief advantage of the use of a mechanical check writer is that it

(A) guards against tearing in handling the check

(B) decreases the possibility of alteration in the amount of the check

(C) tends to prevent the mislaying and loss of checks

(D) facilitates keeping checks in proper order for mailing

22. Of the following, the chief advantage of the use of a dictating machine is that

(A) the stenographer need not take rapid dictation
(B) the person dictating tends to make few errors
(C) the dictator may be dictating letters while the stenographer is busy at some other task
(D) the usual noise in an office is lessened

23. In the absence of specific instructions, the best of the following things for a clerk to do when his/her superior does not wish to interview a visitor is to tell the visitor that

(A) the superior is too busy to see him, and let the visitor go
(B) the superior is out, and ask the visitor to come back another day
(C) the superior will be busy for some time and cannot see him, but that you as his/her secretary will be glad to help in any way you can
(D) the superior is not in, and let him go

24. One of your assignments is the filing of correspondence. You are about to file a letter, addressed to the superintendent and stamped with a receipt date of a week ago, when you realize that the major part of the signature has been torn away. In order to determine under what name the letter is to be filed, the best of the following actions for you to take *first* is to

(A) read the letter for possible clues as to the identity of the writer
(B) show the letter to another clerk in your office and ask what he/she would do
(C) ask the superintendent if he/she remembers the name of the writer of the letter
(D) ask the mail clerk if he/she remembers the name of the writer of the letter

25. Suppose that you have been assigned to proofread a typed copy of a mimeographed report with another clerk. The mimeographed report was prepared in another department, and the copy prepared in your own office. Your supervisor has asked you to make corrections neatly in ink. You are reading aloud from the mimeographed report while the other clerk follows the copy. You notice an obvious spelling error in the mimeographed report that has been repeated in the copy. Of the following, the best action to take is to

(A) correct the spelling error on the mimeographed report only
(B) return the mimeographed report for correction to the department that prepared it
(C) correct the spelling error on both the mimeographed report and copy
(D) leave the spelling error in both the mimeographed report and the copy

26. Assume that you are delivering incoming mail to the office in which you are working. After you have opened a letter addressed to the chief, you discover that the envelope is marked "personal." Of the following, the best action for you to take is to

(A) reseal the letter and say nothing about it in order to avoid any unpleasantness
(B) deliver the letter in the opened envelope and wait to see if anything happens
(C) read the letter and if it does not really seem to be of a personal nature, deliver it without the envelope
(D) deliver the letter in the opened envelope and explain what happened

27. A salesman has a card index file of his customers arranged alphabetically according to their last names. He/she wants to identify for easy reference those of his/her customers residing in each of the five boroughs of New York City. Of the following, the most helpful for the purpose of easy reference would be to

(A) insert in a folder the card of each customer that resides in the same borough
(B) use different-size cards for customers residing in each of the five boroughs
(C) use different-color cards for customers residing in each of the five boroughs
(D) underline the borough in the addresses of customers on each card

28. Assume that you are a storeroom clerk in charge of keeping a card inventory that contains a separate card for each type of article, such as sheets, towels, pillowcases. These articles are obtained from a central purchasing agency under specified code numbers. A single code number usually applies to a rather large group of articles; for example, the above-mentioned items would have a single code number indicating linens. Of the following, the best procedure is to file the cards

(A) first alphabetically, then by code number
(B) first by code number, then alphabetically within each code number
(C) alphabetically, disregarding code number
(D) by code number only

29. One of your duties as a clerk may be to answer routine credit inquiries concerning the employees of your department. These inquiries generally ask for confirmation of employment and salary. However, you have received a letter which, in addition to the usual request, asks for an opinion as to whether or not the credit of the person involved is good. Of the following, the best action for you to take *first* is to

(A) refer the letter of inquiry to your supervisor before making any reply
(B) give a favorable reply, since the employee probably needs the article he wishes to buy
(C) consult the person involved and ask him whether or not he can afford this purchase
(D) ask other employees in the department what they know of this person's financial condition

30. Suppose that a typist in your office has just finished typing a report prepared by you. You are about to proofread the copy with her. She suggests that she read aloud from the original while you check the copy. Compared with the alternative of your reading from the original while the typist checks her own work, this procedure is

(A) more desirable; the typist will have an opportunity to detect errors in the original report
(B) less desirable; the typist should have the opportunity to discover her own errors
(C) less desirable; you are given the opportunity to review your own report once more
(D) more desirable; whenever possible, a person's work should be checked by someone else, rather than by himself/herself

31. Suppose that you are a clerk assigned to the employment office of a hospital. One of your duties is to conduct preliminary interviews with people seeking low-salaried jobs, such as laundry workers and kitchen helpers. You know that at the present time such help is hard to get. An applicant tells you that he has worked at the hospital before. You look up his record and find that he was frequently absent from work. Of the following, the best action for you to take is to

(A) tell him that his past record prevents further employment
(B) refer him to the head of the division in which he seeks employment, after explaining the circumstances to the division head

(C) tell him to report for work immediately

(D) tell him to seek employment at some other institution

32. Suppose that you have been adding a typed list of amounts of money, extending over several pages. You have computed a subtotal at the end of each page. The grand total you have found should check with an amount given to you by your supervisor, but is too large by seven dollars. Of the following, the step you should take *first* in order to detect your error in the computation is to

(A) check the addition of the subtotals

(B) verify the accuracy of each subtotal

(C) add all the figures, disregarding the subtotals

(D) add the column immediately left of the decimal point, since that is where the error occurs

33. Your supervisor has given you instructions concerning the method to be used in doing a certain job. You do not understand the reasons for these instructions. For you to ask your supervisor to explain his reasons would be

(A) wise; you will probably do a better job if you understand the whole picture

(B) unwise; a supervisor is not required to explain the reasons for his/her instructions

(C) wise; you will probably gain the confidence of your supervisor

(D) unwise; you will be wasting your supervisor's time

34. Suppose that you are a clerk assigned to the information desk in your department. Your function is to give information to members of the public who telephone or call in person. It is a busy period of the year. There is a line of seventeen people waiting to speak to you. Because you are constantly being interrupted by telephone calls for information, however, you are unable to give any attention to the people waiting in line. The line is increasing in length. Of the following, the best action for you to take is to

(A) explain courteously to the people in line that you will probably be unable to help them

(B) advise the people at the end of the line that you will probably not reach them for some time and suggest that they come back when you are less busy

(C) ask the switchboard operator to answer telephone requests for information herself/himself instead of putting the calls on your extension

(D) ask your supervisor to assign another clerk to answer telephone calls so that you can give your full attention to the people in line

(E) take care of all of the people in the line before answering any more telephone calls

35. One of your duties as a clerk may be to deliver mimeographed copies of administrative orders to administrators in your department. It is not necessary for an administrator to sign a receipt for his/her copy of an order. One of the administrators to whom you are requested to deliver a copy of an order is not at his desk when you make your usual tour of the offices. Of the following, the best action for you to take is to

(A) keep this order until a later order is issued and then deliver both orders at the same time

(B) wait until you meet the administrator in the corridor and give him his copy in person

(C) leave a note on the administrator's desk requesting him to call at the mail room for his copy

(D) wait at the administrator's desk until he returns

(E) leave the administrator's copy of the order on his desk

36. One of your duties as a clerk may be to deliver interoffice mail to all of the offices in the department in which you work. Of the following, the best procedure for you to follow before you deliver the letters is, in general, to arrange them on the basis of the

(A) offices to which the letters are to be delivered

(B) dates on which the letters were written

(C) specific persons by whom the letters were signed

(D) offices from which the letters come

(E) dates on which the letters were received in the mail room

37. Suppose that your supervisor has asked you to type a copy of a statistical table. In general, the best method for checking the copy to make certain that it is absolutely accurate is to

(A) type a second copy of the table and compare the two copies

(B) have another clerk read the original table aloud to you while you read the copy

(C) compare all totals in the two tables, for if the totals check the copy is probably accurate

(D) check the one or two points in the table at which an error is most likely to be made

(E) examine the copy to determine whether all entries look reasonable

38. Of the following, the most important caution to observe before beginning work on a new task assigned to you by your supervisor is that

(A) you understand fully the relationship of that task to the general function of your department

(B) you know precisely how long the task will take to complete

(C) you will be able to finish the task within a week or two

(D) you understand fully your supervisor's instructions for doing the task

(E) the other clerk in the office knows what your assignment is

39. As a clerk, you may be assigned the duty of opening and sorting the mail coming to your department. The one of the following that is the best reason for not discarding the envelopes in which letters come from members of the public until you have glanced at the letters is that

(A) it is sometimes necessary to return a letter to the writer in the original envelope

(B) the subject of a letter can, of course, be determined only from the letter itself

(C) the envelopes should usually be filed together with the letters

(D) members of the public frequently neglect to include a return address in their letters

(E) the precise bureau in the department to which a letter should be forwarded sometimes cannot be determined from the envelope

40. Suppose that your supervisor has asked you and another clerk to proofread a stencil. The other clerk is reading rapidly to you from the original copy while you are checking the stencil. For you to interrupt his reading and make an immediate notation of each error you find is

(A) wise; you might otherwise forget to note the error
(B) foolish; such action slows down the reading
(C) foolish; such action demonstrates that the copy is not accurate
(D) wise; such action demonstrates that the rate of reading may be increased
(E) foolish; interruptions waste time

41. One of the administrators in your department cannot find an important letter left on his desk. He believes that the letter may accidentally have been placed among a group of letters sent to you for filing. You look in the file and find the letter filed in its correct place. Of the following, the best suggestion for you to make to your supervisor in order to avoid repetition of such incidents is that

(A) file clerks should be permitted to read material they are requested to file
(B) correspondence files should be cross-indexed
(C) a periodic check should be made of the files to locate material inaccurately filed
(D) material sent to the file clerk for filing should be marked "O.K. for filing"
(E) only authorized persons should be permitted to take materials from the files

42. One of your duties as a clerk is to keep a file of administrative orders by date. Your supervisor often asks you to find the order concerning a particular subject. Since you are rarely able to remember the date of the order, it is necessary for you to search through the entire file. Of the following the best suggestion for you to make to your supervisor for remedying this situation is that

(A) each order bear conspicuously in its upper lefthand corner the precise date on which it is issued
(B) old orders be taken from the file and destroyed as soon as they are superseded by new orders, so that the file will not be overcrowded
(C) an alphabetic subject index of orders be prepared so that orders can be located easily by content as well as date
(D) dates be eliminated entirely from orders
(E) the content of each order be summarized briefly at the end of the order

43. As a clerk, you are regularly assigned to the information desk of your department. When you report for work at 9 A.M. one morning, you find four people waiting to speak to you. When the first person, Mr. Williams, explains his problem, you realize that his case is unusual and that it will be necessary to make an exhaustive search of record files in other parts of the building. There is no other clerk available to help you. For you to explain the situation to Mr. Williams and to ask him to be seated until you have had an opportunity to speak to the other persons who are waiting would be wise chiefly because

(A) to answer the questions of the other persons may requre a very brief time
(B) Mr. Williams was probably not the first to arrive, although he was the first to speak to you
(C) every person seeking information from the department should be asked to wait a short time
(D) one of the other persons waiting may be able to supply the information in which Mr. Williams is interested
(E) unusual problems should not be given preference over routine matters

44. Assume that, as a clerk, you are assigned to the information desk of your department. A man makes a request on which, according to your instructions, action cannot be taken unless a detailed application form has been filled out and

filed. You therefore hand a blank form to this person and request that he fill it out. He looks briefly at the form and then tells you that he does not have the necessary information immediately available. His records, he tells you, are at home. For you to advise him to fill out the form at home and to mail it to the department, instead of asking him to attempt to guess at the necessary information, would be wise chiefly because

(A) he may not be able to determine accurately, by only a brief inspection, whether the necessary information is immediately available
(B) inaccurate information on an application form may lead to a considerable waste of time
(C) mail is generally acceptable as a way of delivering official documents
(D) needless work would be created if the application must be returned to the man for additional information
(E) the department would gain an additional day or two to act on his request

45. Suppose that you are assigned to the mail room in your department. It is your duty to open incoming letters and to route them to the appropriate offices. Of the following, the best reason for you to become thoroughly acquainted with the functions and procedures of the various offices in your department is that

(A) many letters are addressed to the department rather than to a specific office or individual
(B) routine letters should be answered without referring them to another office
(C) an accurate directory of departmental employees is an invaluable aid to the mail clerk
(D) letters concerning important matters of policy should be acknowledged before they are referred to another office
(E) it would require too much time for the clerk to open every letter before forwarding it to the proper office

46. You are assigned the duty of receiving applications filed in person at your department. Applications filed by mail are handled by another clerk. The one of the following that is the best reason for glancing through an application being filed in person, before accepting that application, is that

(A) the person filing the application may not be the applicant
(B) false information on the application may be detected
(C) obvious mistakes in filling out the form should be brought to the attention of the person filing the application before he/she leaves
(D) there may be sections of the application uncompleted
(E) each applicant should be held strictly accountable for the number of forms wasted because of careless or avoidable errors

47. Usually, the use of a money order is preferable to sending currency in ordinary mail because

(A) money orders bear interest at the rate of 2 percent
(B) money orders may be deposited or cashed in banks
(C) there is less chance of theft
(D) proof of identity is not required in cashing a money order at a post office

48. While you are working at the information desk of your department, a man requests certain application forms which, he claims, are being distributed by your department. As far as you know, no such forms are being distributed by your department. For you to question the man as to the reason for his request would be

(A) wise; such information may indicate that he should contact another department

(B) unwise; he is obviously well-informed concerning the availability of the forms

(C) unwise; valuable time will be wasted if he is mistaken

(D) unwise; his reason for requesting the forms is immaterial in view of the fact that the forms are not available

(E) unwise; he may wish to obtain the forms for a friend or relative

49. One of the duties to which you as a clerk may be assigned is the distribution of mail from the central mail room to the various departmental offices. Of the following, the best reason for waiting until all of the mail has been sorted before you begin to distribute the mail is that

(A) more mail can be carried at any one time

(B) you can devote time to other duties

(C) mail can be distributed immediately on being received in the mail room

(D) fewer trips to the departmental offices will be required

(E) no office will receive more mail than it can handle at any one time

50. Suppose that your supervisor has asked you to work on five long-range assignments simultaneously. In general, for you to change regularly every two or three hours from one assignment to another would be

(A) wise; greater variety would be introduced into your work

(B) unwise; getting ready and putting away the material necessary for each assignment would consume excessive time

(C) wise; approaching a new task with a fresh mind would enable you to work more efficiently

(D) unwise; you would be unable to devote equal time to each assignment

(E) wise; no one assignment could be completed before the others

Answer Key for Judgment in Office Work Practice Test

1. C	18. C	35. E
2. B	19. D	36. A
3. A	20. D	37. B
4. D	21. B	38. D
5. D	22. C	39. D
6. C	23. C	40. A
7. D	24. A	41. D
8. C	25. C	42. C
9. D	26. D	43. A
10. C	27. C	44. B
11. C	28. B	45. A
12. A	29. A	46. C
13. B	30. D	47. C
14. B	31. B	48. A
15. C	32. A	49. D
16. C	33. A	50. B
17. B	34. D	

FILING

The following information and tests on basic filing practices will give you a good start toward adequate preparation for this portion of clerical examinations. Study this information thoroughly before doing the practice tests that follow.

Methods of Filing

Modern, efficient filing systems and supplies are designed to facilitate the handling and the finding of necessary correspondence and records when required for future reference. Proper understanding of this material will help you greatly on your examination.

Alphabetic Filing

This is by far the most important method, and besides, it is fundamental to the proper operation of all the other methods.

When alphabetic filing is employed, the papers are sorted according to the letters of the alphabet. The following are the most important rules governing alphabetic filing:

1. Consider the surname first, then the given name, then the middle initial, and last the title.

   Bonomo, Henry J.
   Bonomo, Leo
   Caudwell, Fred
   Charters, John D. (Dr.)

   If the surnames are the same, then the given names are considered; and if the given names are the same, then the middle name or initial is the deciding factor in filing the name. All material must be arranged in A–Z sequence of letters down to the last letter of the item.
2. Many names are pronounced exactly alike but are spelled differently. They must be filed exactly as spelled.
3. Mac and Mc are filed exactly as they are spelled, Mc coming after Mac.
4. In filing a group of names, all of which have the same surname, the following must be kept in mind: (A) the name consisting of the surname only (without initials or given name indicated) comes first. (B) names consisting of the surname and one or more initials only, come before the same surname with full given names that begin with the same letter as the initial after the preceding surname.

   King
   King, D
   King, Dorothy

5. Hyphenated surnames are indexed as though the hypen joined the two parts making one.

Lytton-Strachey, John
Lyttonte, Amadeus

6. Foreign names are filed as spelled, and prefixes are not considered separately. Likewise, foreign-language articles (Le, La, Les, El, etc.) are considered part of the name when they appear: L'Aiglon; Les Miserables.

Da Costa, Carl
D'Agnota, Ugo
Des Verney, Elizabeth
De Takacs, Maria

7. When the same names appear with different addresses, arrange them alphabetically to town or city, considering state only where there is a duplication of town or city names.

American Tobacco Co.
Norfolk, Va.
American Tobacco Co.
Osceola, Fla.

8. Names of firms, corporations, and institutions are indexed as written, except where they include the full names of individuals, in which case the surnames are considered first, the Christian names next, the middle initial next, and then the remainder of the title.

Rice, A.
Rice, B., & Co.
Rice, Bernard
Rice and Co.
Rice, Edward and Bros.
Rice, Henry, and Son

9. Names that begin with numbers should be indexed as if spelled out. The numeral is treated as one word.

8th Avenue Bookshop
Fifth Street Church
4th National Bank
7th Avenue Restaurant

10. Abbreviations are alphabetized as though they were spelled out in full.

Indus. Bros. of America
Indus. and Loan Assoc.

11. Hyphenated firm names are treated as separate words.

Oil-O-Matic Heating Company
Oilimatic Heating Company

12. Words that may be spelled either as one word or two words are treated as one word.

North Pole Expedition
North East Grocery Corporation

13. Compound geographic names are always treated as two words.

West Chester
West Milton
Westinghouse

14. Parts of names that are omitted in indexing and filing are the following:
    (A) The article *the,* unless, as indicated above, it occurs in a foreign name.
    (B) Phrases such as *dep't. of, board of,* etc. applied to municipal, state, and federal agencies are placed in parentheses after the words they modify and are disregarded in filing.
    (C) *and, &, of,* abbreviations such as *Jr., 2nd.* Titles or degrees of individuals, except a foreign title with one name and a title forming the first word of a firm name—*Bailey and Allen, Jonson, Ben (Jr.), Peabody, C. W. (Prof.), Prince Henry*
    (D) Apostrophe s ('s) indicating the possessive case.
15. Parts of names that are included in filing are the following:

    Ltd.
    Inc.
    Co.
    Son
    Bros.
    Mfg.
    Corp.

    When abbreviated, these words are treated as though spelled in full and as though they were first names.
16. Institutions or societies beginning with a first name should be filed under the surname with the first name following.

    Franklin, Benjamin, Hotel
    Hopkins, Johns, University
    Gibbs, Katharine, School
    Sage, Russell, College
    Roosevelt, Theodore, High School

Geographical Filing

When geographical filing is employed, the matter to be filed is grouped first according to states; then according to cities or towns; and last, according to alphabetic arrangement of names of correspondents in each city or town.

This method of filing is used when there is a need to keep material from particular localities in one place. Thus, a firm sponsoring a radio program might wish to keep together all letters of criticism from individual states so that the feeling of a state might be the more easily gauged. To facilitate the use of a geographical file, an alphabetic card file is kept, so that letters from a particular correspondent may be located even if the correspondent's address has been forgotten.

Numerical Filing

This method is less popular now than it used to be. Its greatest use is in courts and professional offices where it is desirable to have a quick indication as to when a case was received. Numbers are assigned to cases as they come in. Thus, a later case will receive a higher number. An alphabetic card index is kept, and by looking up the name of the case, one obtains the number. The cases are filed in numerical order, so it is a simple matter to find one if the number is known.

If letters are to be filed numerically, then a number is assigned to each correspondent with whom the firm does business. Any letter that comes in is placed in the folder assigned to the correspondent. As the firm acquires new correspondents, new numbers are assigned. Unless the clerk knows all of the numbers by heart, he/she must consult the card index each time he/she wants to file or find a letter. This makes the system rather cumbersome. It is useful where two or three cases may be filed under the same name, and it is necessary to make a quick distinction between the cases. If three cases—167, 1169, 1584—have been filed against one man in a court, it is quickly apparent that cases 1169 and 1584 have been filed later than 167; and when the number is used in referring to each case, the clerk knows immediately which one is meant.

Subject Filing

This method is used in cases where there is a large volume of correspondence on many subjects between a small number of people. The main difficulty lies in building up a logical, inclusive, and consistent subject classification and adhering to it strictly. Supervision over the subject of filing is usually placed in the hands of a responsible person who reads each letter and writes on it the subject under which it is to be filed.

Answer Sheet for Filing Practice Tests

Test 1

1 Ⓐ Ⓑ Ⓒ Ⓓ Ⓔ   11 Ⓐ Ⓑ Ⓒ Ⓓ Ⓔ   21 Ⓐ Ⓑ Ⓒ Ⓓ Ⓔ
2 Ⓐ Ⓑ Ⓒ Ⓓ Ⓔ   12 Ⓐ Ⓑ Ⓒ Ⓓ Ⓔ   22 Ⓐ Ⓑ Ⓒ Ⓓ Ⓔ
3 Ⓐ Ⓑ Ⓒ Ⓓ Ⓔ   13 Ⓐ Ⓑ Ⓒ Ⓓ Ⓔ   23 Ⓐ Ⓑ Ⓒ Ⓓ Ⓔ
4 Ⓐ Ⓑ Ⓒ Ⓓ Ⓔ   14 Ⓐ Ⓑ Ⓒ Ⓓ Ⓔ   24 Ⓐ Ⓑ Ⓒ Ⓓ Ⓔ
5 Ⓐ Ⓑ Ⓒ Ⓓ Ⓔ   15 Ⓐ Ⓑ Ⓒ Ⓓ Ⓔ   25 Ⓐ Ⓑ Ⓒ Ⓓ Ⓔ
6 Ⓐ Ⓑ Ⓒ Ⓓ Ⓔ   16 Ⓐ Ⓑ Ⓒ Ⓓ Ⓔ   26 Ⓐ Ⓑ Ⓒ Ⓓ Ⓔ
7 Ⓐ Ⓑ Ⓒ Ⓓ Ⓔ   17 Ⓐ Ⓑ Ⓒ Ⓓ Ⓔ   27 Ⓐ Ⓑ Ⓒ Ⓓ Ⓔ
8 Ⓐ Ⓑ Ⓒ Ⓓ Ⓔ   18 Ⓐ Ⓑ Ⓒ Ⓓ Ⓔ   28 Ⓐ Ⓑ Ⓒ Ⓓ Ⓔ
9 Ⓐ Ⓑ Ⓒ Ⓓ Ⓔ   19 Ⓐ Ⓑ Ⓒ Ⓓ Ⓔ   29 Ⓐ Ⓑ Ⓒ Ⓓ Ⓔ
10 Ⓐ Ⓑ Ⓒ Ⓓ Ⓔ   20 Ⓐ Ⓑ Ⓒ Ⓓ Ⓔ   30 Ⓐ Ⓑ Ⓒ Ⓓ Ⓔ

Test 2

1 Ⓐ Ⓑ Ⓒ Ⓓ   11 Ⓐ Ⓑ Ⓒ Ⓓ   21 Ⓐ Ⓑ Ⓒ Ⓓ
2 Ⓐ Ⓑ Ⓒ Ⓓ   12 Ⓐ Ⓑ Ⓒ Ⓓ   22 Ⓐ Ⓑ Ⓒ Ⓓ
3 Ⓐ Ⓑ Ⓒ Ⓓ   13 Ⓐ Ⓑ Ⓒ Ⓓ   23 Ⓐ Ⓑ Ⓒ Ⓓ
4 Ⓐ Ⓑ Ⓒ Ⓓ   14 Ⓐ Ⓑ Ⓒ Ⓓ   24 Ⓐ Ⓑ Ⓒ Ⓓ
5 Ⓐ Ⓑ Ⓒ Ⓓ   15 Ⓐ Ⓑ Ⓒ Ⓓ   25 Ⓐ Ⓑ Ⓒ Ⓓ
6 Ⓐ Ⓑ Ⓒ Ⓓ   16 Ⓐ Ⓑ Ⓒ Ⓓ   26 Ⓐ Ⓑ Ⓒ Ⓓ
7 Ⓐ Ⓑ Ⓒ Ⓓ   17 Ⓐ Ⓑ Ⓒ Ⓓ   27 Ⓐ Ⓑ Ⓒ Ⓓ
8 Ⓐ Ⓑ Ⓒ Ⓓ   18 Ⓐ Ⓑ Ⓒ Ⓓ   28 Ⓐ Ⓑ Ⓒ Ⓓ
9 Ⓐ Ⓑ Ⓒ Ⓓ   19 Ⓐ Ⓑ Ⓒ Ⓓ   29 Ⓐ Ⓑ Ⓒ Ⓓ
10 Ⓐ Ⓑ Ⓒ Ⓓ   20 Ⓐ Ⓑ Ⓒ Ⓓ   30 Ⓐ Ⓑ Ⓒ Ⓓ

Test 3

1 Ⓐ Ⓑ Ⓒ Ⓓ   12 Ⓐ Ⓑ Ⓒ Ⓓ   23 Ⓐ Ⓑ Ⓒ Ⓓ   33 Ⓐ Ⓑ Ⓒ Ⓓ
2 Ⓐ Ⓑ Ⓒ Ⓓ   13 Ⓐ Ⓑ Ⓒ Ⓓ   24 Ⓐ Ⓑ Ⓒ Ⓓ   34 Ⓐ Ⓑ Ⓒ Ⓓ
3 Ⓐ Ⓑ Ⓒ Ⓓ   14 Ⓐ Ⓑ Ⓒ Ⓓ   25 Ⓐ Ⓑ Ⓒ Ⓓ   35 Ⓐ Ⓑ Ⓒ Ⓓ
4 Ⓐ Ⓑ Ⓒ Ⓓ   15 Ⓐ Ⓑ Ⓒ Ⓓ   26 Ⓐ Ⓑ Ⓒ Ⓓ   36 Ⓐ Ⓑ Ⓒ Ⓓ
5 Ⓐ Ⓑ Ⓒ Ⓓ   16 Ⓐ Ⓑ Ⓒ Ⓓ   27 Ⓐ Ⓑ Ⓒ Ⓓ   37 Ⓐ Ⓑ Ⓒ Ⓓ
6 Ⓐ Ⓑ Ⓒ Ⓓ   17 Ⓐ Ⓑ Ⓒ Ⓓ   28 Ⓐ Ⓑ Ⓒ Ⓓ   38 Ⓐ Ⓑ Ⓒ Ⓓ
7 Ⓐ Ⓑ Ⓒ Ⓓ   18 Ⓐ Ⓑ Ⓒ Ⓓ   29 Ⓐ Ⓑ Ⓒ Ⓓ   39 Ⓐ Ⓑ Ⓒ Ⓓ
8 Ⓐ Ⓑ Ⓒ Ⓓ   19 Ⓐ Ⓑ Ⓒ Ⓓ   30 Ⓐ Ⓑ Ⓒ Ⓓ   40 Ⓐ Ⓑ Ⓒ Ⓓ
9 Ⓐ Ⓑ Ⓒ Ⓓ   20 Ⓐ Ⓑ Ⓒ Ⓓ   31 Ⓐ Ⓑ Ⓒ Ⓓ   41 Ⓐ Ⓑ Ⓒ Ⓓ
10 Ⓐ Ⓑ Ⓒ Ⓓ   21 Ⓐ Ⓑ Ⓒ Ⓓ   32 Ⓐ Ⓑ Ⓒ Ⓓ   42 Ⓐ Ⓑ Ⓒ Ⓓ
11 Ⓐ Ⓑ Ⓒ Ⓓ   22 Ⓐ Ⓑ Ⓒ Ⓓ

Test 4

1 Ⓐ Ⓑ Ⓒ Ⓓ Ⓔ	11 Ⓐ Ⓑ Ⓒ Ⓓ Ⓔ	21 Ⓐ Ⓑ Ⓒ Ⓓ Ⓔ	31 Ⓐ Ⓑ Ⓒ Ⓓ Ⓔ
2 Ⓐ Ⓑ Ⓒ Ⓓ Ⓔ	12 Ⓐ Ⓑ Ⓒ Ⓓ Ⓔ	22 Ⓐ Ⓑ Ⓒ Ⓓ Ⓔ	32 Ⓐ Ⓑ Ⓒ Ⓓ Ⓔ
3 Ⓐ Ⓑ Ⓒ Ⓓ Ⓔ	13 Ⓐ Ⓑ Ⓒ Ⓓ Ⓔ	23 Ⓐ Ⓑ Ⓒ Ⓓ Ⓔ	33 Ⓐ Ⓑ Ⓒ Ⓓ Ⓔ
4 Ⓐ Ⓑ Ⓒ Ⓓ Ⓔ	14 Ⓐ Ⓑ Ⓒ Ⓓ Ⓔ	24 Ⓐ Ⓑ Ⓒ Ⓓ Ⓔ	34 Ⓐ Ⓑ Ⓒ Ⓓ Ⓔ
5 Ⓐ Ⓑ Ⓒ Ⓓ Ⓔ	15 Ⓐ Ⓑ Ⓒ Ⓓ Ⓔ	25 Ⓐ Ⓑ Ⓒ Ⓓ Ⓔ	35 Ⓐ Ⓑ Ⓒ Ⓓ Ⓔ
6 Ⓐ Ⓑ Ⓒ Ⓓ Ⓔ	16 Ⓐ Ⓑ Ⓒ Ⓓ Ⓔ	26 Ⓐ Ⓑ Ⓒ Ⓓ Ⓔ	36 Ⓐ Ⓑ Ⓒ Ⓓ Ⓔ
7 Ⓐ Ⓑ Ⓒ Ⓓ Ⓔ	17 Ⓐ Ⓑ Ⓒ Ⓓ Ⓔ	27 Ⓐ Ⓑ Ⓒ Ⓓ Ⓔ	37 Ⓐ Ⓑ Ⓒ Ⓓ Ⓔ
8 Ⓐ Ⓑ Ⓒ Ⓓ Ⓔ	18 Ⓐ Ⓑ Ⓒ Ⓓ Ⓔ	28 Ⓐ Ⓑ Ⓒ Ⓓ Ⓔ	38 Ⓐ Ⓑ Ⓒ Ⓓ Ⓔ
9 Ⓐ Ⓑ Ⓒ Ⓓ Ⓔ	19 Ⓐ Ⓑ Ⓒ Ⓓ Ⓔ	29 Ⓐ Ⓑ Ⓒ Ⓓ Ⓔ	39 Ⓐ Ⓑ Ⓒ Ⓓ Ⓔ
10 Ⓐ Ⓑ Ⓒ Ⓓ Ⓔ	20 Ⓐ Ⓑ Ⓒ Ⓓ Ⓔ	30 Ⓐ Ⓑ Ⓒ Ⓓ Ⓔ	40 Ⓐ Ⓑ Ⓒ Ⓓ Ⓔ

Test 1

TIME: 30 minutes. 30 questions.

DIRECTIONS: In each of the following questions there is a name enclosed in a box, and a series of four other names in proper alphabetic order. The spaces between the names are lettered (A), (B), (C), (D), and (E). Decide where the boxed name belongs in proper alphabetic order in that series, then blacken the capital letter of your choice on your answer sheet.

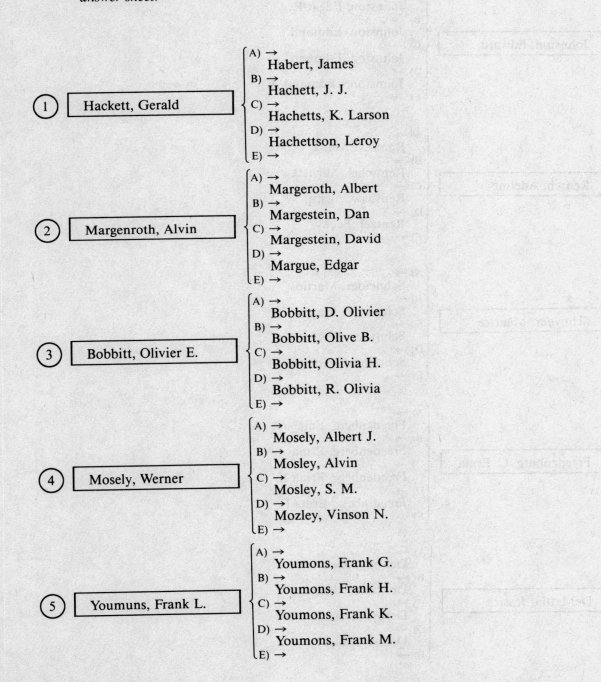

1. Hackett, Gerald
- A) →
- Habert, James
- B) →
- Hachett, J. J.
- C) →
- Hachetts, K. Larson
- D) →
- Hachettson, Leroy
- E) →

2. Margenroth, Alvin
- A) →
- Margeroth, Albert
- B) →
- Margestein, Dan
- C) →
- Margestein, David
- D) →
- Margue, Edgar
- E) →

3. Bobbitt, Olivier E.
- A) →
- Bobbitt, D. Olivier
- B) →
- Bobbitt, Olive B.
- C) →
- Bobbitt, Olivia H.
- D) →
- Bobbitt, R. Olivia
- E) →

4. Mosely, Werner
- A) →
- Mosely, Albert J.
- B) →
- Mosley, Alvin
- C) →
- Mosley, S. M.
- D) →
- Mozley, Vinson N.
- E) →

5. Youmuns, Frank L.
- A) →
- Youmons, Frank G.
- B) →
- Youmons, Frank H.
- C) →
- Youmons, Frank K.
- D) →
- Youmons, Frank M.
- E) →

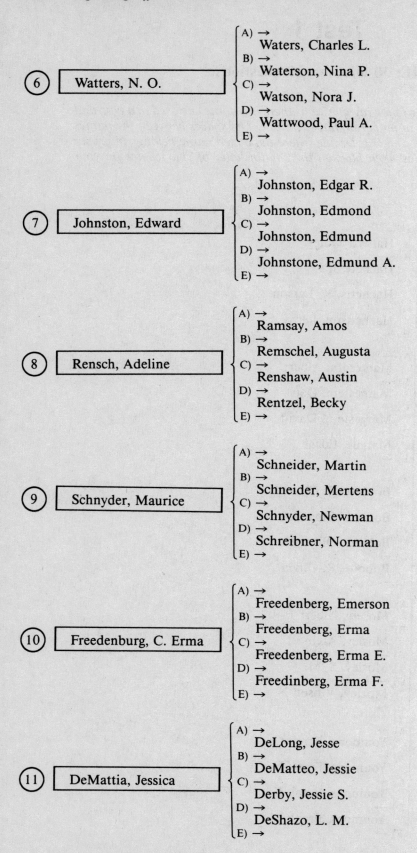

6 Watters, N. O.
A) →
Waters, Charles L.
B) →
Waterson, Nina P.
C) →
Watson, Nora J.
D) →
Wattwood, Paul A.
E) →

7 Johnston, Edward
A) →
Johnston, Edgar R.
B) →
Johnston, Edmond
C) →
Johnston, Edmund
D) →
Johnstone, Edmund A.
E) →

8 Rensch, Adeline
A) →
Ramsay, Amos
B) →
Remschel, Augusta
C) →
Renshaw, Austin
D) →
Rentzel, Becky
E) →

9 Schnyder, Maurice
A) →
Schneider, Martin
B) →
Schneider, Mertens
C) →
Schnyder, Newman
D) →
Schreibner, Norman
E) →

10 Freedenburg, C. Erma
A) →
Freedenberg, Emerson
B) →
Freedenberg, Erma
C) →
Freedenberg, Erma E.
D) →
Freedinberg, Erma F.
E) →

11 DeMattia, Jessica
A) →
DeLong, Jesse
B) →
DeMatteo, Jessie
C) →
Derby, Jessie S.
D) →
DeShazo, L. M.
E) →

(12) | Theriault, Louis

- A) →
  Therien, Annette
- B) →
  Therien, Elaine
- C) →
  Thibeault, Gerald
- D) →
  Thiebeault, Pierre
- E) →

(13) | Gaston, M. Hubert

- A) →
  Gaston, Dorothy M.
- B) →
  Gaston, Henry N.
- C) →
  Gaston, Isabel
- D) →
  Gaston, M. Melvin
- E) →

(14) | SanMiguel, Carlos

- A) →
  SanLuis, Juana
- B) →
  Santilli, Laura
- C) →
  Stinnett, Nellie
- D) →
  Stoddard, Victor
- E) →

(15) | DeLaTour, Hall F.

- A) →
  Delargy, Harold
- B) →
  DeLathouder, Hilda
- C) →
  Lathrop, Hillary
- D) →
  LaTour, Hulbert E.
- E) →

(16) | O'Bannon, M. J.

- A) →
  O'Beirne, B. B.
- B) →
  Oberlin, E. L.
- C) →
  Oberneir, L. P.
- D) →
  O'Brian, S. F.
- E) →

(17) | Entsminger, Jacob

- A) →
  Ensminger, J.
- B) →
  Entsminger, J. A.
- C) →
  Entsminger, Jack
- D) →
  Entsminger, James
- E) →

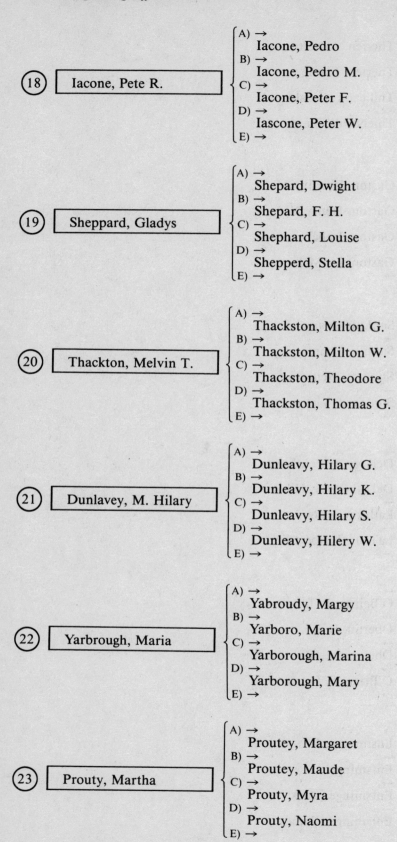

(18) Iacone, Pete R.

A) →
  Iacone, Pedro
B) →
  Iacone, Pedro M.
C) →
  Iacone, Peter F.
D) →
  Iascone, Peter W.
E) →

(19) Sheppard, Gladys

A) →
  Shepard, Dwight
B) →
  Shepard, F. H.
C) →
  Shephard, Louise
D) →
  Shepperd, Stella
E) →

(20) Thackton, Melvin T.

A) →
  Thackston, Milton G.
B) →
  Thackston, Milton W.
C) →
  Thackston, Theodore
D) →
  Thackston, Thomas G.
E) →

(21) Dunlavey, M. Hilary

A) →
  Dunleavy, Hilary G.
B) →
  Dunleavy, Hilary K.
C) →
  Dunleavy, Hilary S.
D) →
  Dunleavy, Hilery W.
E) →

(22) Yarbrough, Maria

A) →
  Yabroudy, Margy
B) →
  Yarboro, Marie
C) →
  Yarborough, Marina
D) →
  Yarborough, Mary
E) →

(23) Prouty, Martha

A) →
  Proutey, Margaret
B) →
  Proutey, Maude
C) →
  Prouty, Myra
D) →
  Prouty, Naomi
E) →

24 Pawlowicz, Ruth M.
- A) →
  Pawalek, Edward
- B) →
  Pawelek, Flora G.
- C) →
  Pawlowski, Joan M.
- D) →
  Pawtowski, Wanda
- E) →

25 Vanstory, George
- A) →
  Vanover, Eva
- B) →
  VanSwinderen, Floyd
- C) →
  VanSyckle, Harry
- D) →
  Vanture, Laurence
- E) →

26 Fitzsimmons, Hugh
- A) →
  Fitts, Harold
- B) →
  Fitzgerald, June
- C) →
  FitzGibbon, Junius
- D) →
  FitzSimons, Martin
- E) →

27 D'Amato, Vincent
- A) →
  Daly, Steven
- B) →
  D'Amboise, S. Vincent
- C) →
  Daniel, Vail
- D) →
  DeAlba, Valentina
- E) →

28 Schaeffer, Roger D.
- A) →
  Schaffert, Evelyn M.
- B) →
  Schaffner, Margaret M.
- C) →
  Schafhirt, Milton G.
- D) →
  Shafer, Richard E.
- E) →

29 White-Lewis, Cecil
- A) →
  Whitelaw, Cordelia
- B) →
  White-Leigh, Nancy
- C) →
  Whitely, Rodney
- D) →
  Whitlock, Warren
- E) →

(30) | VanDerHeggen, Don |

A) →

VanDemark, Doris

B) →

Vandenberg, H. E.

C) →

VanDercook, Marie

D) →

vanderLinden, Robert

E) →

Test 2

TIME: 30 minutes. 30 questions.

DIRECTIONS: *Each of the following exercises consists of a capitalized word that is to be filed correctly. Indicate the word* **before** *which the capitalized word should be filed by blackening the letter preceding that word on your sheet.*
In the following example the correct answer is (B).

Example
HARMONY
(A) Growth (B) Hegemony (C) Holdout (D) Indicator

1. BIOGRAPHY:
   (A) Bible (B) Bibliography (C) Bilge (D) Biology

2. DRAMA:
   (A) Drawing (B) Drayton (C) Dreyfus (D) Drugs

3. INQUISITION:
   (A) Industry (B) Insurance (C) International (D) Interne

4. LUGUBRIOUS:
   (A) Lucretius (B) Lumber (C) Luther (D) Lutheran

5. OCEANIC:
   (A) Occult (B) Ohio (C) Oklahoma (D) Optics

6. ENGLAND:
   (A) Engineering (B) English (C) Engraving (D) Entomology

7. IRRIGATION:
   (A) Ireland (B) Irish (C) Iron (D) Irving

8. MARINE:
   (A) Margolin (B) Marketing (C) Mary (D) Maryland

9. PALEONTOLOGY:
   (A) Pacific (B) Painting (C) Palestine (D) Paltry

10. ASIATIC:
    (A) Ascetic (B) Assyriology (C) Astronomy (D) Astrophysics

11. ENTOMOLOGY:
    (A) Endocrine (B) Erasmus (C) Eskimo (D) Etching

12. GREAT BRITAIN:

    (A) Grant   (B) Greece   (C) Greek   (D) Greeley

13. JAPAN:

    (A) Jackson   (B) James   (C) Japanese   (D) Java

14. MENUS:

    (A) Melville   (B) Mennonites   (C) Merchandising   (D) Meredith

15. PEDAGOGY:

    (A) Peace   (B) Pediatrics   (C) Penman   (D) Penology

16. ARCHIVES:

    (A) Archaeology   (B) Architecture   (C) Arctic   (D) Arkansas

17. HAGIOGRAPHY:

    (A) Hamilton   (B) Hardy   (C) Hawaiiana   (D) Hays

18. LEGEND:

    (A) Legacy   (B) Legal   (C) Legislation   (D) Legislative

19. METALLURGY:

    (A) Metal   (B) Mete   (C) Meteorology   (D) Methodist

20. PHILIPPINE:

    (A) Philately   (B) Philology   (C) Philosopher   (D) Philosophy

21. MONTAIGNE:

    (A) Monastic   (B) Money   (C) Montana   (D) Mountain

22. LANGUAGES:

    (A) Land   (B) Landscape   (C) Lanier   (D) Lantern

23. ANATOMY:

    (A) Anabaptistica   (B) Anarchism   (C) Annuals   (D) Anthropology

24. CONFEDERATE:

    (A) Congregational   (B) Connecticut   (C) Conrad   (D) Contamination

25. FOOD:

    (A) Florida   (B) Folklore   (C) Foreign   (D) Forestry

26. LITERATURE:

    (A) Lincoln   (B) Lithograph   (C) Lithuanian   (D) Liturgy

27. MICROSCOPY:

    (A) Michigan   (B) Middle   (C) Military   (D) Milton

28. PHYSICS:

    (A) Physiocrat   (B) Physical   (C) Physician   (D) Psychical

29. CATHOLIC:

    (A) Catacombs   (B) Catalogs   (C) Catechisms   (D) Cattle

30. FRANCE:

    (A) Franciscan   (B) Franklin   (C) Fraternity   (D) Free

Test 3

TIME: 12 minutes. 42 questions.

DIRECTIONS: For each of the following questions, select the choice that best answers the question or completes the statement.

1. The system of filing most generally used is the

   (A) alphabetic file
   (B) geographic file
   (C) numeric file
   (D) Dewey decimal classification

2. When filing papers that are to be held together, the best procedure to follow is to

   (A) clip the papers together before filing
   (B) staple the papers together before filing
   (C) tear the corners of the papers and hold them together by turning down the torn corners
   (D) pin the papers together

3. Everyone should know something about filing in order to

   (A) become a file clerk
   (B) write checks
   (C) find information readily
   (D) make out an income tax blank

4. Indexing information under two or more headings is called

   (A) out-charging
   (B) transferring
   (C) cross-referencing
   (D) sorting

5. The marking of a letter to show how it is to be filed is called

   (A) sorting   (B) filing   (C) coding   (D) transferring

6. A letter from the Brooklyn Home for Children marked "The first of next month" should be placed in a

   (A) subject file   (B) follow-up file   (C) geographic file   (D) numeric file

7. A good file clerk allows no paper to be removed from the file unless replaced by

   (A) an out-card
   (B) an expansion folder
   (C) a cross-reference card
   (D) a tab folder

8. If a letter from the Better Printing Co. of N.Y.C. has the word *Printing* underlined, the letter is to be filed by the

(A) alphabetic method
(B) numeric method
(C) subject method
(D) geographic method

9. Names in the classified telephone directory are first arranged according to

(A) alphabetic filing
(B) occupation or business
(C) location
(D) numerical filing

10. Confusion regarding the exact location of certain papers missing from files can probably best be avoided by

(A) using colored tabs
(B) using the Dewey Decimal System
(C) making files available to few persons
(D) consistently using "out" guides

11. When correspondence is to be filed according to both subject matter and the name of the writer, the file clerk should prepare

(A) a double file
(B) a tickler
(C) an index of names and subject matter
(D) a cross-reference sheet

12. Generally speaking, the best arrangement of folder tabs, for easy location of material in the files, is

(A) staggered from left to right
(B) zigzagged in alternate positions
(C) staggered from right to left
(D) placed in one center position, one tab directly behind the other

13. In filing, a requisition card is

(A) a card showing where material related to a subject may be located under another title
(B) a card or form recording material requested to be taken from the files, identifying its location
(C) a card of a different color from the other cards in the file, flagging a matter needing attention
(D) a card in an alphabetic file, giving the index to the numbers in a numeric file

14. A *tickler file* is used chiefly for

(A) unsorted papers that the file clerk has not had time to file
(B) personnel records
(C) pending matters that should receive attention at some particular time
(D) index to cross-referenced material

15. The papers in a filing folder are arranged with the most recently dated one in front, and a clerk has been instructed to arrange them according to date in a binder but with the paper of most recent date at the back. The most efficient of the following methods that the clerk might use in performing this task is to

(A) begin at the back of the folder and remove the papers in groups of convenient size for binding, laying each group face down on top of the group pulled just before

(B) begin at the back of the folder and pull the papers one by one, laying each paper face up on top of the one pulled just before

(C) begin at the front of the folder and pull the papers one by one, laying each paper face up on top of the one pulled just before

(D) begin at the front of the folder and pull the papers one by one, laying each paper face down on top of the one pulled just before

16. Of the following, for which reason are cross-references necessary in filing?

(A) There is a choice of terms under which the correspondence may be filed.

(B) The only filing information contained in the correspondence is the name of the writer

(C) Records are immediately visible without searching through the files

(D) Persons other than file clerks can easily locate material

17. In filing terminology, coding means

(A) making a preliminary arrangement of names according to caption before bringing them together in final order of arrangement

(B) reading correspondence and determining the proper caption under which it is to be filed

(C) marking a card or paper with symbols or other means of identification to indicate where it is to be placed in the files according to a predetermined plan

(D) placing a card or paper in the files showing where correspondence may be located under another name or title

18. Of the following, which practice is undesirable in the operation of files?

(A) handling guides by sides instead of tabs

(B) mending torn papers before placing them in the files

(C) using clips for fastening papers belonging together

(D) placing headings of papers to the left, face forward in the file drawer

19. Of the following, in which situation would the subject filing system furnish an advantage?

(A) Speed is required in preparing material for the files

(B) Only inexperienced file clerks are available

(C) All the papers relating to a given topic or transaction are usually wanted at the same time

(D) It is considered undesirable to keep an index to the files

20. Of the following, which statement presents the only *disadvantage* in maintaining a central file department?

(A) The elimination of duplicate copies of the original correspondence is effected

(B) One person has sole responsibility for the records

(C) Elimination of doubt as to the place of filing material of interest to several bureaus is effected

(D) The variety of needs of different bureaus calls for different arrangements of records

21. In alphabetic filing the first of the names to be filed is

(A) Book & Co.   (B) Book and Son   (C) Brook and Co.   (D) The Brook Co.

22. In alphabetic filing the last of the names to file is

    (A) G. Jones   (B) George T. Jones   (C) David A. Jones   (D) George Jones

23. The name filed first is

    (A) 520 West 18th St. Corp.
    (B) 400 West 208 St., Corp.
    (C) The Howard Publishing Co.
    (D) New York Realty Corp.

24. Dr. John J. Hood should be indexed as

    (A) Hood J. John (Dr.)
    (B) John J. Hood (Dr.)
    (C) Hood, John J. (Dr.)
    (D) Dr. John J. Hood

25. The name Board of Education, Philadelphia, should be filed as

    (A) Philadelphia, Education, Board of
    (B) Board of Education, Philadelphia
    (C) Education, Board of, Philadelphia
    (D) Philadelphia, Board of Education

26. Dr. L. Carlton Brown should be indexed as

    (A) Carlton L. Brown (Dr.)
    (B) Brown, L. Carlton (Dr.)
    (C) Brown, Carlton, L. (Dr.)
    (D) Dr. L. Carlton Brown

27. Of the following which statement of a numeric system of filing is true?

    (A) It renders a more rapid location of papers than an alphabetic system
    (B) It must be limited to a given number of digits
    (C) It is more applicable to filing by firm names than by subject matter
    (D) It necessitates an alphabetic card index to operate it

28. The correct alphabetical filing order of the following names is

    (A) Sanford, C.M.; Sanford, Charles B.; St. John, Philip
    (B) Sanford, Charles B.; Sanford, C. M.; St. John, Philip
    (C) St. John, Philip; Sanford, C. M.; Sanford, Charles B.
    (D) St. John, Philip; Sanford, Charles B.; Sanford, C. M.

29. In alphabetic filing the name filed first is

    (A) Mrs. O. Bradon (B) Dr. O. Brandon (C) A. Brandon (D) Prof. P. Bradon

30. In alphabetic filing the name filed last is

    (A) John Eton   (B) J. Allen Gould   (C) J. A. Gould   (D) J. B. Clinton

31. In subject filing (alphabetic by subject) the name filed first is

    (A) The Howard Publishing Co.
    (B) The Elliot Book Co.
    (C) Faber Camera Co.
    (D) Greater Auto Co.

32. In alphabetical filing, abbreviations such as "Wm." or "Chas." are

   (A) disregarded entirely
   (B) treated as if spelled out
   (C) disregarded except for first letter
   (D) placed in parentheses and disregarded

33. The correct alphabetical filing order of the following names is

   (A) Burns Hat Company, Chicago, Ill.; Burns Hat Company, New Haven, Conn.; Burns Community Shops
   (B) Burns Hat Company, New Haven, Conn.; Burns Hat Company, Chicago, Ill.; Burns Community Shops
   (C) Burns Community Shops; Burns Hat Company, New Haven, Conn.; Burns Hat Company, Chicago, Ill.
   (D) Burns Community Shops; Burns Hat Company, Chicago, Ill.; Burns Hat Company, New Haven, Conn.

34. A new file clerk who has not become thoroughly familiar with the files is unable to locate "McLeod" in the correspondence files under "Mc" and asks your help. Of the following, the best reply to give her is that

   (A) there probably is no correspondence in the files for that person
   (B) she probably has the name spelled wrong and should verify the spelling
   (C) she will probably find the correspondence under "MacLeod" as the files are arranged with the prefix "Mc" considered as "Mac" (as if the name were spelled "MacLeod")
   (D) the correspondence folder for "McLeod" has evidently been misplaced or borrowed from the files

35. Of the following, which procedure would most likely result in the efficient operation of a filing system?

   (A) permitting access to the files by employees other than file clerks
   (B) permitting personal conversation among file clerks while filing papers
   (C) noting papers taken from the files for quick reference but not removed from the file room
   (D) using shortcuts obtained by time and motion studies

36. Of the following, which statement is false?

   (A) An advantage of using a card record system is that flexibility is permitted by the insertion of cards for new records or the transferring of cards of existing records
   (B) In planning the installation of a filing system, the most effective procedure is to select the filing equipment first and then adapt the filing system to the equipment
   (C) When it is necessary to use a comparatively inexperienced assistant in a large file room, it is better practice to have him/her remove records from the file rather than to file them
   (D) Papers misfiled often may be found in the folder preceding or following the one in which they belong

Four Methods of Filing

(A) Name   (B) Subject   (C) Geographic   (D) Numeric

DIRECTIONS: Questions 37–42 list seven filing situations that a clerk may meet. On the basis of the information contained in the above box write, in the proper place to the right of each situation: (A) if you would file the letter by name; (B) if you would file the letter by subject; (C) if you would file the letter by the use of a geographic scheme; (D) if you would file the letter by the use of a numeric scheme.

37. Mr. Jones has written a letter to the Department of Docks, where you are employed.

38. The U.S. Employment Service has requested in writing information concerning Mr. John J. Smith.

39. An anonymous letter is sent asking that traffic lights be erected on a certain avenue.

40. The department in which you are employed has written a letter to a Mr. Isaac Stein.

41. A letter is received by a certain company from a Mr. Reilly, one of its representatives in a certain city. This company has a tremendous turnover in the personnel of its representatives and has representatives in each of 273 cities, which are located so as to cover the country completely.

42. A letter is received from a certain company stating that a very high grade of bond paper is available at a low price. The offices of this company are located in Westchester County. The organization for which you are employed already possesses files labeled "desks, typewriters."

Test 4

TIME: 13 minutes. 40 questions.

DIRECTIONS: One of the five classes of employment, lettered (A) to (E), may be applied to each of the individuals listed below. Place on the answer sheet the capital letter of the class in which that name may best be placed.

Class of Work

(A) Clerical   (B) Educational   (C) Professional   (D) Mechanical   (E) Art

Name and Occupation

1.	John M. Devine	Stenographer
2.	G. D. Wahl	Lawyer
3.	Harry B. Allen	Typewriter repairman
4.	M. C. Walton	Elevator maintainer
5.	Lewis E. Reigner	Typist
6.	John G. Cook	Electrician
7.	H. B. Allen	Civil engineer
8.	Walter E. Jenkins	Physician
9.	Clifford H. Wrenn	Telephone operator
10.	H. A. Schwartz	Plumber
11.	Harry Gruber	Locksmith
12.	Ely Fairbanks	Sculptor
13.	Abraham Hohing	Radio repairman
14.	Samuel Tapft	Laundry driver
15.	William M. Murray	Advertising layout person
16.	Hyman E. Oral	Motion picture operator
17.	L. A. Kurtz	Director of a nursery school
18.	Richard H. Hunter	Painter of miniatures
19.	Lewis F. Kosch	Saxophone player
20.	Marion L. Young	Assistant director of a university extension program
21.	Karl W. Hisgen	Printer
22.	E. T. Williams	Administrative Assistant
23.	H. B. Enderton	Mechanical Engineer
24.	Robert F. Hallock	Proofreader
25.	Joseph L. Hardin	Dentist
26.	E. B. Gjelsteen	Chemist
27.	Carter B. Magruder	Coppersmith
28.	Wilber R. Pierce	Flutist
29.	Russell G. Smith	Carpenter
30.	Wilber S. Nye	Singer
31.	David Larr	Instructor in barbering
32.	Oliver M. Barton	Band Leader
33.	E. Oliver Parmly	Word processor
34.	C. Parul Summerall	Blacksmith
35.	Louis Friedersdorff	Research scientist
36.	Daniel E. Healy	Director of worker's education in an industrial union
37.	Howard Kessinger	Player of tympani
38.	John B. Horton	Secretary
39.	Frank S. Kirkpatrick	Supervisor of a filing system
40.	William H. Bertsch	Oil burner Installer

Answer Key For Filing Practice Tests

Test 1

1. E	7. D	13. D	19. D	25. B
2. A	8. C	14. B	20. E	26. D
3. D	9. C	15. C	21. A	27. B
4. B	10. D	16. A	22. E	28. A
5. E	11. C	17. D	23. C	29. C
6. D	12. A	18. C	24. C	30. D

Test 2

1. D	7. D	13. C	19. B	25. C
2. A	8. B	14. C	20. B	26. B
3. B	9. C	15. B	21. C	27. B
4. B	10. B	16. C	22. C	28. A
5. B	11. B	17. A	23. C	29. D
6. B	12. B	18. C	24. A	30. A

Test 3

1. A	7. A	13. B	19. C	25. A	31. D	37. A
2. B	8. C	14. C	20. D	26. B	32. B	38. A
3. C	9. B	15. C	21. A	27. D	33. D	39. B
4. C	10. D	16. A	22. B	28. C	34. C	40. A
5. C	11. D	17. C	23. A	29. A	35. D	41. C
6. B	12. A	18. C	24. C	30. B	36. B	42. B

Test 4

1. A	6. D	11. D	16. D	21. D	26. C	31. B	36. B
2. C	7. C	12. E	17. B	22. A	27. D	32. E	37. E
3. D	8. C	13. D	18. E	23. C	28. E	33. A	38. A
4. D	9. A	14. D	19. E	24. A	29. D	34. D	39. A
5. A	10. D	15. E	20. B	25. C	30. E	35. C	40. D

MATHEMATICS REFRESHER COURSE

Before we begin a systematic discussion of mathematics necessary to Arithmetic Reasoning and Mathematics Knowledge, let us quickly list a few basic rules that must be mastered for speed and accuracy in performing Numerical Operations. You should memorize these rules:

Any number multiplied by 0 = 0.
  $5 \times 0 = 0$.
Zero divided by any number = 0.
  $0 \div 2 = 0$
If 0 is added to any number, that number does not change.
  $7 + 0 = 7$
If 0 is subtracted from any number, that number does not change.
  $4 - 0 = 4$
If a number is multiplied by 1, that number does not change.
  $3 \times 1 = 3$
If a number is divided by 1, that number does not change.
  $6 \div 1 = 6$
A number added to itself is doubled.
  $4 + 4 = 8$
If a number is subtracted from itself, the answer is 0.
  $9 - 9 = 0$
If a number is divided by itself, the answer is 1.
  $8 \div 8 = 1$

If you have memorized these rules, you should be able to write the answers to the questions in the following exercise as fast as you can read the questions.

Exercise 1.

1. $1 - 1 =$
2. $3 \div 1 =$
3. $6 \times 0 =$
4. $6 - 0 =$
5. $0 \div 8 =$
6. $9 \times 1 =$
7. $5 + 0 =$
8. $4 - 0 =$
9. $2 \div 1 =$
10. $7 - 7 =$
11. $8 \times 0 =$
12. $0 \div 4 =$
13. $1 + 0 =$
14. $3 - 0 =$
15. $5 \times 1 =$
16. $9 \div 1 =$
17. $6 + 6 =$
18. $4 - 4 =$
19. $5 \div 5 =$
20. $6 \times 1 =$

The more rules, procedures, and formulas you are able to memorize, the easier it will be to solve mathematical problems on your exam and throughout life. Become thoroughly familiar with the following rules and try to commit to memory as many as possible.

When multiplying a number by 10, 100, 1,000, etc., move the decimal point to the right a number of spaces equal to the number of zeros in the multiplier. If the number being multiplied is a whole number, push the decimal point to the *right* by inserting the appropriate number of zeros.

$$.36 \times 100 = 36.$$
$$1.2 \times 10 = 12.$$
$$5. \times 10 = 50.$$
$$60.423 \times 100 = 6,042.3$$

When dividing a number by 10, 100, 1,000, etc., again count the zeros, but this time move the decimal point to the *left*.

$$123. \div 100 = 1.23$$
$$352.9 \div 10 = 35.28$$
$$16. \div 100 = .16$$
$$7. \div 1,000 = .007$$

Exercise 2.

1. $18 \times 10 =$
2. $5 \div 100 =$
3. $1.3 \times 1,000 =$
4. $3.62 \times 10 =$
5. $9.86 \div 10 =$

6. $.12 \div 100 =$
7. $4.5 \times 10 =$
8. $83.28 \div 1,000 =$
9. $761 \times 100 =$
10. $68.86 \div 10 =$

When adding or subtracting decimals, it is most important to keep the decimal points in line. Once the decimal points are aligned, proceed with the problem in exactly the same way as with whole numbers, simply maintaining the location of the decimal point.

```
    36.08            If you find it easier,        036.0800
   745.              you may fill in the           745.0000
 +   4.362           spaces with zeros.          + 004.3620
    58.6             The answer will be            058.6000
      .0061          unchanged.                    000.0061
   --------                                        --------
   844.0481                                         844.0481

    82.1                                82.100
 -   7.928                            -  7.928
   --------                            --------
    74.172                               74.172
```

Exercise 3.

1. $1.52 + .389 + 42.9 =$
2. $.6831 + .01 + 4.26 + 98 =$
3. $84 - 1.9 =$
4. $3.25 + 5.66 + 9.1 =$
5. $17 - 12.81 =$
6. $46.33 - 12.1 =$

7. $51 + 7.86 + 42.003 =$
8. $35.4 - 18.21 =$
9. $.85 - .16 =$
10. $7.6 + .32 + 830 =$

When multiplying decimals, you can ignore the decimal points until you reach the product. Then the placement of the decimal point is dependent on the sum of the places to the right of the decimal point in both the multiplier and number being multiplied.

$$
\begin{array}{r}
1.482 \text{ (3 places to right of decimal point)} \\
\times \quad .16 \text{ (2 places to right of decimal point)} \\
\hline
8892 \\
14820 \\
\hline
.23712 \text{ (5 places to right of decimal point)}
\end{array}
$$

You cannot divide by a decimal. If the divisor is a decimal, you must move the decimal point to the right until the divisor becomes a whole number, an integer. Count the number of spaces by which you moved the decimal point to the right and move the decimal point in the dividend (the number being divided) the same number of spaces to the right. The decimal point in the answer should be directly above the decimal point in the dividend.

$$
\begin{array}{r}
70.2 \text{ Decimal point moves two spaces} \\
.06\overline{)4.21\ 2} \text{ to the right.}
\end{array}
$$

Exercise 4.

1. $3.62 \times 5.6 =$
2. $92 \times .11 =$
3. $18 \div .3 =$
4. $1.5 \times .9 =$
5. $7.55 \div 5 =$

6. $6.42 \div 2.14 =$
7. $12.01 \times 3 =$
8. $24.82 \div 7.3 =$
9. $.486 \div .2 =$
10. $.21 \times 12 =$

When fractions are to be added or subtracted they must have the same denominator, a *common denominator*. The common denominator is a number into which the denominators of all the fractions in the problem can be divided without a remainder. The common denominator of ⅜, ⅚, ¼, and ⅔ is 24. If you want to add these fractions, they must all be converted to fractions with the denominator 24. Convert each fraction by dividing 24 by the denominator and multiplying the numerator by the quotient.

$$\frac{3}{8} = \frac{(24 \div 8) \times 3}{24} = \frac{3 \times 3}{24} = \frac{9}{24}$$

$$\frac{5}{6} = \frac{(24 \div 6) \times 5}{24} = \frac{4 \times 5}{24} = \frac{20}{24}$$

$$\frac{1}{4} = \frac{(24 \div 4) \times 1}{24} = \frac{6 \times 1}{24} = \frac{6}{24}$$

$$\frac{2}{3} = \frac{(24 \div 3) \times 2}{24} = \frac{8 \times 2}{24} = \frac{16}{24}$$

Now you can add the fractions:

$$\frac{3}{8} = \frac{9}{24}$$

$$\frac{5}{6} = \frac{20}{24}$$

$$\frac{1}{4} = \frac{6}{24}$$

$$\frac{2}{3} = \frac{16}{24}$$

$$\frac{51}{24}$$

The answer, $\frac{51}{24}$, is an improper fraction; that is, its numerator is greater than its denominator. To convert the answer to a mixed number, divide the numerator by the denominator and express the remainder as a fraction.

$$\frac{51}{24} = 51 \div 24 = 2\frac{3}{24} = 2\frac{1}{8}$$

Exercise 5. Express your answers as simple mixed numbers.

1. $\frac{2}{3} + \frac{3}{5} + \frac{1}{2} =$ 6. $\frac{1}{2} + \frac{1}{4} + \frac{2}{3} =$

2. $\frac{6}{8} = \frac{2}{4} =$ 7. $\frac{5}{6} - \frac{1}{2} =$

3. $\frac{1}{3} + \frac{1}{2} =$ 8. $\frac{5}{8} - \frac{1}{3} =$

4. $\frac{4}{5} - \frac{3}{5} =$ 9. $\frac{5}{12} + \frac{3}{4} =$

5. $\frac{7}{8} + \frac{3}{4} + \frac{1}{3} =$ 10. $\frac{8}{9} - \frac{2}{3} =$

When multiplying fractions, multiply numerators by numerators and denominators by denominators.

$$\frac{3}{5} \cdot \frac{4}{7} \cdot \frac{1}{5} = \frac{3 \times 4 \times 1}{5 \times 7 \times 5} = \frac{12}{175}$$

In multiplying fractions, try to work with numbers that are as small as possible. You can make numbers smaller by *canceling*. Cancel by dividing the numerator of any one fraction and the denominator of any one fraction by the same number.

$$\frac{\overset{1}{\cancel{3}}}{\underset{2}{\cancel{4}}} \cdot \frac{\overset{1}{\cancel{2}}}{\underset{3}{\cancel{9}}} = \frac{1 \times 1}{2 \times 3} = \frac{1}{6}$$

In this case the numerator of the first fraction and the denominator of the other fraction were divided by 3, while the denominator of the first fraction and the numerator of the other fraction were divided by 2.

To divide by a fraction, invert the fraction following the division sign and multiply.

$$\frac{3}{16} \div \frac{1}{8} = \frac{3}{\cancel{10}_{2}} \times \frac{\cancel{8}^{1}}{1} = \frac{3}{2} = 1\frac{1}{2}$$

Exercise 6. Cancel wherever possible and express your answer in the simplest terms possible.

1. $\frac{4}{5} \cdot \frac{3}{6} =$

2. $\frac{2}{4} \cdot \frac{8}{12} \cdot \frac{7}{1} =$

3. $\frac{3}{4} \div \frac{3}{8} =$

4. $\frac{5}{2} \div \frac{3}{6} =$

5. $\frac{8}{9} \cdot \frac{3}{4} \cdot \frac{1}{2} =$

6. $\frac{7}{8} \div \frac{2}{3} =$

7. $\frac{4}{6} \cdot \frac{8}{12} \cdot \frac{10}{3} =$

8. $\frac{1}{6} \cdot \frac{7}{6} \cdot \frac{12}{3} =$

9. $\frac{3}{7} \div \frac{9}{4} =$

10. $\frac{2}{3} \div \frac{2}{3} =$

The line in a fraction means "divided by." To change a fraction to a decimal follow through on the division.

$$\frac{4}{5} = 4 \div 5 = .8$$

To change a decimal to a percent, move the decimal point two places to the right and add a percent sign.

$$.8 = 80\%$$

Exercise 7. Change each fraction first to a decimal to three places and then to a percent.

1. $\frac{2}{4}$

2. $\frac{7}{8}$

3. $\frac{5}{6}$

4. $\frac{6}{8}$

5. $\frac{3}{4}$

6. $\frac{2}{3}$

7. $\frac{3}{5}$

8. $\frac{4}{10}$

9. $\frac{1}{4}$

10. $\frac{2}{5}$

To find a percent of a number, change the percent to a decimal and multiply the number by it.

$$5\% \text{ of } 80 = 80 \times .05 = 4$$

To find out what a number is when a percent of it is given, change the percent to a decimal and divide the given number by it.

5 is 10% of what number?

$$5 \div .10 = 50$$

To find what percent one number is of another number, create a fraction by putting the part over the whole. Reduce the fraction if possible, then convert it to a decimal (remember: the line means *divide by,* so divide the numerator by the denominator) and change to a percent by multiplying by 100, moving the decimal point two places to the right.

4 is what percent of 80?

$$\frac{4}{80} = \frac{1}{20} = .05 = 5\%$$

Exercise 8.

1. 10% of 32 =
2. 8 is 25% of what number?
3. 12 is what percent of 24?
4. 20% of 360 is
5. 5 is what percent of 60?
6. 12 is 8% of what number?
7. 6% of 36 =
8. 25 is 5% of what number?
9. 70 is what percent of 140?
10. What percent of 100 is 19?

An equation is an equality. The values on either side of the equal sign in an equation must be equal. In order to learn the value of an unknown in an equation, do the same thing to both sides of the equation so as to leave the unknown on one side of the equal sign and its value on the other side.

$$X - 2 = 8$$

Add 2 to both sides of the equation.

$$X - 2 + 2 = 8 + 2; \ X = 10$$
$$5X = 25$$

Divide both sides of the equation by 5.

$$\frac{\overset{1}{\cancel{5}}X}{\underset{1}{\cancel{5}}} = \frac{25}{5}; \ X = 5$$

$$Y + 9 = 15$$

Subtract 9 from both sides of the equation.

$$Y + 9 - 9 = 15 - 9; Y = 6$$
$$A \div 4 = 48$$

Multiply both sides of the equation by 4.

$$\frac{\overset{1}{\cancel{4}A}}{\underset{1}{\cancel{4}}} = 48 \times 4; A = 192$$

Sometimes more than one step is required to solve an equation.

$$6A \div 4 = 48$$

First, multiply both sides of the equation by 4.

$$\frac{6A}{\underset{1}{\cancel{4}}} \times \frac{\overset{1}{\cancel{4}}}{1} = 48 \times 4; 6A = 192$$

Then divide both sides of the equation by 6.

$$\frac{\overset{1}{\cancel{6}A}}{\underset{1}{\cancel{6}}} = \frac{192}{6}; A = 32$$

Exercise 9. Solve for X.

1. $X + 13 = 25$
2. $4X = 84$
3. $X - 5 = 28$
4. $X \div 9 = 4$
5. $3X + 2 = 14$
6. $\frac{X}{4} - 2 = 4$
7. $10X - 27 = 73$
8. $2X \div 4 = 13$
9. $8X + 9 = 81$
10. $2X \div 11 = 6$

Answers to Math Refresher Course Exercises

Exercise 1

1. 0
2. 3
3. 0
4. 6
5. 0
6. 9
7. 5
8. 4
9. 2
10. 0

11. 0
12. 0
13. 1
14. 3
15. 5
16. 9
17. 12
18. 0
19. 1
20. 6

Exercise 2

1. 180
2. .05
3. 1,300
4. 36.2
5. .986

6. .0012
7. 45
8. .08328
9. 76,100
10. 6.886

Exercise 3

1. 44.809
2. 102.9531
3. 82.1
4. 18.01
5. 4.19

6. 34.23
7. 100.863
8. 17.19
9. .69
10. 837.92

Exercise 4

1. 20.272
2. 10.12
3. 60
4. 1.35
5. 1.51

6. 3
7. 36.03
8. 3.4
9. 2.43
10. 2.52

Exercise 5

1. $\frac{32}{20} = 1\frac{12}{20} = 1\frac{3}{5}$

2. $\frac{2}{8} = \frac{1}{4}$

3. $\frac{5}{6}$

4. $\frac{1}{5}$

5. $\frac{47}{24} = 1\frac{23}{24}$

6. $\frac{17}{12} = 1\frac{5}{12}$

7. $\frac{2}{6} = \frac{1}{3}$

8. $\frac{7}{24}$

9. $\frac{14}{12} = 1\frac{2}{12} = 1\frac{1}{6}$

10. $\frac{2}{9}$

Exercise 6

1. $\frac{2}{5}$

2. $2\frac{1}{3}$

3. 2

4. $\frac{15}{3} = 5$

5. $\frac{1}{3}$

6. $\frac{21}{16} = 1\frac{5}{16}$

7. $1\frac{13}{27}$

8. $\frac{7}{9}$

9. $\frac{4}{21}$

10. 1

Exercise 7

1. $.50 = 50\%$

2. $.875 = 87\frac{1}{2}\%$

3. $.833 = 83\frac{1}{3}\%$

4. $.75 = 75\%$

5. $.75 = 75\%$

6. $.666 = 66\frac{2}{3}\%$

7. $.60 = 60\%$

8. $.40 = 40\%$

9. $.25 = 25\%$

10. $.40 = 40\%$

Exercise 8

1. $32 \times .10 = 3.2$

2. $8 \div .25 = 32$

3. $\frac{12}{24} = \frac{1}{2} = .50 = 50\%$

4. $360 \times .20 = 72$

5. $\frac{5}{60} = \frac{1}{12} = .0833 = 8\frac{1}{3}\%$

6. $12 \div .08 = 150$

7. $36 \times .06 = 2.16$

8. $25 \div .05 = 500$

9. $\frac{70}{140} = \frac{1}{2} = .50 = 50\%$

10. $\frac{19}{100} = .19 = 19\%$

Exercise 9

1. $X = 12$
2. $X = 21$
3. $X = 33$
4. $X = 36$
5. $X = 4$

6. $X = 24$
7. $X = 10$
8. $X = 26$
9. $X = 9$
10. $X = 33$

ARITHMETIC COMPUTATIONS

To add valuable points to your exam score you must master arithmetical computations. And by this we mean doing them quickly and with absolute accuracy. The computations themselves will be simple, although the form in which they are presented may rattle you if you're not prepared. In addition to calculation, they measure your ability to interpret and act on directions. Thus this chapter provides practice through a series of tests modeled on the different question types that have actually appeared on examinations. An important tip from our years of experience with the self-tutored test-taker: Study the Directions! We have included those you are most likely to meet on your exam. Control over them will gain precious minutes for you. This doesn't mean you can skip reading directions on your actual exam. It does mean that you will be ahead of the game for knowing the language examiners use. Then you can afford to play it cool. A misunderstood direction can lead to a run of incorrect answers. Avoid this costly carelessness.

To Score High on Math Tests

1. *Schedule your study.* Set a definite time, and stick to it. Enter Arithmetic Computations on your study schedule.
2. *Plan* on taking different types of Computation Tests in each study period. Keep alert to the differences and complications. That will help keep you bright and interested.
3. *Do your best* and work fast to complete each test before looking at our Correct Answers. Keep pushing yourself.
4. *Record* time taken for each test next to your score. Your schedule may allow you to take the tests again. And you may want to see how your speed and accuracy have improved.
5. *Review your errors.* This is a must for every study session. Allow time for redoing every incorrect answer. The good self-tutor is a good self-critic. He learns most from his mistakes. And never makes them again.
6. *Don't guess at answers.* Because each practice test, like the actual examination, requires a multiple-choice answer, you might be tempted to pick up speed by approximating the answers. This is fatal. Carefully work out your answer to each question. Then choose the right answer. Any other way is certain to create confusion, slow you down, lower your score.
7. *Clarity & order.* Write all your figures clearly, in neat rows and columns. And this includes the figures you have to carry over from one column to another. Don't make mistakes because of lack of space and cramped writing. Use scratch paper wherever necessary.
8. *Skip the puzzlers.* If a single question gives you an unusual amount of trouble, go on to the next question. Come back to the tough one after you have done all the others, and still have time left.
9. *Study the sample solutions.* Note how carefully we have worked out each step. Get into this habit in doing all the practice tests. You'll quickly find that it's a time-saver . . . a high-scoring habit.

Sample Questions and Detailed Solutions

DIRECTIONS: Each question has five suggested answers lettered (A), (B), (C), (D), and (E). Suggested answer (E) is NONE OF THESE. Blacken space E only if your answer for a question does not exactly agree with any of the first four suggested answers. When you have finished the two questions, compare your answers with the correct answers.

Example 1:

Divide:

$$4.6\overline{)233.404}$$

(A) 50.74
(B) 52.24
(C) 57.30
(D) 58.24
(E) None of these

SOLUTION I.

$$
\begin{array}{r}
50.74 \\
4.6\overline{)233.404} \\
\underline{230} \\
3\ 40 \\
\underline{3\ 22} \\
184 \\
\underline{184} \\
\end{array}
$$

Since the answer is clearly 50.74, blacken A on the answer sheet. Do not mark any of the other letter choices. There is only one correct answer.

Example 2:

Multiply:

$$
\begin{array}{r}
2946 \\
\times\ 7.007 \\
\end{array}
$$

(A) 21,642.622
(B) 20,642.622
(C) 41,244.001
(D) 20,641.622
(E) None of these

SOLUTION II.

$$
\begin{array}{r}
2946 \\
\times\ 7.007 \\
\hline
20\ 622 \\
00\ 00 \\
000\ 0 \\
20\ 622 \\
\hline
20{,}642.622 \\
\end{array}
$$

The answer is 20,642.622, which is answer choice (B). This answer is similar to answer choices (A) and (D), but it is not the same. So you must be careful not to let the (A) and (D) choices confuse you. Blacken only B on your answer sheet.

Example 3:

A certain kind of stencil can be bought for 20 cents each or in packages of 12 for $2. How much more would it cost to buy 240 stencils singly than to buy them in the 12-stencil packages?

(A) $0.40
(B) $8
(C) $40
(D) $48
(E) none of these

SOLUTION III.

"How *much more* would it cost to buy 240 stencils singly than to buy them in the 12-stencil packages?" asks the question, and you are given clues to work with. The first step is to figure the cost of both methods and find the difference. Buying 240 stencils singly at 20 cents each would cost $48 ($0.20 × 240 = $48). Buying the stencils in packages of 12 would mean buying 20 packages (240 ÷ 12 = 20); at $2 a package they would cost $40 ($2 × 20 = $40). The difference is $8 ($48 − $40 = $8), and the answer is B.

Answer Sheet For Arithmetic Computations Practice Tests

Test 1

1 Ⓐ Ⓑ	11 Ⓐ Ⓑ	21 Ⓐ Ⓑ	31 Ⓐ Ⓑ	41 Ⓐ Ⓑ
2 Ⓐ Ⓑ	12 Ⓐ Ⓑ	22 Ⓐ Ⓑ	32 Ⓐ Ⓑ	42 Ⓐ Ⓑ
3 Ⓐ Ⓑ	13 Ⓐ Ⓑ	23 Ⓐ Ⓑ	33 Ⓐ Ⓑ	43 Ⓐ Ⓑ
4 Ⓐ Ⓑ	14 Ⓐ Ⓑ	24 Ⓐ Ⓑ	34 Ⓐ Ⓑ	44 Ⓐ Ⓑ
5 Ⓐ Ⓑ	15 Ⓐ Ⓑ	25 Ⓐ Ⓑ	35 Ⓐ Ⓑ	45 Ⓐ Ⓑ
6 Ⓐ Ⓑ	16 Ⓐ Ⓑ	26 Ⓐ Ⓑ	36 Ⓐ Ⓑ	46 Ⓐ Ⓑ
7 Ⓐ Ⓑ	17 Ⓐ Ⓑ	27 Ⓐ Ⓑ	37 Ⓐ Ⓑ	47 Ⓐ Ⓑ
8 Ⓐ Ⓑ	18 Ⓐ Ⓑ	28 Ⓐ Ⓑ	38 Ⓐ Ⓑ	48 Ⓐ Ⓑ
9 Ⓐ Ⓑ	19 Ⓐ Ⓑ	29 Ⓐ Ⓑ	39 Ⓐ Ⓑ	49 Ⓐ Ⓑ
10 Ⓐ Ⓑ	20 Ⓐ Ⓑ	30 Ⓐ Ⓑ	40 Ⓐ Ⓑ	50 Ⓐ Ⓑ

Test 2

1 Ⓐ Ⓑ	21 Ⓐ Ⓑ	41 Ⓐ Ⓑ	61 Ⓐ Ⓑ
2 Ⓐ Ⓑ	22 Ⓐ Ⓑ	42 Ⓐ Ⓑ	62 Ⓐ Ⓑ
3 Ⓐ Ⓑ	23 Ⓐ Ⓑ	43 Ⓐ Ⓑ	63 Ⓐ Ⓑ
4 Ⓐ Ⓑ	24 Ⓐ Ⓑ	44 Ⓐ Ⓑ	64 Ⓐ Ⓑ
5 Ⓐ Ⓑ	25 Ⓐ Ⓑ	45 Ⓐ Ⓑ	65 Ⓐ Ⓑ
6 Ⓐ Ⓑ	26 Ⓐ Ⓑ	46 Ⓐ Ⓑ	66 Ⓐ Ⓑ
7 Ⓐ Ⓑ	27 Ⓐ Ⓑ	47 Ⓐ Ⓑ	67 Ⓐ Ⓑ
8 Ⓐ Ⓑ	28 Ⓐ Ⓑ	48 Ⓐ Ⓑ	68 Ⓐ Ⓑ
9 Ⓐ Ⓑ	29 Ⓐ Ⓑ	49 Ⓐ Ⓑ	69 Ⓐ Ⓑ
10 Ⓐ Ⓑ	30 Ⓐ Ⓑ	50 Ⓐ Ⓑ	70 Ⓐ Ⓑ
11 Ⓐ Ⓑ	31 Ⓐ Ⓑ	51 Ⓐ Ⓑ	71 Ⓐ Ⓑ
12 Ⓐ Ⓑ	32 Ⓐ Ⓑ	52 Ⓐ Ⓑ	72 Ⓐ Ⓑ
13 Ⓐ Ⓑ	33 Ⓐ Ⓑ	53 Ⓐ Ⓑ	73 Ⓐ Ⓑ
14 Ⓐ Ⓑ	34 Ⓐ Ⓑ	54 Ⓐ Ⓑ	74 Ⓐ Ⓑ
15 Ⓐ Ⓑ	35 Ⓐ Ⓑ	55 Ⓐ Ⓑ	75 Ⓐ Ⓑ
16 Ⓐ Ⓑ	36 Ⓐ Ⓑ	56 Ⓐ Ⓑ	76 Ⓐ Ⓑ
17 Ⓐ Ⓑ	37 Ⓐ Ⓑ	57 Ⓐ Ⓑ	77 Ⓐ Ⓑ
18 Ⓐ Ⓑ	38 Ⓐ Ⓑ	58 Ⓐ Ⓑ	78 Ⓐ Ⓑ
19 Ⓐ Ⓑ	39 Ⓐ Ⓑ	59 Ⓐ Ⓑ	79 Ⓐ Ⓑ
20 Ⓐ Ⓑ	40 Ⓐ Ⓑ	60 Ⓐ Ⓑ	80 Ⓐ Ⓑ

Test 3

1 Ⓐ Ⓑ Ⓒ Ⓓ	11 Ⓐ Ⓑ Ⓒ Ⓓ	21 Ⓐ Ⓑ Ⓒ Ⓓ
2 Ⓐ Ⓑ Ⓒ Ⓓ	12 Ⓐ Ⓑ Ⓒ Ⓓ	22 Ⓐ Ⓑ Ⓒ Ⓓ
3 Ⓐ Ⓑ Ⓒ Ⓓ	13 Ⓐ Ⓑ Ⓒ Ⓓ	23 Ⓐ Ⓑ Ⓒ Ⓓ
4 Ⓐ Ⓑ Ⓒ Ⓓ	14 Ⓐ Ⓑ Ⓒ Ⓓ	24 Ⓐ Ⓑ Ⓒ Ⓓ
5 Ⓐ Ⓑ Ⓒ Ⓓ	15 Ⓐ Ⓑ Ⓒ Ⓓ	25 Ⓐ Ⓑ Ⓒ Ⓓ
6 Ⓐ Ⓑ Ⓒ Ⓓ	16 Ⓐ Ⓑ Ⓒ Ⓓ	26 Ⓐ Ⓑ Ⓒ Ⓓ
7 Ⓐ Ⓑ Ⓒ Ⓓ	17 Ⓐ Ⓑ Ⓒ Ⓓ	27 Ⓐ Ⓑ Ⓒ Ⓓ
8 Ⓐ Ⓑ Ⓒ Ⓓ	18 Ⓐ Ⓑ Ⓒ Ⓓ	28 Ⓐ Ⓑ Ⓒ Ⓓ
9 Ⓐ Ⓑ Ⓒ Ⓓ	19 Ⓐ Ⓑ Ⓒ Ⓓ	29 Ⓐ Ⓑ Ⓒ Ⓓ
10 Ⓐ Ⓑ Ⓒ Ⓓ	20 Ⓐ Ⓑ Ⓒ Ⓓ	30 Ⓐ Ⓑ Ⓒ Ⓓ

Test 4

1 Ⓐ Ⓑ Ⓒ Ⓓ	4 Ⓐ Ⓑ Ⓒ Ⓓ	7 Ⓐ Ⓑ Ⓒ Ⓓ	10 Ⓐ Ⓑ Ⓒ Ⓓ
2 Ⓐ Ⓑ Ⓒ Ⓓ	5 Ⓐ Ⓑ Ⓒ Ⓓ	8 Ⓐ Ⓑ Ⓒ Ⓓ	11 Ⓐ Ⓑ Ⓒ Ⓓ
3 Ⓐ Ⓑ Ⓒ Ⓓ	6 Ⓐ Ⓑ Ⓒ Ⓓ	9 Ⓐ Ⓑ Ⓒ Ⓓ	12 Ⓐ Ⓑ Ⓒ Ⓓ

Test 5

1 Ⓐ Ⓑ Ⓒ Ⓓ Ⓔ	7 Ⓐ Ⓑ Ⓒ Ⓓ Ⓔ	13 Ⓐ Ⓑ Ⓒ Ⓓ Ⓔ	19 Ⓐ Ⓑ Ⓒ Ⓓ Ⓔ
2 Ⓐ Ⓑ Ⓒ Ⓓ Ⓔ	8 Ⓐ Ⓑ Ⓒ Ⓓ Ⓔ	14 Ⓐ Ⓑ Ⓒ Ⓓ Ⓔ	20 Ⓐ Ⓑ Ⓒ Ⓓ Ⓔ
3 Ⓐ Ⓑ Ⓒ Ⓓ Ⓔ	9 Ⓐ Ⓑ Ⓒ Ⓓ Ⓔ	15 Ⓐ Ⓑ Ⓒ Ⓓ Ⓔ	21 Ⓐ Ⓑ Ⓒ Ⓓ Ⓔ
4 Ⓐ Ⓑ Ⓒ Ⓓ Ⓔ	10 Ⓐ Ⓑ Ⓒ Ⓓ Ⓔ	16 Ⓐ Ⓑ Ⓒ Ⓓ Ⓔ	22 Ⓐ Ⓑ Ⓒ Ⓓ Ⓔ
5 Ⓐ Ⓑ Ⓒ Ⓓ Ⓔ	11 Ⓐ Ⓑ Ⓒ Ⓓ Ⓔ	17 Ⓐ Ⓑ Ⓒ Ⓓ Ⓔ	23 Ⓐ Ⓑ Ⓒ Ⓓ Ⓔ
6 Ⓐ Ⓑ Ⓒ Ⓓ Ⓔ	12 Ⓐ Ⓑ Ⓒ Ⓓ Ⓔ	18 Ⓐ Ⓑ Ⓒ Ⓓ Ⓔ	24 Ⓐ Ⓑ Ⓒ Ⓓ Ⓔ

Test 6

1 Ⓐ Ⓑ Ⓒ Ⓓ Ⓔ	6 Ⓐ Ⓑ Ⓒ Ⓓ Ⓔ	11 Ⓐ Ⓑ Ⓒ Ⓓ Ⓔ	16 Ⓐ Ⓑ Ⓒ Ⓓ Ⓔ
2 Ⓐ Ⓑ Ⓒ Ⓓ Ⓔ	7 Ⓐ Ⓑ Ⓒ Ⓓ Ⓔ	12 Ⓐ Ⓑ Ⓒ Ⓓ Ⓔ	17 Ⓐ Ⓑ Ⓒ Ⓓ Ⓔ
3 Ⓐ Ⓑ Ⓒ Ⓓ Ⓔ	8 Ⓐ Ⓑ Ⓒ Ⓓ Ⓔ	13 Ⓐ Ⓑ Ⓒ Ⓓ Ⓔ	18 Ⓐ Ⓑ Ⓒ Ⓓ Ⓔ
4 Ⓐ Ⓑ Ⓒ Ⓓ Ⓔ	9 Ⓐ Ⓑ Ⓒ Ⓓ Ⓔ	14 Ⓐ Ⓑ Ⓒ Ⓓ Ⓔ	19 Ⓐ Ⓑ Ⓒ Ⓓ Ⓔ
5 Ⓐ Ⓑ Ⓒ Ⓓ Ⓔ	10 Ⓐ Ⓑ Ⓒ Ⓓ Ⓔ	15 Ⓐ Ⓑ Ⓒ Ⓓ Ⓔ	20 Ⓐ Ⓑ Ⓒ Ⓓ Ⓔ

Test 7

1 Ⓐ Ⓑ Ⓒ Ⓓ
2 Ⓐ Ⓑ Ⓒ Ⓓ
3 Ⓐ Ⓑ Ⓒ Ⓓ
4 Ⓐ Ⓑ Ⓒ Ⓓ
5 Ⓐ Ⓑ Ⓒ Ⓓ
6 Ⓐ Ⓑ Ⓒ Ⓓ
7 Ⓐ Ⓑ Ⓒ Ⓓ
8 Ⓐ Ⓑ Ⓒ Ⓓ
9 Ⓐ Ⓑ Ⓒ Ⓓ
10 Ⓐ Ⓑ Ⓒ Ⓓ
11 Ⓐ Ⓑ Ⓒ Ⓓ
12 Ⓐ Ⓑ Ⓒ Ⓓ
13 Ⓐ Ⓑ Ⓒ Ⓓ
14 Ⓐ Ⓑ Ⓒ Ⓓ
15 Ⓐ Ⓑ Ⓒ Ⓓ
16 Ⓐ Ⓑ Ⓒ Ⓓ
17 Ⓐ Ⓑ Ⓒ Ⓓ
18 Ⓐ Ⓑ Ⓒ Ⓓ
19 Ⓐ Ⓑ Ⓒ Ⓓ
20 Ⓐ Ⓑ Ⓒ Ⓓ
21 Ⓐ Ⓑ Ⓒ Ⓓ
22 Ⓐ Ⓑ Ⓒ Ⓓ
23 Ⓐ Ⓑ Ⓒ Ⓓ
24 Ⓐ Ⓑ Ⓒ Ⓓ
25 Ⓐ Ⓑ Ⓒ Ⓓ

26 Ⓐ Ⓑ Ⓒ Ⓓ
27 Ⓐ Ⓑ Ⓒ Ⓓ
28 Ⓐ Ⓑ Ⓒ Ⓓ
29 Ⓐ Ⓑ Ⓒ Ⓓ
30 Ⓐ Ⓑ Ⓒ Ⓓ
31 Ⓐ Ⓑ Ⓒ Ⓓ
32 Ⓐ Ⓑ Ⓒ Ⓓ
33 Ⓐ Ⓑ Ⓒ Ⓓ
34 Ⓐ Ⓑ Ⓒ Ⓓ
35 Ⓐ Ⓑ Ⓒ Ⓓ
36 Ⓐ Ⓑ Ⓒ Ⓓ Ⓔ
37 Ⓐ Ⓑ Ⓒ Ⓓ Ⓔ
38 Ⓐ Ⓑ Ⓒ Ⓓ Ⓔ
39 Ⓐ Ⓑ Ⓒ Ⓓ Ⓔ
40 Ⓐ Ⓑ Ⓒ Ⓓ Ⓔ
41 Ⓐ Ⓑ Ⓒ Ⓓ Ⓔ
42 Ⓐ Ⓑ Ⓒ Ⓓ Ⓔ
43 Ⓐ Ⓑ Ⓒ Ⓓ Ⓔ
44 Ⓐ Ⓑ Ⓒ Ⓓ Ⓔ
45 Ⓐ Ⓑ Ⓒ Ⓓ
46 Ⓐ Ⓑ Ⓒ Ⓓ
47 Ⓐ Ⓑ Ⓒ Ⓓ
48 Ⓐ Ⓑ Ⓒ Ⓓ
49 Ⓐ Ⓑ Ⓒ Ⓓ

50 Ⓐ Ⓑ Ⓒ Ⓓ Ⓔ
51 Ⓐ Ⓑ Ⓒ Ⓓ Ⓔ
52 Ⓐ Ⓑ Ⓒ Ⓓ Ⓔ
53 Ⓐ Ⓑ Ⓒ Ⓓ Ⓔ
54 Ⓐ Ⓑ Ⓒ Ⓓ Ⓔ
55 Ⓐ Ⓑ Ⓒ Ⓓ Ⓔ
56 Ⓐ Ⓑ Ⓒ Ⓓ Ⓔ
57 Ⓐ Ⓑ Ⓒ Ⓓ Ⓔ
58 Ⓐ Ⓑ Ⓒ Ⓓ Ⓔ
59 Ⓐ Ⓑ Ⓒ Ⓓ Ⓔ
60 Ⓐ Ⓑ Ⓒ Ⓓ
61 Ⓐ Ⓑ Ⓒ Ⓓ
62 Ⓐ Ⓑ Ⓒ Ⓓ
63 Ⓐ Ⓑ Ⓒ Ⓓ
64 Ⓐ Ⓑ Ⓒ Ⓓ
65 Ⓐ Ⓑ Ⓒ Ⓓ
66 Ⓐ Ⓑ Ⓒ Ⓓ
67 Ⓐ Ⓑ Ⓒ Ⓓ
68 Ⓐ Ⓑ Ⓒ Ⓓ
69 Ⓐ Ⓑ Ⓒ Ⓓ
70 Ⓐ Ⓑ Ⓒ Ⓓ
71 Ⓐ Ⓑ Ⓒ Ⓓ
72 Ⓐ Ⓑ Ⓒ Ⓓ
73 Ⓐ Ⓑ Ⓒ Ⓓ

Test 1

TIME: 25 minutes. 25 questions.

DIRECTIONS: In this test you are asked to do two of the fundamental operations in arithmetic: addition and multiplication. They are closely related in that multiplication is really a succession of additions. Blacken space A if the given answer is correct. Blacken space B if the answer is incorrect.

MULTIPLICATION   **WORK SPACE**   **ADDITION**   **WORK SPACE**

1) 39 × 7 = 273   2) 73 × 4 = 282

3) 44 × 6 = 264   4) 27 × 2 = 54

5) 94 × 8 = 752   6) 25 × 7 = 185

7) 47 × 3 = 131   8) 36 × 8 = 298

9) 64 × 7 = 448   10) 72 × 9 = 658

11) 13 + 68 + 34 + 25 = 140   12) 56 + 88 + 44 + 19 = 207

13) 89 + 29 + 56 + 36 = 200   14) 48 + 69 + 42 + 26 = 185

15) 13 + 21 + 96 + 47 = 177   16) 85 + 64 + 93 + 79 = 331

17) 38 + 56 + 47 + 21 = 162   18) 75 + 63 + 78 + 47 = 263

19) 40 + 35 + 64 + 68 = 207   20) 26 + 62 + 25 + 37 = 160

MULTIPLICATION

21) 21   22) 16   23) 27
   × 7   × 9   × 4
   157   144   118

24) 39   25) 78   26) 44
   × 3   × 2   × 5
   107   156   220

27) 56   28) 17   29) 21
   × 7   × 8   × 5
   382   146   104

30) 24   31) 28   32) 36
   × 9   × 2   × 3
   216   56   108

33) 45   34) 52   35) 64
   × 4   × 8   × 6
   180   426   374

WORK SPACE

ADDITION

36) 17   37) 17   38) 43
     92   50   85
     11   86   24
   + 46   + 21   + 94
    166   174   256

39) 25   40) 69   41) 91
     92   23   56
     74   53   32
   + 31   + 19   + 35
    232   164   214

42) 12   43) 10   44) 12
     17   94   60
     78   29   63
   + 53   + 27   + 38
    160   170   183

45) 14   46) 31   47) 29
     57   89   56
     21   77   58
   + 13   + 55   + 95
    105   252   228

48) 45   49) 37   50) 56
     37   75   95
     97   49   53
   + 33   + 23   + 77
    222   194   281

Test 2

TIME: 40 minutes. 40 questions.

DIRECTIONS: Subtraction and division are two of the basic operations in arithmetic. This test will help you gain proficiency in both these diminution processes, and thereby in many others. Blacken space A if the given answer is correct. Blacken space B if the answer is incorrect. We suggest that you do all the division problems before going on to subtraction. Although the processes are related, you should be able to work more accurately and quickly if you do the test this way.

SUBTRACTION   **WORK SPACE**   **DIVISION**   **WORK SPACE**

1) $\begin{array}{r} 16 \\ -11 \\ \hline 5 \end{array}$ 2) $\begin{array}{r} 23 \\ -18 \\ \hline 15 \end{array}$

3) $\begin{array}{r} 45 \\ -29 \\ \hline 16 \end{array}$ 4) $\begin{array}{r} 61 \\ -32 \\ \hline 39 \end{array}$

5) $\begin{array}{r} 32 \\ -19 \\ \hline 13 \end{array}$ 6) $\begin{array}{r} 77 \\ -51 \\ \hline 26 \end{array}$

7) $\begin{array}{r} 48 \\ -39 \\ \hline 9 \end{array}$ 8) $\begin{array}{r} 53 \\ -25 \\ \hline 38 \end{array}$

9) $\begin{array}{r} 86 \\ -47 \\ \hline 49 \end{array}$ 10) $\begin{array}{r} 66 \\ -52 \\ \hline 14 \end{array}$

11) $\begin{array}{r} 38 \\ -17 \\ \hline 21 \end{array}$ 12) $\begin{array}{r} 94 \\ -43 \\ \hline 51 \end{array}$

13) $\begin{array}{r} 69 \\ -31 \\ \hline 38 \end{array}$ 14) $\begin{array}{r} 99 \\ -19 \\ \hline 70 \end{array}$

15) $\begin{array}{r} 57 \\ -32 \\ \hline 15 \end{array}$ 16) $\begin{array}{r} 35 \\ -14 \\ \hline 21 \end{array}$

17) $5\overline{)30}$ quotient 6 18) $2\overline{)18}$ quotient 8

19) $5\overline{)25}$ quotient 4 20) $7\overline{)35}$ quotient 5

21) $4\overline{)12}$ quotient 4 22) $8\overline{)24}$ quotient 4

23) $6\overline{)24}$ quotient 4 24) $7\overline{)49}$ quotient 7

25) $4\overline{)32}$ quotient 9 26) $5\overline{)35}$ quotient 7

27) $9\overline{)81}$ quotient 8 28) $7\overline{)42}$ quotient 7

29) $7\overline{)28}$ quotient 4 30) $5\overline{)40}$ quotient 8

31) $8\overline{)16}$ quotient 2 32) $4\overline{)16}$ quotient 3

SUBTRACTION

33) $\begin{array}{r} 61 \\ -19 \\ \hline 42 \end{array}$ 34) $\begin{array}{r} 78 \\ -51 \\ \hline 26 \end{array}$ 35) $\begin{array}{r} 64 \\ -28 \\ \hline 26 \end{array}$

36) $\begin{array}{r} 36 \\ -16 \\ \hline 20 \end{array}$ 37) $\begin{array}{r} 83 \\ -38 \\ \hline 55 \end{array}$ 38) $\begin{array}{r} 43 \\ -12 \\ \hline 31 \end{array}$

39) $\begin{array}{r} 87 \\ -79 \\ \hline 8 \end{array}$ 40) $\begin{array}{r} 55 \\ -31 \\ \hline 23 \end{array}$ 41) $\begin{array}{r} 80 \\ -14 \\ \hline 76 \end{array}$

42) $\begin{array}{r} 93 \\ -40 \\ \hline 53 \end{array}$ 43) $\begin{array}{r} 79 \\ -64 \\ \hline 5 \end{array}$ 44) $\begin{array}{r} 28 \\ -12 \\ \hline 16 \end{array}$

45) $\begin{array}{r} 70 \\ -34 \\ \hline 46 \end{array}$ 46) $\begin{array}{r} 98 \\ -83 \\ \hline 15 \end{array}$ 47) $\begin{array}{r} 69 \\ -37 \\ \hline 42 \end{array}$

48) $\begin{array}{r} 47 \\ -33 \\ \hline 14 \end{array}$ 49) $\begin{array}{r} 60 \\ -49 \\ \hline 11 \end{array}$ 50) $\begin{array}{r} 73 \\ -28 \\ \hline 45 \end{array}$

51) $\begin{array}{r} 21 \\ -16 \\ \hline 4 \end{array}$ 52) $\begin{array}{r} 88 \\ -77 \\ \hline 11 \end{array}$ 53) $\begin{array}{r} 97 \\ -59 \\ \hline 39 \end{array}$

54) $\begin{array}{r} 53 \\ -29 \\ \hline 25 \end{array}$ 55) $\begin{array}{r} 31 \\ -19 \\ \hline 12 \end{array}$ 56) $\begin{array}{r} 77 \\ -49 \\ \hline 28 \end{array}$

WORK SPACE

DIVISION

57) $7\overline{)21}$ = 4   58) $2\overline{)14}$ = 7   59) $7\overline{)56}$ = 8

60) $5\overline{)45}$ = 8   61) $9\overline{)72}$ = 9   62) $7\overline{)14}$ = 2

63) $5\overline{)20}$ = 4   64) $7\overline{)63}$ = 9   65) $3\overline{)12}$ = 4

66) $5\overline{)15}$ = 2   67) $4\overline{)20}$ = 4   68) $9\overline{)63}$ = 7

69) $8\overline{)32}$ = 3   70) $8\overline{)56}$ = 7   71) $4\overline{)24}$ = 6

72) $9\overline{)54}$ = 5   73) $8\overline{)40}$ = 6   74) $4\overline{)28}$ = 7

75) $6\overline{)54}$ = 9   76) $6\overline{)18}$ = 4   77) $8\overline{)48}$ = 7

78) $3\overline{)18}$ = 6   79) $6\overline{)36}$ = 7   80) $9\overline{)27}$ = 4

Test 3

TIME: 30 minutes. 30 questions.

DIRECTIONS The sample arithmetic questions below are similar to the questions on your test. Use the space around each question for figuring. Each question has four suggested answers lettered A, B, C, and D. In most questions, suggested answer D is none of these. Blacken space D only if your answer for such a question does not exactly agree with any of the first three suggested answers.

1. Add:
   285
   946
   + 327

   Answers
   (A) 1,448
   (B) 1,548
   (C) 1,558
   (D) none of these

2. Add:
   456
   973
   + 514

   (A) 1,933
   (B) 2,034
   (C) 2,039
   (D) none of these

3. Subtract:
   704
   − 636

   (A) 68
   (B) 78
   (C) 168
   (D) none of these

4. Subtract:
   685
   − 288

   (A) 307
   (B) 397
   (C) 413
   (D) none of these

5. Multiply:
   378
   × 607

   (A) 25,326
   (B) 169,446
   (C) 229,446
   (D) none of these

6. Multiply:
   587
   × 49

   (A) 28,763
   (B) 28,853
   (C) 28,963
   (D) none of these

7. Divide:

   73)38,544

   (A) 529
   (B) 542
   (C) 543
   (D) none of these

8. Divide:

$$246\overline{)16{,}974}$$

(A) 62.1
(B) 67.9
(C) 69.0
(D) none of
these

9. Add:
7.6 + .85 + 44.0 =

(A) 45.61
(B) 52.45
(C) 601
(D) none of
these

10. Add:
.48 + 2.7 + .009 =

(A) 3.189
(B) 7.59
(C) 84
(D) none of
these

11. Add:
.006 + .05 + .74 =

(A) .7456
(B) .796
(C) 1.84
(D) none of
these

12. Subtract:
85.67 − 63.5 =

(A) 22.62
(B) 25.32
(C) 79.32
(D) none of
these

13. Subtract:
3.64 − .236 =

(A) 2.306
(B) 3.306
(C) 3.404
(D) none of
these

14. Subtract:
74.3 − 6.58 =

(A) 8.5
(B) 67.72
(C) 77.88
(D) none of
these

15. Multiply:
69.27
× .38

(A) 26.3226
(B) 263.226
(C) 2,632.26
(D) none of
these

16. Multiply:
70.4
× 4.55

(A) 6.336
(B) 32.032
(C) 319.320
(D) none of
these

17. Multiply:
    2946
    × 7.007

    (A) 20,642.622
    (B) 22,684.200
    (C) 41,244.000
    (D) none of
         these

18. Divide:

    $.87\overline{)6.438}$

    (A) .74
    (B) 7.4
    (C) 74.0
    (D) none of
         these

19. Divide:

    $4.6\overline{)233.404}$

    (A) 50.74
    (B) 52.24
    (C) 57.30
    (D) none of
         these

20. Divide:

    $.009\overline{)000522}$

    (A) .00058
    (B) .0058
    (C) .058
    (D) none of
         these

21. 39.8 increased by 3% =

    (A) 1.119
    (B) 40.994
    (C) 51.74
    (D) none of
         these

22. 24.7 decreased by 6% =

    (A) 1.482
    (B) 9.88
    (C) 20.6
    (D) none of
         these

23. What is 8% of 4.56?

    (A) .57
    (B) 3.99
    (C) 4.1952
    (D) none of
         these

24. 63% of 637 =

    (A) 10.111
    (B) 57.33
    (C) 401.31
    (D) none of
         these

25. 3.7% of 951 =

    (A) 25.703
    (B) 35.187
    (C) 257.027
    (D) none of
         these

26. $\dfrac{2.0976}{23.0}$

    expressed as a
    percent =

    (A) .0912%
    (B) .912%
    (C) 9.12%
    (D) none of
        these

27. $^{14}/_{32}$, changed to
    a decimal, =

    (A) .4375
    (B) 4.375
    (C) 43.75
    (D) none of
        these

28. What is the sum of

    .941 and $3^{2}/_{5}$,

    written as a
    decimal?

    (A) 4.141
    (B) 4.341
    (C) 4.441
    (D) none of
        these

29. Which of the suggested an-
    swers is the *largest* number?

    (A) $^{195}/_{20}$
    (B) $^{196}/_{98}$
    (C) 5.0025
    (D) .750

30. Which of the suggested an-
    swers is the *smallest*
    number?

    (A) .78
    (B) $^{40}/_{45}$
    (C) .87%
    (D) $^{7}/_{8}$

Test 4

Time: 12 minutes. 12 questions.

DIRECTIONS: Each problem in this test involves a certain amount of logical reasoning and thinking on your part, besides the usual simple computations, to help you in finding the solution. Read each problem carefully and choose the correct answer from choices that follow.

1. Find 5 1/2% of $2,800

    (A) $140   (B) $154   (C) $160   (D) $172

2. Add 10 1/6, 2 7/12, 7 2/3

    (A) 12 1/2   (B) 15 2/3   (C) 18 5/6   (D) 20 5/12

3. Subtract $27.95 from $50

    (A) $22.05   (B) $25.95   (C) $26.05   (D) $27.95

4. Divide 3 3/4 by 2

    (A) 1 3/16   (B) 1 3/4   (C) 1 7/8   (D) 2 5/8

5. Multiply $2.04 by 60.5

    (A) $96.20   (B) $104.40   (C) $114.80   (D) $123.42

6. Divide .768 by .32

    (A) 2.4   (B) 4.9   (C) 6.8   (D) 9.4

7. Add 6 1/2, 8 3/4, 5 1/8

    (A) 18 1/4   (B) 19 1/2   (C) 20 3/8   (D) 21 7/8

8. Subtract 14 2/3 from 56

    (A) 41 1/3   (B) 44 2/3   (C) 46 1/3   (D) 48 2/3

9. Add $124.00, $48.25, $.98, $8.09 and $9.67

    (A) $140.62   (B) $152.81   (C) $188.24   (D) $190.99

10. Find 3 1/3 ÷ 2/3

    (A) 2   (B) 3   (C) 4   (D) 5

11. Divide 2.064 by .24

    (A) 6.9   (B) 8.6   (C) 9.1   (D) 9.9

12. Multiply $1.04 by 8 1/4

    (A) $6.44   (B) $7.39   (C) $8.58   (D) $9.46

Test 5

Time: 24 minutes. 24 questions.

DIRECTIONS: The following arithmetic word problems have been devised to make you think with numbers. In each question, the arithmetic is simple, but the objective is to comprehend what you have to do with the numbers and/or quantities. Read the problem carefully and choose the correct answer from the five choices that follow each question.

1. The fraction 7/16 expressed as a decimal is

   (A) .1120   (B) .4375   (C) .2286   (D) .4850   (E) None of these

2. If .10 is divided by 50, the result is

   (A) .002   (B) .02   (C) .2   (D) 2.   (E) None of these

3. The number 60 is 40% of

   (A) 24   (B) 84   (C) 96   (D) 150   (E) None of these

4. If 3/8 of a number is 96, the number is

   (A) 132   (B) 36   (C) 256   (D) 156   (E) None of these

5. The sum of 637.894, 8352.16, 4.8673 and 301.5 is, most nearly,

   (A) 8989.5   (B) 9021.35   (C) 9294.9   (D) 9296.4   (E) None of these

6. If 30 is divided by .06, the result is

   (A) 5   (B) 50   (C) 500   (D) 5000   (E) None of these

7. The sum of the fractions 1/3, 4/6, 3/4, 1/2, and 1/12 is

   (A) 1/4   (B) 1/3   (C) 1/6   (D) 1 11/12   (E) None of these

8. If 96,934.42 is divided by 53.496, the result is most nearly

   (A) 181   (B) 552   (C) 1819   (D) 5520   (E) None of these

9. If 25% of a number is 48, the number is

   (A) 12   (B) 60   (C) 144   (D) 192   (E) None of these

10. The number 88 is 2/5 of

    (A) 123   (B) 141   (C) 221   (D) 440   (E) None of these

11. If the product of 8.3 multiplied by .42 is subtracted from the product of 156 multiplied by .09, the result is most nearly

    (A) 10.6   (B) 13.7   (C) 17.5   (D) 20.8   (E) None of these

12. Add the following lengths: 4 yards, 2 feet, 3 inches; 4 feet, 11 inches; 6 yards, 8 inches; 6 yards; and give the answer in feet and fractions thereof.

   (A) 39′   (B) 38 1/2′   (C) 38 3/4′   (D) 39 1/4′   (E) None of these

13. What is the net amount of a bill of $428 after a discount of 6% has been allowed?

   (A) $401.10
   (B) $401.23
   (C) $402.32
   (D) $402.23
   (E) None of these

14. What number decreased by 3/7 of itself is equal to 56?

   (A) 97   (B) 100   (C) 96   (D) 91   (E) None of these

15. The length of time from 8:23 A.M. to 2:53 P.M. is

   (A) 6 hours 16 minutes
   (B) 6 hours 30 minutes
   (C) 7 hours 16 minutes
   (D) 6 hours 40 minutes
   (E) None of these

16. The sum of 9/16, 11/32, 15/64 and 1 3/32 is most nearly

   (A) 2.234   (B) 2.134   (C) 2.334   (D) 2.214   (E) None of these

17. At 4 cents each, the cost of 144 fuses would be

   (A) $.48   (B) $5.76   (C) $4.00   (D) $8.00   (E) None of these

18. Milk sells at 42 1/2 cents a quart. The cost of 4 gallons of milk is

   (A) $6.50   (B) $6.60   (C) $6.70   (D) $6.80   (E) None of these

19. The sum of the numbers 38,806, 2,074, 48,761, 9,632, 7,899, 4,628, is

   (A) 111,800   (B) 112,000   (C) 14,900   (D) 111,700   (E) None of these

20. If a piece of wood measuring 4 feet 2 inches is divided into three equal parts, each part is

   (A) 1 foot 4 2/3 inches
   (B) 1 foot 4 inches
   (C) 1 foot 2 1/3 inches
   (D) 1 foot 7/18 inches
   (E) None of these

21. If gaskets are sold at the rate of 3 for 7 cents, then 21 gaskets will cost

   (A) 21 cents   (B) 50 cents   (C) 70 cents   (D) $1.41   (E) None of these

22. A worker receives $36.70 per day. After working 13 days his total earnings should be

    (A) $477.30   (B) $477.20   (C) $477.10   (D) $477.40   (E) None of these

23. 1/7 changed to a two-place decimal is

    (A) .15   (B) 14.29   (C) 15.00   (D) .14   (E) None of these

24. A square has an area of 49 sq. in. The number of inches in its perimeter is

    (A) 7   (B) 28   (C) 14   (D) 98   (E) None of these

Test 6

Time: 20 minutes. 20 questions.

DIRECTIONS: Each problem in this test involves a certain amount of logical reasoning and thinking on your part, besides the usual simple computations, to help you in finding the solution. Read each problem carefully and choose the correct answer from the five choices that follow. Mark E as your answer if none of the suggested answers agrees with your answer.

1. Find the interest on $25,800 for 144 days at 6% per annum. Base your calculations on a 360-day year.

   (A) $619.20   (B) $619.02   (C) $691.02   (D) $691.20   (E) None of these

2. A court clerk estimates that the untried cases on the docket will occupy the court for 150 trial days. If new cases are accumulating at the rate of 1.6 trial days per day (Saturday and Sunday excluded) and the court sits 5 days a week, how many days' business will remain to be heard at the end of 60 trial days?

   (A) 168 trial days
   (B) 185 trial days
   (C) 188 trial days
   (D) 186 trial days
   (E) None of these

3. The visitors section of a courtroom seats 105 people. The court is in session 6 hours of the day. On one particular day 486 people visited the court and were given seats. What is the average length of time spent by each visitor in the court? Assume that as soon as a person leaves his seat it is immediately filled and that at no time during the day is one of the 105 seats vacant. Express your answer in hours and minutes.

   (A) 1 hr. 20 min.
   (B) 1 hr. 18 min.
   (C) 1 hr. 30 min
   (D) 2 hr.
   (E) None of these

4. If paper costs $2.92 per ream and 5% discount is allowed for cash, how many reams can be purchased for $138.70 cash? Do not discard fractional part of a cent in your calculations.

   (A) 49 reams
   (B) 60 reams
   (C) 50 reams
   (D) 53 reams
   (E) None of these

5. How much time is there between 8:30 a.m. today and 3:15 a.m. tomorrow.

   (A) 17 3/4 hrs.
   (B) 18 hrs.
   (C) 18 2/3 hrs.

(D) 18 1/2 hrs.
(E) None of these

6. How many days are there between September 19th and December 25th, both inclusive?

(A) 98 days   (B) 96 days   (C) 89 days   (D) 90 days   (E) None of these

7. A clerk is requested to file 800 cards. If he can file cards at the rate of 80 cards an hour, the number of cards remaining to be filed after 7 hours of work is

(A) 40   (B) 250   (C) 140   (D) 260   (E) None of these

8. An officer's weekly salary is increased from $200.00 to $225.00. The percent of increase is

(A) 10%   (B) 11 1/9%   (C) 12 1/2%   (D) 14 1/7%   (E) None of these

9. If there are 245 sections in the city, the average number of sections for each of the 5 boroughs is

(A) 50 sections
(B) 49 sections
(C) 47 sections
(D) 59 sections
(E) None of these

10. If a section had 45 miles of street to plow after a snowstorm and 9 plows are used, each plow would cover an average of how many miles?

(A) 7 miles   (B) 6 miles   (C) 8 miles   (D) 5 miles   (E) None of these

11. If a crosswalk plow engine is run 5 minutes a day for 10 days in a given month, it would run how long in the course of this month?

(A) 50 min.   (B) 1 1/2 hr.   (C) 1 hrs.   (D) 30 min.   (E) None of these

12. If the department uses 1,500 men in manual street cleaning and half as many more to load and drive trucks, the total number used is

(A) 2200 men
(B) 2520 men
(C) 2050 men
(D) 2250 men
(E) None of these

13. If an inspector issued 186 summonses in the course of 7 hours, his hourly average of summonses issued was

(A) 23 summonses
(B) 26 summonses
(C) 25 summonses
(D) 28 summonses
(E) None of these

14. If, of 186 summonses issued, one hundred were issued to first offenders, then there were how many summonses issued to other than first offenders?

(A) 68   (B) 90   (C) 86   (D) 108   (E) None of these

15. A truck going at a rate of 20 miles an hour will reach a town 40 miles away in how many hours?

    (A) 3 hrs.   (B) 1 hrs.   (C) 4 hr.   (D) 5 hrs.   (E) None of these

16. If a barrel has a capacity of 100 gallons, it will contain how many gallons when it is two-fifths full?

    (A) 20 gal.   (B) 60 gal.   (C) 40 gal.   (D) 80 gal.   (E) None of these

17. If a salary of $12,000 is subject to a 20 percent deduction, the net salary is

    (A) $8,000   (B) $9,600   (C) $10,000   (D) $10,400   (E) None of these

18. If $1,000 is the cost of repairing 100 square yards of pavement, the cost of repairing one square yard is

    (A) $10   (B) $150   (C) $100   (D) $300   (E) None of these

19. If a man's base pay is $9000 and it is increased by a bonus of $1050 and a seniority increment of $750, his total salary is

    (A) $10,800   (B) $10,500   (C) $9,000   (D) $11,100   (E) None of these

20. If an annual salary of $8640 is increased by a bonus of $2880 and by a service increment of $480, the total pay rate is

    (A) $11,840   (B) $15,840   (C) $10,760   (D) $12,000   (E) None of these

Test 7

Time: 1 1/2 hours. 73 questions.

DIRECTIONS: The questions on this test have been scientifically designed to demonstrate all the tricks and difficulties you may encounter on your test. Try to work quickly and accurately. Each question is followed by four or five suggested answers. Blacken the capital letter preceding your answer choice on your answer sheet.

1. A real estate dealer buys a house and lot for $44,000. He pays $1,250 for painting, $1,750 for plumbing, and $1,000 for grading and walks. At what price must he sell the property to make a profit of 12 1/2%?

   (A) $60,000 (B) $54,000 (C) $56,000 (D) $58,000

2. An automobile cost $12,000. It depreciated in value 45% the first year, 20% of the reduced value the second year, and 20% of the second reduced value the third year. What was it worth at the end of the third year?

   (A) $4250 (B) $4328 (C) $1800 (D) $4224

3. If the income of a certain city is $6,950,000, and .018¢ of each dollar is expended for parks, libraries, and museums, the total amount spent for parks, libraries, and museums will be

   (A) $25,795 (B) $135,795 (C) $125,000 (D) $12,579

4. A desk has a marked price of $100. Discounts of 20% and 25% are allowed. The dealer's profit is 30% of the selling price, and his cost of doing business is 10% of the selling price. What is the cost of the desk to the dealer?

   (A) $40 (B) $50 (C) $24 (D) $36

5. What is the sum of 8 1/3, 4/5, 5 1/4, and 4 3/8?

   (A) 18 91/120 (B) 17 91/120 (C) 18 17/24 (D) 17 5/24

6. If 1/3 gallon of milk is added to 4/5 gallon, how many quarts of milk will there be?

   (A) 4 2/15 qts. (B) 4 1/30 qts. (C) 4 8/15 qts. (D) 4 3/5 qts.

7. A man invests $500 at the rate of 6%. How much interest is due him at the end of 3 years and 60 days? (Consider a year as 360 days.)

   (A) $125 (B) $105 (C) $85 (D) $95

8. A mortgage on a house in the amount of $4,000 provides for quarterly payments of $200 plus interest on the unpaid balance at 4 1/2%. The total second payment to be made is

   (A) $371 (B) $285.50 (C) $242.75 (D) $240.00

9. A man borrowed $1,200 at 6% on June 1, 1979; on September 25, 1980, he paid the note in full with interest. What was the amount of payment made? (Consider a month as 30 days.)

   (A) $1,295.40 (B) $1,289.55 (C) $1,298.35 (D) $1,295.00

10. A certain property is assessed at $55,000, and the tax rate is $4.85 per $1,000. What is the amount of the tax to be paid on this property?

    (A) $256.75   (B) $276.75   (C) $286.75   (D) $266.75

11. $120,000 worth of land is assessed at 115% of its value. If the tax rate is $2.80 per $1,000, the amount of tax to be paid is

    (A) $384.60   (B) $386.40   (C) $368.80   (D) $384.25

12. Blocks of real estate in a certain area are assessed at $20,000 each. The tax rate is 90¢ per $500. What amount of tax is due on each block?

    (A) $54.00   (B) $48.00   (C) $36.00   (D) $28.00

13. The number of cubic feet of soil it takes to fill a flower box 3 ft. long, 8 in. wide, and 1 ft. deep is

    (A) 2   (B) 4 2/3   (C) 12   (D) 24

14. If a man can get 1/3 bushel of berries per cubic foot, how many bushels can he get into a box measuring 5 ft. square by 1 ft. deep?

    (A) 5   (B) 9 1/2   (C) 9 1/3   (D) 8 1/3

15. A carton is 10 ft. long, 4 ft. wide, and 6 in. deep. When packed with machine parts, the carton weighs 60 lbs. How many pounds of machine parts can be packed into a cubic foot of the carton?

    (A) 10   (B) 3   (C) 6   (D) 8

16. A certain highway intersection has had A accidents over a 10-year period, resulting in B deaths. What is the yearly average death rate for the intersection?

    (A) $A + B - 10$ (B) $B/10$ (C) $10 - A/B$ (D) $A/10$

17. A typist can address approximately R envelopes in a 7-hour day. A list containing S addresses is submitted with a request that all the envelopes be typed within T hours. The number of typists needed to complete this task would be

    (A) $\dfrac{7RS}{T}$ (B) $\dfrac{S}{7RT}$ (C) $\dfrac{R}{7ST}$ (D) $\dfrac{S}{\frac{R}{7} \times T}$

18. Clerk X earns $L per year. Clerk Y earns $R less per month. Both earn yearly increments of $T up to S years. At the end of P years, which is less than S years, the excess of Clerk X's earnings over Clerk Y's will be

    (A) 12PR
    (B) 12P(L minus R)
    (C) 12PT(L plus R)
    (D) P(T plus L minus R)

19. A car traveling a distance of 900 miles averages 50 m.p.h. the first 3 hours of travel, 45 m.p.h. for the 4th and 5th hours, and 40 m.p.h. for the remainder of the trip. How long did it take the car to go 900 miles?

    (A) 16 1/2 hours   (B) 18 1/2 hours   (C) 21 1/2 hours   (D) 23 hours

20. An airplane on a transatlantic flight took 9 hours to get from New York to its destination, a distance of 3,000 miles. To avoid a storm, however, the pilot went

off his course, adding a distance of 200 miles to the flight. How fast did the plane travel?

(A) 349.6 m.p.h.   (B) 326.8 m.p.h.   (C) 332.6 m.p.h.   (D) 355.6 m.p.h.

21. Two cars start toward each other along a road between two cities that are 450 miles apart. The speed of the first car is 35 m.p.h. and that of the second is 48 m.p.h. How much time will elapse before they meet?

(A) 5.42 hours   (B) 6.01 hours   (C) 4.98 hours   (D) 5.25 hours

22. A city pumping station can pump 3,600,000 gallons of water in 24 hours. The pump is operated on an average of 14 hours a day. The population of the city is 15,000. What is the average number of gallons of water pumped every day for each resident of the city?

(A) 145 gals.   (B) 140 gals.   (C) 132 gals.   (D) 1,200 gals.

23. Two men working together can build a cabinet in 2 1/2 days. The first man, working alone, can build the cabinet in 6 days. How long would it take the second man to build the cabinet working alone?

(A) 5 1/7 days   (B) 3 7/8 days   (C) 4 2/7 days   (D) 4 3/10 days

24. One man can load a truck in 25 minutes, a second can load it in 50 minutes, and a third can load it in 10 minutes. How long would it take the three together to load the truck?

(A) 5 3/11 min.   (B) 8 1/3 min.   (C) 6 1/4 min.   (D) 10 min.

25. If 4 typists can type 600 letters in 3 days, how many letters can 2 typists complete in one day?

(A) 100 letters   (B) 120 letters   (C) 90 letters   (D) 150 letters

26. If 12 factory workers produce 120 units in 20 days, how many units can 18 workers produce in 50 days?

(A) 375   (B) 350   (C) 325   (D) 450

27. If 15 workers complete 2,800 work units in 18 days, how many will 8 workers complete in 25 days?

(A) 2,900   (B) 2,074   (C) 1,843   (D) 2,650

28. Population figures for a certain area show there are 1 1/2 times as many single men as single women in the area. Total population is 18,000. There are 1,122 married couples, with 756 children. How many single men are there in the area?

(A) 5,893   (B) 9,874   (C) 3,498   (D) 9,000

29. A dairyman has 4 gallons of milk worth 50¢ a quart. How much water must he add to make it worth 36¢ a quart?

(A) 1.2 gallons   (B) 3.7 quarts   (C) 6.2 quarts   (D) 3 gallons

30. A car dealer sold 3 different makes of cars. The price of the first make was $5,400; the second, $6,600; and the third, $7,800. The income from these sales was $79,200. If the number of each make sold was the same, how many cars were sold?

    (A) 12   (B) 10   (C) 8   (D) 6

31. If it takes 3 men 56 minutes to fill a trench $4' \times 6' \times 5'$, and two of the men work twice as rapidly as the third, the number of minutes that it will take the two faster men alone to fill this trench is

    (A) 70 minutes
    (B) 50 minutes
    (C) 60 minutes
    (D) impossible to determine from the above data

32. Your office wishes to purchase an adding machine. Company X offers you a standard model, less discounts of 10% and 5%. Company Y offers you the same model at the same list price, less discounts of 5% and 10%. Of the two plans, the total discount given by Company X, compared to that given by Company Y, is

    (A) much larger   (B) slightly larger   (C) equal   (D) slightly less

33. The dimensions of an office are 25 feet by 15 feet. It is to be fitted with desks 4 feet by 3 feet. The distance between the front of one desk and the rear of another would be 3 feet, and the distance between the sides of 2 desks should be 4 feet. Assuming that no desk is placed closer than 1 ft. from any wall, the optimum number that can be placed in the office is

    (A) 6   (B) 8   (C) 10   (D) 12

34. Two pieces of meat that together weighed 40 lbs. were sold for the same sum. What did the $1.20 piece weigh if they were worth $1.80 and $1.20 a pound?

    (A) 24   (B) 20   (C) 30   (D) 40

35. How many houses worth $120,000 each can a real estate agent buy for 1,000 bungalows worth $9,000 each?

    (A) 75   (B) 74   (C) 73   (D) 72

36. Suppose that the loss of water pressure in a hose due to friction is uniformly L pounds per square inch for every foot of hose. Of the following, the best estimate of the total loss in terms of pressure per square inch in a hose H feet long is

    (A) H plus L pounds
    (B) H times L pounds
    (C) H divided by L pounds
    (D) L divided by H pounds
    (E) None of the foregoing

37. Suppose that the amount of money that the fire department has saved the citizens of a city in 1980 is estimated at P dollars. If this sum is to be increased at least 100% in 1981, then the saving in 1980 must be at least

    (A) equivalent to the ratio between P and 100
    (B) commensurate with a sum derived by arithmetic manipulation involving P, 100, and a third value not given in the problem
    (C) 100 times P dollars

(D) twice P dollars

(E) a sum of money not accurately described in any of the foregoing options

38. The velocity of a fire engine traveling to a fire is computed by

(A) multiplying distance by time
(B) dividing distance by time
(C) squaring the force with which the earth attracts the engine
(D) means of the moment of inertia
(E) use of the Pythagorean Theorem

39. Suppose that R persons were rescued from burning buildings by firemen in 1980. Suppose also that P persons perished in burning buildings in 1980. If R is less than S but greater than T and P is less than both M and N, it may safely be concluded that

(A) the sum of R and T is greater than S
(B) the sum of M and N is greater than P
(C) R is between M and N times as great as P
(D) R exceeds P to an indeterminate degree lying somewhere between S and N
(E) none of the foregoing options is correct

40. In an experiment, a sprinkler system discharging W gallons of water per hour extinguished a fire covering a floor of A square yards in T minutes. The amount of water actually used to put out the fire was

(A) W times T divided by 60
(B) 60 times W divided by T
(C) 60 times W times T
(D) T divided by the fraction whose numerator is W and denominator 60
(E) none of the foregoing

41. Suppose that a ladder consists of four sections, each R feet in length. When the ladder is extended, adjacent sections overlap for a distance of S feet to strengthen the interlocking. The total overall length of the ladder, when fully opened, is

(A) 4 R feet
(B) 4 R minus 3 S feet
(C) 4 R minus 4 S feet
(D) 4 R minus 6 S feet
(E) none of the foregoing

42. In the fire department of a city there are A firemen, D lieutenants, E captains, and G chiefs of various ranks. Suppose that, for comparative purposes, promotional opportunities are evaluated as the ratio of the number of promotional positions to the number of positions at the entrance level. In accordance with this method, promotional opportunities in the uniformed force of the fire department in the city are evaluated as

(A) G divided by the sum of A plus D plus E
(B) the sum of D plus E plus G divided by the number of firemen
(C) A divided by the sum of D plus E plus G
(D) the sum of A plus D divided by the sum of E plus G
(E) a fraction about which it is known only that the numerator is greater than the denominator

43. Suppose that the number of fires occurring in a particular type of dwelling decreased C% in 1979, as compared with 1978, but then increased C% in 1980, as compared with 1979. Then the number of fires occurring in that type of dwelling during 1980, as compared with 1978, is

   (A) decreased by the percentage equal to C squared divided by 100
   (B) unchanged
   (C) increased by the percentage equal to the fraction whose numerator is 100 minus C and denominator is 100
   (D) decreased by the percentage equal to the square of the fraction C over 100
   (E) dependent on the temporal distance between 1978 and 1979 as contrasted with that between 1979 and 1980

44. In the year 1980, fires occurred in K "Type Z" multiple dwellings. It is known that L% of the M multiple dwellings in New York City are of "Type Z." The fraction of "Type Z" multiple dwellings in which fires occurred during 1980 is

   (A) K divided by L times M
   (B) L times M divided by 100 K
   (C) K divided by the quantity 100 times L times M
   (D) 100 K divided by the quantity L times M
   (E) none of the foregoing

45. Suppose that the amount of money spent for supplies in 1980 for a division in a city department was $15,650. This represented an increase of 12% over the amount spent for supplies for this division in 1979. The amount of money spent for supplies for this division in 1979 was most nearly

   (A) $13,973   (B) $13,772   (C) $14,346   (D) $13,872

46. Suppose that a group of five clerks has been assigned to insert 24,000 letters into envelopes. The clerks perform this work at the following rates of speed: Clerk A, 1,100 letters an hour; Clerk B, 1,450 letters an hour; Clerk C, 1,200 letters an hour; Clerk D, 1,300 letters an hour; Clerk E, 1,250 letters an hour. At the end of 2 hours of work, Clerks C and D are assigned to another task. From the time that Clerks C and D were taken off the assignment, the number of hours required for the remaining clerks to complete this assignment is

   (A) less than 3 hours
   (B) 3 hours
   (C) more than 3 hours, but less than 4 hours
   (D) more than 4 hours

47. Six gross of special drawing pencils were purchased for use in a city department. If the pencils were used at the rate of 24 a week, the maximum number of weeks that the six gross of pencils would last is

   (A) 6 weeks   (B) 12 weeks   (C) 24 weeks   (D) 36 weeks

48. A stock clerk had 600 pads on hand. He then issued 3/8 of his supply of pads to Division X, 1/4 to Division Y, and 1/6 to Division Z. The number of pads remaining in stock is

   (A) 48   (B) 125   (C) 240   (D) 475

49. If a certain job can be performed by 18 clerks in 26 days, the number of clerks needed to perform the job in 12 days is

    (A) 24 clerks   (B) 30 clerks   (C) 39 clerks   (D) 52 clerks

50. A department vehicle has completed the first 5 miles of a 10-mile trip in 10 minutes. To complete the entire trip at an average rate of 45 miles per hour, the vehicle must travel the remaining 5 miles in

    (A) 3 minutes
    (B) 5 minutes
    (C) 10 minutes
    (D) 15 minutes
    (E) 20 minutes

51. Assume that the average time required for a department vehicle to reach the scene of an emergency is M minutes. Solely on the basis of this fact, the one of the following that is the most reasonable inference is that in

    (A) no case did a vehicle reach the scene of an emergency in less than M minutes
    (B) no case did a vehicle reach the scene of an emergency in more than M minutes
    (C) every case a vehicle reached the scene of an emergency in exactly M minutes
    (D) some cases vehicles reached the scene of an emergency after M minutes had elapsed
    (E) a majority of cases vehicles reached the scene of an emergency in a period of time equal to M divided by 2

52. "A proper record shall be kept of the dimension and capacity of each bin or space in quarters that is used for the storage of coal." Suppose that it is necessary to determine the capacity of a bin measuring 12 feet by 10 feet by 6 feet. The additional information required is

    (A) the weight of a cubic foot of coal
    (B) the volume of the bin
    (C) the area of the base of the bin
    (D) which dimension is the height
    (E) the corresponding volume of coal required to fill the bin

53. Suppose that the average number of violations per day during a period of P days is M. The total number of violations during the period of P days is expressed as

    (A) M
    (B) P
    (C) the product of P and M
    (D) the sum of M and P
    (E) the quotient M divided by P

54. The fraction corresponding to the decimal .40 is

    (A) 1/25   (B) 1/4   (C) 1/8   (D) 2/5   (E) 1/40

55. When 5.1 is divided by 0.017 the quotient is

    (A) 30   (B) 300   (C) 3,000   (D) 30,000   (E) 300,000

56. One percent of $23,000 is

    (A) $.023   (B) $2.30   (C) $23   (D) $230   (E) $2,300

57. The sum of $82.79, $103.06, and $697.88 is, most nearly,

    (A) $1628   (B) $791   (C) $873   (D) $1395   (E) $885

58. A clerk is requested to file 800 cards. If he can file cards at the rate of 80 cards an hour, the number of cards remaining to be filed after 7 hours of work is

    (A) 40   (B) 140   (C) 240   (D) 260   (E) 560

59. An accountant's weekly salary is increased from $320.00 to $360.00. The increase is, most nearly,

    (A) 10%   (B) 11 1/9%   (C) 12 1/2%   (D) 14 1/7%   (E) 20%

60. If an engine pumps G gallons of water per minute, then the number of gallons pumped in half an hour may be found by

    (A) taking one-half of G
    (B) dividing 60 by G
    (C) multiplying G by 60 and then dividing the product by two
    (D) dividing 30 by G

61. Suppose there were 69 employees on the payroll of your department on June 1, 1980. This is a decrease of 8% from the number of employees on the payroll June 1, 1979. The number of employees on the payroll on June 1, 1979 was

    (A) 75   (B) 74   (C) 76   (D) 77

62. If change is made of three dollars in nickels and dimes, giving twice as many nickels as dimes, it will consist of

    (A) $1.50 in nickels and $1.50 in dimes
    (B) $1.00 in nickels and $2.00 in dimes
    (C) $2.00 in nickels and $1.00 in dimes
    (D) $1.80 in nickels and $1.20 in dimes

63. A cashier having $2.00 in nickels, $1.00 in dimes, and $2.00 in quarters, has

    (A) twice as many nickels as dimes
    (B) twice as many quarters as dimes
    (C) five times as many nickels as quarters
    (D) the same number of nickels as quarters

64. To say that the number of arrests made by members of the uniformed force has been increased by 50 percent means that the number of arrests has been

    (A) increased by 1/2   (B) doubled   (C) multiplied by 5   (D) multiplied by 50

65. It is estimated that 10 workers can do a certain job in 10 hours. If only 5 workers are available, the job will probably take

    (A) 5 hours   (B) 10 hours   (C) 15 hours   (D) 20 hours

66. If the number of officers in a uniformed force is to be increased by 150, and this increase represents an increase of 5 per cent over the present force, then the number of officers in the force at present is most nearly

    (A) 1500   (B) 3000   (C) 5000   (D) 7500

67. If a vehicle is to complete a 20 mile trip at an average rate of 30 miles per hour, it must complete the trip in

    (A) 20 minutes   (B) 30 minutes   (C) 40 minutes   (D) 50 minutes

68. Suppose that a uniformed force, during a certain period of time, has made 150 arrests and has issued 400 summonses. If the number of arrests were doubled and the number of summonses reduced by one-half, the ratio of arrests to summonses would be

    (A) 1 to 3   (B) 4 to 1   (C) 1 1/2 to 1   (D) 2 1/2 to 4

69. A stolen vehicle traveling at 60 miles per hour passes by a police car, which is standing still with the engine running. The police car immediately starts out in pursuit, and one minute later, having covered a distance of half a mile, it reaches a speed of 90 miles per hour, and continues at this speed. In how many minutes after the stolen vehicle passes the police car will the police car overtake it?

    (A) 1 minute   (B) 1 1/2 minutes   (C) 2 minutes   (D) 3 minutes

70. A police officer found his 42-hour work week was divided as follows: 1/6 of his time in investigating incidents on his patrol post; 1/2 of his time patrolling his post; and 1/8 of his time in special traffic duty. The rest of his time was devoted to assignments at precinct headquarters. The percentage of his work week which was spent at precinct headquarters is most nearly

    (A) 10%   (B) 15%   (C) 20%   (D) 25%

71. In 1980 a Department of Sanitation towed away 8,430 cars which were abandoned or illegally parked on city streets. If the value of the abandoned cars was $1,038,200 and that of the illegally parked cars was $6,234,800, then the average value of one of the towed away cars was most nearly

    (A) $400   (B) $720   (C) $860   (D) $1,100

72. Two percent of all school children are problem children. Some 80% of these problem children become delinquents, and about 80% of the delinquent children become criminals. If the school population is 1,000,000 children, the number of this group who will eventually become criminals, according to this analysis, is

    (A) 12,800   (B) 1,280   (C) 640   (D) 128

73. A patrol car began a trip with 12 gallons of gasoline in the tank and ended with 7 1/2 gallons. The car traveled 17.3 miles for each gallon of gasoline. During the trip gasoline was bought for $9.28 at a cost of $1.16 per gallon. The total number of miles traveled during this trip was most nearly

    (A) 79   (B) 196   (C) 216   (D) 229

Answer Key For Arithmetic Computations Practice Tests

Test 1

1. A	11. A	21. B	31. A	41. A
2. B	12. A	22. A	32. A	42. A
3. A	13. B	23. B	33. A	43. B
4. A	14. A	24. B	34. B	44. B
5. A	15. A	25. A	35. B	45. A
6. B	16. B	26. A	36. A	46. A
7. B	17. A	27. B	37. A	47. B
8. B	18. A	28. B	38. B	48. B
9. A	19. A	29. B	39. B	49. B
10. B	20. B	30. A	40. A	50. A

Test 2

1. A	21. B	41. B	61. B
2. B	22. B	42. A	62. A
3. B	23. A	43. B	63. A
4. B	24. A	44. A	64. A
5. A	25. B	45. B	65. A
6. A	26. A	46. A	66. B
7. A	27. B	47. B	67. B
8. B	28. B	48. A	68. A
9. B	29. A	49. A	69. B
10. A	30. A	50. A	70. A
11. A	31. A	51. B	71. A
12. A	32. B	52. A	72. B
13. A	33. A	53. B	73. B
14. B	34. B	54. A	74. A
15. B	35. B	55. A	75. A
16. A	36. A	56. A	76. B
17. A	37. B	57. B	77. B
18. B	38. A	58. A	78. A
19. B	39. A	59. A	79. B
20. A	40. B	60. B	80. B

Test 3

1. C	5. C	9. B	13. C	17. A	21. B	25. B	28. B
2. D	6. A	10. A	14. B	18. B	22. D	26. C	29. A
3. A	7. D	11. B	15. A	19. A	23. D	27. A	30. C
4. B	8. C	12. D	16. D	20. C	24. C		

Test 4

1. B	3. A	5. D	7. C	9. D	11. B
2. D	4. C	6. A	8. A	10. D	12. C

Test 5

1. B	4. C	7. E	10. E	13. C	16. A	19. A	22. C
2. A	5. D	8. E	11. A	14. E	17. B	20. A	23. D
3. D	6. C	9. D	12. E	15. B	18. D	21. E	24. B

Test 6

1. A	6. A	11. A	16. C
2. D	7. E	12. D	17. B
3. B	8. C	13. B	19. A
4. C	9. B	14. C	19. A
5. E	10. D	15. E	20. D

Test 7

1. B	11. B	21. A	31. A	41. B	51. D	61. A	71. C
2. D	12. C	22. B	32. C	42. B	52. A	62. A	72. A
3. C	13. A	23. C	33. B	43. A	53. C	63. C	73. C
4. D	14. D	24. C	34. A	44. D	54. D	64. A	
5. A	15. B	25. A	35. A	45. A	55. B	65. D	
6. C	16. B	26. D	36. B	46. B	56. D	66. B	
7. D	17. D	27. B	37. D	47. D	57. E	67. C	
8. A	18. A	28. D	38. B	48. B	58. C	68. C	
9. D	19. C	29. C	39. B	49. C	59. C	69. C	
10. D	20. D	30. A	40. A	50. B	60. C	70. C	

CORRECT ENGLISH USAGE

Every test of English usage tests your understanding of English grammar. This grammar and usage review is meant to serve as a quick refresher course. It should "bring back" the rules, hints, and suggestions supplied by many teachers over the years.

Parts of Speech

A **noun** is the name of a person, place, thing, or idea: teacher city desk democracy

Pronouns substitute for nouns: he they ours those

An **adjective** describes a noun: warm quick tall blue

A **verb** expresses action or state of being: yell interpret feel are

An **adverb** modifies a verb, an adjective, or another adverb: fast slowly friendly well

Conjunctions join words, sentences, and phrases: and but or

A **preposition** shows position in time or space: in during after behind

Nouns

There are different kinds of nouns:

Common nouns are general: house girl street city
Proper nouns are specific: White House Jane Main Street New York
Collective nouns name groups: team crowd organization Congress

Nouns have *cases:*

Nominative—the subject, noun of address, or predicate noun
Objective—the direct object, indirect object, or object of the preposition
Possessive—the form that shows possession

Pronouns

Antecedent of the pronoun—the noun to which a pronoun refers. A pronoun must agree with its antecedent in gender, person, and number. There are several kinds of pronouns. (Pronouns also have cases.)

Demonstrative pronoun: this, that, these, those

Indefinite pronoun: all, any, anybody
Interrogative pronoun: who, which, what

Personal pronoun:			Nominative Case	Objective Case	Possessive Case
Singular	1st person		I	me	mine
	2nd person		you	you	yours
	3rd person		he, she, it	him, her, it	his, hers, its
Plural	1st person		we	us	ours
	2nd person		you	you	your
	3rd person		they	them	theirs

Adjectives

Adjectives answer the questions "Which one?", "What kind?", and "How many?"

There are three uses of adjectives:

A **noun modifier** is usually placed directly before the noun it describes: He is a *tall* man.
A **predicate adjective** follows an inactive verb and modifies the subject: He is *happy*. I feel *terrible*.
An **article** or **noun marker** are other names for these adjectives: the, a, an

Adverbs

Adverbs answer the questions "Why?", "How?", "Where?", "When?", and "To what degree?". Adverbs should NOT be used to modify nouns. Adverbs modify verbs, adjectives, and other adverbs.

Verbs

Verbs are the most important part of speech. A verb may stand alone, as an imperative sentence such as "Stop!" Conversely, no group of words can function as a sentence without a verb.

Attributes of a Verb

Mood
I *laugh.* (indicative—factual)
If I were laughing . . . (subjunctive—wishful)
Laugh! (imperative—forceful)

Voice
I *moved the chair.* (active)
The chair was moved by me. (passive)

Agreement of Persons and Number	*We don't know.* (1st person plural subject and verb) *He doesn't know.* (3rd person singular subject and verb)
Tense	*I laugh.* (present) *We had laughed.* (past perfect) *She will be laughing.* (future progressive)

Types of Verbs

Transitive	completed by a noun or pronoun *We invited our friends.*
Intransitive	completed in itself or by an adverb *She fell. She fell down.*
Copulative	a form of *is* or a sensory/seeming verb *She is pretty. We felt bad. He appeared depressed.*

Principal Parts of a Verb

	Present	Past	Present Perfect
Regular	walk bathe	walked bathed	have walked have bathed
Irregular	ring eat	rang ate	have rung have eaten

English Verb Time Lines

Simple Tenses	Past	Present	Future
Simple Progressive Emphatic	I walked I was walking I did walk	I walk I am walking I do walk	I shall walk I shall be walking

Perfect Tenses	Past Perfect	Present Perfect	Future Perfect
	I had walked	I have walked	I will have walked
	I had walked three miles by the time you met me.	I have walked three miles to get here.	I will have walked three miles by the time you catch up with me.
	activity begun and completed in the past before some other past action	activity begun in the past, completed in the present	activity begun at any time and completed in the future.

Selected Rules of Grammar

1. The subject of a verb is in the nominative case even if the verb is understood and not expressed.

   Example: They are as old as *we*. (As we are)

2. The word *who* is in the nominative case. *Whom* is in the objective case.

   Example: The trapeze artist who ran away with the clown broke the lion tamer's heart. (*Who* is the subject of the verb *ran*.)

   Example: The trapeze artist whom he loved ran away with the circus clown. (*Whom* is the object of the verb *loved*.)

3. The word *whoever* is in the nominative case. *Whomever* is in the objective case.

   Example: Whoever comes to the door is welcome to join the party. (*Whoever* is the subject of the verb *comes*.)

   Example: Invite whomever you wish to accompany you. (*Whomever* is the object of the verb *invite*.)

4. Nouns or pronouns connected by a form of the verb *to be* should always be in the nominative case.

   Example: It is *I*. (Not *me*)

5. A pronoun that is the object of a preposition or of a transitive verb must be in the objective case.

   Example: It would be impossible for *me* to do that job alone. (*Me* is the object of the preposition *for*.)

   Example: The attendant gave *me* the keys to the locker. (*Me* is the indirect object of the verb *gave*.)

6. *Each, either, neither, anyone, anybody, somebody, someone, every, everyone, one, no one,* and *nobody* are singular pronouns. Each of these words takes a singular verb and a singular pronoun.

   Example: *Neither likes* the pets of the other.
   Everyone must wait *his* turn.
   Each of the patients *carries* insurance.
   Neither of the women *has* completed *her* assignment.

7. When the correlative conjunctions *either/or* and *neither/nor* are used, the number of the verb agrees with the number of the last subject.

   Example: Neither John nor *Greg eats* meat.

   Example: Either the cat or the *mice take* charge in the barn.

8. A subject consisting of two or more nouns joined by a coordinating conjunction takes a plural verb.

   Example: Paul *and* Sue *were* the last to arrive.

9. The number of the verb is not affected by the addition to the subject of words introduced by *with, together with, no less than, as well as,* etc.

Example: The *captain,* together with the rest of the team, *was* delighted by the victory celebration.

10. A verb agrees in number with its subject. A verb should not be made to agree with a noun that is part of a phrase following the subject.

    Example: *Mount Snow,* one of my favorite ski areas, *is* in Vermont.

    Example: The *mountains* of Colorado, like those of Switzerland, *offer* excellent skiing.

11. A verb should agree in number with the subject, not with the predicate noun or pronoun.

    Example: Poor study *habits are* the leading cause of unsatisfactory achievement in school.

    Example: The leading *cause* of unsatisfactory achievement in school *is* poor study habits.

12. A pronoun agrees with its antecedent in person, number, gender, and case.

    Example: Since you were absent on Tuesday, you will have to ask Mary or Beth for her notes on the lecture. (Use *her,* not *their,* because two singular antecedents joined by *or* take a singular pronoun.)

13. *Hardly, scarcely, barely, only,* and *but* (when it means *only*) are negative words. Do NOT use another negative in conjunction with any of these words.

    Example: He *didn't have but* one hat. (WRONG)
              He *had but* one hat. OR He had *only* one hat.

    Example: I *can't hardly* read the small print. (WRONG)
              I *can hardly* read the small print. OR I *can't* read the small print.

14. *As* is a conjunction introducing a subordinate clause; *like* is a preposition. The object of a preposition is a noun or phrase.

    Example: I expect him to behave *as* a gentleman *should.* (*Gentleman* is the subject of the clause; *should* is its verb.)

    Example: He behaves *like* a gentleman.

    Example: The gambler accepts only hard currency *like* gold coins.

15. When modifying the words *kind* and *sort,* the words *this* and *that* always remain in the singular.

    Example: *This kind* of apple makes the best pie.

    Example: *That sort* of behavior will result in severe punishment.

16. In sentences beginning with *there is* and *there are,* the verb should agree in number with the noun that follows it.

    Example: There isn't an unbroken bone in her body. (The singular subject *bone* takes the singular verb *is.*)

    Example: There are many choices to be made. (The plural subject *choices* takes the plural verb *are.*)

17. A noun or pronoun modifying a gerund should be in the possessive case.

Example: Is there any criticism of Arthur's going? (*Going* is a gerund. It must be modified by Arthur's, not by Arthur.)

18. Do NOT use the possessive case when referring to an inanimate object.

Example: He had difficulty with the *store's* management. (WRONG)
He had difficulty with the management *of the store*.

19. When expressing a condition contrary to fact or a wish, use the subjunctive form *were*.

Example: I wish I *were* a movie star.

20. Statements equally true in the past and in the present are usually expressed in the present tense. The contents of a book are also expressed in the present tense.

Example: He said that Venus is a planet. (Even though he made the statement in the past, the fact remains that Venus *is* a planet.)

Example: In the book *Peter Pan,* Wendy says, "I can fly." (Every time one reads the book, Wendy *says* it again.)

Antecedents and Modifiers

1. *It*, when used as a relative pronoun, refers to the nearest noun. In your writing, you must be certain that the grammatical antecedent is indeed the intended antecedent.

Example: Since the mouth of the cave was masked by underbrush, *it* provided an excellent hiding place. (Do you really mean that the underbrush is an excellent hiding place, or do you mean the cave?)

2. *Which* is another pronoun that causes reference problems. In fact, whenever using pronouns, you must ask yourself whether or not the reference of the pronoun is clear.

Example: The first chapter awakens your interest in cloning, *which* continues to the end of the book. (What continues, cloning or your interest?)

Example: Jim told Bill that he was about to be fired. (Who is about to be fired? This sentence can be interpreted to mean that Jim was informing Bill about Bill's impending termination or about his, Jim's, own troubles.)

In your writing, you may find that the most effective way to clear up an ambiguity is to recast the sentence.

Example: The first chapter awakens your interest in cloning. The following chapters build upon this interest and maintain it throughout the book.

Example: Jim told Bill, "I am about to be fired." OR   Jim told Bill, "You are about to be fired."

3. Adjectives modify only nouns and pronouns. Adverbs modify verbs, adjectives, and other adverbs.

Example: One can swim in a lake as *easy* as in a pool. (WRONG)
One can swim in a lake as *easily* as in a pool. (The adverb *easily* must modify the verb *can swim*.)

Example: I was *real* happy. (WRONG)
I was *really* happy. (The adverb *really* must be used to modify the adjective happy.)

Sometimes context determines the use of adjective or adverb.

Example: The old man looked *angry*. (*Angry* is an adjective describing the old man. [angry old man])
The old man looked *angrily* out of the window. (*Angrily* is an adverb describing the man's manner of looking out of the window.)

4. Phrases should be placed near the words they modify.

Example: The author says that he intends to influence your life *in the first chapter*. (WRONG)
The author *in the first chapter* says . . .   OR   *In the first chapter,* the author says . . .

Example: He played the part in *Oklahoma* of Jud. (WRONG)
He played the part of Jud in *Oklahoma*.

5. Adverbs should be placed near the words they modify.

Example: The man was *only* willing to sell one horse. (WRONG)
The man was willing to sell *only* one horse.

6. Clauses should be placed near the words they modify.

Example: *He* will reap a good harvest *who sows early*. (WRONG)
He who sows early will reap a good harvest.

7. A modifier must modify something.

Example: Having excellent control, a no-hitter was pitched. (WRONG)
(*Having excellent control* does not modify anything.)
Having excellent control, the pitcher pitched a no-hitter. (*Having excellent control* modifies *the pitcher*.)

Example: The day passed quickly, climbing the rugged rocks. (WRONG)
The day passed quickly as we climbed the rugged rocks.

Example: While away on vacation, the pipes burst. (WRONG) (The pipes were not away on vacation.)
While we were away on vacation, the pipes burst.

Example: To run efficiently, the serviceman should oil the lawnmower. (WRONG)
The serviceman should oil the lawnmower to make it run efficiently.

Note: The best test for the placement of modifiers is to read the sentence literally. If you read a sentence literally and it is literally ridiculous, it is WRONG. The meaning of a sentence must be clear to any reader. The words of the sentence *must make sense.*

Sentence Structure

1. Every sentence must contain a verb. A group of words, no matter how long, without a verb is a sentence fragment, not a sentence. A verb may consist of one, two, three, or four words.

   Examples: The boy *studies* hard.
   The boy *will study* hard.
   The boy *has been studying* hard.
   The boy *should have been studying* hard.

   The words that make up a single verb may be separated.

   Examples: It *is* not *snowing.*
   It *will* almost certainly *snow* tomorrow.

2. Every sentence must have a subject. The subject may be a noun, a pronoun, or a word or group of words functioning as a noun.

   Examples: *Fish* swim. (noun)
   Boats are sailed. (noun)
   She is young. (pronoun)
   Running is good exercise. (gerund)
   To argue is pointless. (infinitive)
   That he was tired was evident. (noun clause)

   In commands, the subject is usually not expressed but is understood to be *you.*

   Example: Mind your own business.

3. A phrase cannot stand by itself as a sentence. A phrase is any group of related words that has no subject or predicate and that is used as a single part of speech. Phrases may be built around prepositions, particles, gerunds, or infinitives.

   Example: The boy *with curly hair* is my brother. (Prepositional phrase used as an adjective modifying *boy*)

   Example: My favorite cousin lives *on a farm.* (Prepositional phrase used as an adverb modifying *lives*)

   Example: *Beyond the double white line* is out of bounds. (Prepositional phrase used as a noun, the subject of the sentence)

   Example: A thunderstorm *preceding a cold front* is often welcome. (Participial phrase used as an adjective modifying *thunderstorm*)

   Example: We eagerly awaited the pay envelopes *brought by the messenger.* (Participial phrase used as an adjective modifying *envelopes*)

   Example: *Running a day camp* is an exhausting job. (Gerund phrase used as a noun, subject of the sentence)

   Example: The director is paid well for *running the day camp.* (Gerund phrase used as a noun, the object of the preposition *for*)

   Example: *To breathe unpolluted air* should be every person's birthright. (Infinitive phrase used as a noun, the subject of the sentence)

   Example: The child began *to unwrap his gift.* (Infinitive phrase used as a noun, the object of the verb *began*)

Example: The boy ran away from home *to become a marine.* (Infinitive phrase used as an adverb modifying *ran away*)

4. A *main, independent,* or *principal* clause can stand alone as a complete sentence or it may be combined with another clause.

Example: The sky darkened ominously and rain began to fall. (Two independent clauses joined by a coordinating conjunction)

A *subordinate* or *dependent* clause must never stand alone. It is not a complete sentence despite the fact that it has a subject and a verb. A subordinate clause usually is introduced by a subordinating conjunction. Subordinate clauses may act as adverbs, adjectives, or nouns. Subordinate adverbial clauses are generally introduced by the subordinating conjunctions *when, while, because, as soon as, if, after, although, as before, since, than, though, until,* and *unless.*

Example: *While we were waiting for the local,* the express roared past.

Example: The woman applied for a new job *because she wanted to earn more money.*

Example: *Although a subordinate clause contains both subject and verb,* it cannot stand alone *because it is introduced by a subordinating word.*

Subordinate adjective clauses may be introduced by the pronouns *who, which,* and *that.*

Example: The play *that he liked best* was a mystery.

Example: I have a neighbor *who served in the Peace Corps.*

Subordinate noun clauses may be introduced by *who, what,* or *that.*

Example: The stationmaster says *that the train will be late.*

Example: I asked the waiter *what the stew contained.*

Example: I wish I knew *who backed into my car.*

5. Two independent clauses cannot share one sentence without some form of connective. If they do, they form a run-on sentence. Two principal clauses may be joined by a coordinating conjunction, by a comma followed by a coordinating conjunction, or by a semicolon. They may form two distinct sentences. Two main clauses may NEVER be joined by a comma without a coordinating conjunction. This error is called a comma splice.

Examples: A college education has never been more important than it is today it has never cost more. (WRONG—run-on sentence)

A college education has never been more important than it is today, it has never cost more. (WRONG—comma splice)

A college education has never been more important than it is today and it has never cost more. (WRONG—the two independent clauses are not equally short, so a comma is required before the coordinating conjunction.)

A college education has never been more important than it is today, and it has never cost more. (correct form)

A college education has never been more important than it is today; and it has never cost more. (WRONG—a semicolon is never used before a coordinating conjunction.)

A college education has never been more important than it is today; it has never cost more. (correct form)

A college education has never been more important than it is today. It has never cost more. (correct form)

A college education has never been more important than it is today. And it has never cost more. (correct form)

Although a college education has never been more important than it is today, it has never cost more. (correct form —introductory subordinate clause is separated from the main clause by a comma.)

6. Direct quotations are bound by all of the rules of sentence formation. Beware of comma splices in divided quotations.

Example: "Your total is wrong," he said, "add the column again." (WRONG)
"Your total is wrong," he said. "Add the column again." (The two independent clauses form two separate sentences.)

Example: "Are you lost?" she asked "may I help you?" (WRONG)
"Are you lost?" she asked. "May I help you?" (Two main clauses; two separate sentences)

7. Comparisons must be logical and complete. Train yourself to concentrate on each sentence so that you can recognize errors.

Example: Wilmington is larger than any city in Delaware. (WRONG)
Wilmington is larger than any *other* city in Delaware.

Example: He is as fat, if not fatter, than his uncle. (WRONG)
He is as fat *as*, if not fatter than, his uncle.

Example: I hope to find a summer job other than a lifeguard. (WRONG)
I hope to find a summer job other than *that of* lifeguard.

Example: Law is a better profession than an accountant. (WRONG)
Law is a better profession than accounting. (Parallel)

8. Avoid "is when" and "is where" constructions.

Example: A limerick is when a short poem has a catchy rhyme. (WRONG)
A limerick is a short poem with a catchy rhyme.

Example: To exile is where a person must live in another place. (WRONG)
To exile a person is to force him to live in another place.

9. Errors in parallelism are often quite subtle, but you should learn to recognize and avoid them.

Example: Skiing and to skate are both winter sports. (WRONG)
Skiing and *skating* are both winter sports.

Example: She spends all her time eating, asleep, and on her studies. (WRONG)
She spends all her time *eating, sleeping,* and *studying.*

Example: The work is neither difficult nor do I find it interesting. (WRONG)
The work is neither difficult nor interesting.

Example:　His heavy drinking and the fact that he gambles makes him a poor role model. (WRONG)
　　　　　His heavy *drinking* and *gambling make* him a poor role model.

10. Avoid needless shifts in point of view. A shift in point of view is a change within the sentence from one tense or mood to another, from one subject or voice to another, or from one person or number to another. Shifts in point of view destroy parallelism within the sentence.

Example:　After he *rescued* the kitten, he *rushes* down the ladder to find its owner. (Shift from past tense to present tense) CHANGE TO: After he rescued the kitten, he rushed down the ladder to find its owner.

Example:　First *stand* at attention and then you *should salute* the flag. (Shift from imperative to indicative mood) CHANGE TO: First *stand* at attention and then *salute* the flag.

Example:　Mary especially likes math, but history is also enjoyed by her. (The subject shifts from *Mary* to *history*; the mood shifts from active to passive.) CHANGE TO: Mary especially likes math, but she also enjoys history.

Example:　George rowed around the island and soon the mainland came in sight. (The subject changes from *George* to *the mainland*.) CANGE TO: George rowed around the island and soon came in sight of the mainland.

Example:　The captain welcomed *us* aboard, and the crew enjoyed showing *one* around the boat. (The object shifts from first to third person. *Us* may be the object of *showing*.)

Example:　*One* should listen to the weather forecast so that *they* may anticipate a hurricane. (The subject shifts from singular to plural.) CHANGE TO: *One* should listen to the weather forecast so that *he or she* may anticipate a hurricane.

Grammar Fundamentals Imparted by the Question and Answer Method

DIRECTIONS: Mark each of the following sentences as correct or incorrect by writing C or I beside its number. As you make your judgments, try to think of the rule that makes the sentence right or wrong. The 42 sentences are followed by explanations.

1. They are as old as us.

2. She is older than him.

3. Whom do you suppose paid us a visit?

4. Punish whomever is guilty.

5. It is me.

6. Can it be them?

7. Can it be her?

8. It would be impossible for you and I.

9. This is the death knell for we individualists.

10. He had a great deal of trouble with the store's management.

11. I, who's older, know better than you.

12. The mans hair is gray.

13. Is there any criticism of Arthur going?

14. Everybody tried their hardest.

15. I do not like these sort of cakes.

16. The government are unanimously agreed upon this action.

17. The government is unanimously agreed upon this action.

18. She don't like to engage in such activity.

19. The use of liquors are dangerous.

20. The district attorney, as well as many of his aides, have been involved in the investigation.

21. Either the fifth or the seventh of the courses they have laid open are to be accepted.

22. The fighting and wrestling of the two men is excellent.

23. The worst feature of the play were the abdominable actors.

24. There is present a child and two dogs.

25. I shall go. You will go. He will go. We shall go. You will go. They will go.

26. I will; I repeat, I will. You shall; I say you shall. He shall; I say he shall. We will; we say we will. You shall; I say you shall. They shall; I say they shall.

27. When he saw me he says his prayers.

28. If I only knowed what the results of my action would be I would have restrained myself.

29. He spoke slow and careful.

30. The sun shines bright on my old Kentucky home.

31. She looks beautiful.

32. A Washington streetcar accident resulted in two deaths.

33. The man gave the wrong reply.

34. The boy answered wrong.

35. He always has and will do it.

36. We hoped that you would have come to the party.

37. I intended to have gone.

38. In the parlor my cousin kept a collection of animals that he shot.

39. He said that Venus was a planet.

40. If he was here, I should be happy.

41. I wish that I was a man.

42. By giving strict obedience to commands, a soldier learns discpline, and consequently would have steady nerves in time of war.

Explanatory Answers

Most of the 42 statements are grammatically incorrect. The errors are those of CASE, AGREEMENT, NUMBER, or PRINCIPAL PARTS. The proper form of each incorrect statement is given below. Following the proper form is a brief explanation of the grammatical principle underlying the correction.

Statements Involving Case

1. They are as old as we (are).

2. She is older than he (is).
   PRINCIPLE: (1,2) The subject of a verb is in the nominative case, even when the verb is remote, or understood (not expressed).
   Note: *Than* and *as* are conjunctions, not prepositions. When they are followed by merely a pronoun, this pronoun is not their object, but part of a clause, the rest of which may be understood. The case of this pronoun is determined by its relation to the rest of the unexpressed clause. Sometimes the understood clause calls for the objective: "I like his brother better than (I like) him."

3. Who do you suppose paid us a visit?
   PRINCIPLE: Guard against the improper attraction of *who* into the objective case by intervening expressions.

4. Punish whoever is guilty.
   PRINCIPLE: Guard against the improper attraction of *who* or *whoever* into the objective case by preceding verbs or prepositions.

5. It is I.

6. Can it be they?

7. Can it be she?
   PRINCIPLE: (5, 6, 7) Nouns or pronouns connected by the verb *to be* (in any of its forms: *is, was, were, be,* etc.) agree in case. *To be* never takes an object because it does not express action.

8. It would be impossible for you and me.

9. This is the death knell for us individualists.
   PRINCIPLE: (8, 9) The objective of a preposition or a verb is in the objective case.

10. He had a great deal of trouble with the management of the store.
    PRINCIPLE: It is usually awkward and slightly illogical to attribute possession to inanimate objects.

11. I, who am older, know better than you.
    PRINCIPLE: A pronoun agrees with its antecedent in person, number, and gender, but not in case.

12. The man's hair is gray.
PRINCIPLE: A noun or pronoun used to express possession is in the possessive case. Do not omit the apostrophe from nouns or from pronouns that require it, such as *one's*.

13. Is there any criticism of Arthur's going?
PRINCIPLE: A noun or pronoun linked with a gerund should be in the possessive case.

Statements Involving Number

14. Everybody tried his hardest.
PRINCIPLE: *Each, every, everyone, everybody, anybody, either, neither, no one, nobody,* and similar words are singular.

15. I do not like this sort of cake.
PRINCIPLE: Do not let *this* or *that,* when modifying *kind* or *sort,* be attracted into the plural by a following noun.

16, 17. Both statements are correct.
PRINCIPLE: (16, 17) Collective nouns may be regarded as singular or plural, according to the meaning intended.

18. She doesn't like to engage in such activity.
PRINCIPLE: Do not use *don't* in the third person singular. Use *doesn't. Don't* is a contraction of *do not.*

19. The use of liquors is dangerous.
PRINCIPLE: A verb agrees in number with the subject. A verb should not agree with a noun that intervenes between it and the subject.

20. The district attorney, as well as many of his aides, has been involved in the investigation.
PRINCIPLE: The number of the verb is not affected by the addition to the subject of words introduced by *with, together with, no less than, as well as,* etc.

21. Either the fifth or the seventh of the courses they have laid open is to be accepted.
PRINCIPLE: Singular subjects joined by *nor* or *or* take a singular verb.

22. The fighting and wrestling of the two men are excellent.
PRINCIPLE: A subject consisting of two or more nouns joined by *and* takes a plural verb.

23. The worst feature of the play was the abominable actors.
PRINCIPLE: A verb should agree in number with the subject, not with a predicate noun.

24. There are present a child and two dogs.
PRINCIPLE: In "there is" and "there are" sentences, the verb should agree in number with the noun that follows it.

25. The conjugation is correct:
PRINCIPLE: To express simple futurity or mere expectation, use *shall* with the first person (both singular and plural) and *will* with the second and third.

26. All of the sentences are correct.
PRINCIPLE: To express resolution or emphatic assurance, reverse the usage: that is, use *will* with the first person (both singular and plural) and *shall* with the second and third.

Statements Involving Principal Parts

27. When he saw me he said his prayers.

28. If only I had known what the results of my action would be, I would have restrained myself.
PRINCIPLE: Use the correct form of the past tense and the past participle. Avoid *come, done, bursted, knowed, says* for the past tense; and *(had) eat, (had) froze, (have) ran, (has) wrote, (are) suppose* for the past participle.
   Note: Memorize the principal parts of the most common "irregular" verbs. The principal parts are the infinitive *(play)*, the first person of the past tense *(played)*, and the past participle *(played)*. This sample *(play)* is a "regular" verb; that is, the past tense and past participle are formed by adding *ed* to the infinitive. This is not the case with irregular verbs. One way to recall the principal parts of irregular verbs is to repeat as follows: today I choose; yesterday I chose; often in the past I have chosen. Thus, the principal parts of *choose* are *choose* (infinitive); *chose* (past tense); and *chosen* (past participle).

29. He spoke slowly and carefully.
PRINCIPLE: Do not use an adjective to modify a verb.

30. The statement is correct because *bright* modifies *sun*.
PRINCIPLE: In such sentences as "He stood firm" and "The cry rang clear," the modifier should be an adjective if it refers to the subject, an adverb if it refers to the verb.

31. Statement is correct grammatically.
PRINCIPLE: After a verb pertaining to the senses, an adjective is used to denote a quality pertaining to the subject. (An adverb is used only when the reference is clearly to the verb.)

32. A streetcar accident in Washington resulted in two deaths.
PRINCIPLE: Use "made" adjectives with caution. When an adjective phrase that normally follows the noun is condensed and placed before the noun as an attributive modifier, the result may be awkward or even confusing.

33, 34. Both are correct.
PRINCIPLE: Certain adverbs do not differ in form from adjectives. When form does not indicate which of the two parts of speech is intended, the word must be classified according to its use in the sentence.

35. He always has done it and always will do it.
PRINCIPLE: Do not use a verb, conjunction, preposition, or noun in a double capacity when one of the uses is ungrammatical.

36. We hoped that you would come to the party. (The principal verb *hoped* indicates a past time. In that past time our hope was that you *would* come, not that you *would have* come.)
    PRINCIPLE: In dependent clauses and infinitives, the tense is to be considered in relation to the time expressed in the principal verb.

37. I intended to go. (The principal verb *intended* indicates a past time. In that past time I intended to do something. What? Did I intend to *go,* or to *have gone*?)

38. In the parlor, my cousin kept a collection of animals that he had shot.
    PRINCIPLE: When narration in the past tense is interrupted for reference to a preceding occurrence, the past perfect tense is used.

39. He said that Venus is a planet.
    PRINCIPLE: General statements equally true in the past and in the present are usually expressed in the present tense.

40. If he were here, I should be happy.

41. I wish that I were a man.
    PRINCIPLE: The subjunctive mode of the verb to be is used to express a condition contrary to fact, or a wish.

42. By giving strict obedience to commands, a soldier learns discipline and consequently *will have* steady nerves in time of war.
    PRINCIPLE: Use the correct auxiliary. Make sure that the tense, mode, or aspect of successive verbs is not altered without reason.

How To Answer English Usage Questions

The key to answering English usage questions is careful reading and complete understanding of the directions. If directions ask you to choose from a group of four or five sentences, are you looking for the one that is incorrect or for the one that is correct? What elements are to be considered in your choice: usage? grammar? spelling? punctuation and capitalization? sentence structure? awkwardness?

The most common English usage question type presents four sentences, and asks you to select the one sentence that is grammatically *incorrect*. Example 1 illustrates this question type.

Example 1

DIRECTIONS: *In the following group of sentences, select the one sentence that is gramatically incorrect.*

1. (A) No employee considered to be indispensable will be assigned to the new office.

   (B) Mr. Green thought the procedure would facilitate his work; he knows better now.

   (C) Ms. Ross has demonstrated that she is as courageous, if not more courageous, than Mr. Langley.

   (D) The successful completion of the project depends on the manager's accepting our advisory opinion.

EXPLANATION: Sentences (A), (B), and (D) are correct. Sentence (C) contains two grammatical errors: an incomplete comparison and a misplaced comma. The sentence is correctly stated as follows: Ms. Ross has demonstrated that she is as courageous *as,* if not more courageous *than,* Mr. Langley. To indicate this answer, you should have blackened (C) on the answer strip.

Sometimes the process is reversed, and you are presented with four sentences from which you must choose the one sentence that is *correct*. Example 2 provides an example of this question type.

Example 2

DIRECTIONS: *In the following question, the same idea is expressed in four different ways. Select the sentence that is preferable with respect to grammar and usage. Mark your answer sheet for the letter of the correct sentence.*

2. (A) Double parking is when you park your car alongside one that is already having been parked.

   (B) When one double-parks, you park your car alongside one that is already parked.

   (C) Double parking is parking alongside a car already parked.

   (D) To double-park is alongside a car already parked.

EXPLANATION: Sentence (C) is the best expression of the idea. Sentence (A) has two grammatical errors: the use of *when* to introduce a definition and the unacceptable verb form *is already having been parked*. Sentence (B) incorrectly shifts subjects from *one* to *you*. Sentence (D) does not make sense.

Other usage questions present a single sentence and ask you to identify the type of error it contains. In such cases you will be provided with a scheme for classifying the error. Examples 3 and 4 illustrate two different schemes that are commonly used.

Example 3

DIRECTIONS: *The following sentence may be classified under one of the lettered categories below. Read the sentence carefully, then select your answer as follows:*

(A) The sentence is faulty because of incorrect grammar or word usage.

(B) The sentence is faulty because of incorrect punctuation.

(C) The sentence is faulty because of incorrect capitalization.

(D) The sentence is correct.

3. After he had finished the test, he hurries off to catch the last train home.

EXPLANATION: This sentence is faulty because of incorrect grammar. The past perfect tense (*had finished*) in the opening clause should be followed by the past tense (*hurried*) in the main clause. According to the marking scheme, you should choose answer (A) for this question.

Example 4

DIRECTIONS: *Study the sentence below and select your answer as follows:*

(A) if the sentence is correct

(B) if the sentence contains only a spelling error

(C) if the sentence contains only a grammatical or word usage error

(D) if the sentence contains more than one error of any kind

4. He will not loan me the book, I'll have to buy it.

EXPLANATION: This sentence contains two errors. The use of the noun *loan* is a grammatical error; the correct word is the verb *lend*. The use of the comma is a punctuation error; two independent clauses require a period, a semicolon, or a conjunction between them. According to the marking scheme, the correct answer to this question is (D).

Because there are so many different marking schemes for this type of English usage question, paying close attention to the directions on your test is especially important.

The exercises that follow illustrate many different question styles. All of these question styles and the questions themselves have appeared on civil service exams. Read the directions carefully before starting each exercise. Then answer each question to the best of your ability. Explanations of the correct answers follow each exercise so that you will learn from your errors and apply new information to the next exercise.

Answer Sheet For English Usage
Practice Tests

Test 1

1 Ⓐ Ⓑ Ⓒ Ⓓ	4 Ⓐ Ⓑ Ⓒ Ⓓ	7 Ⓐ Ⓑ Ⓒ Ⓓ	10 Ⓐ Ⓑ Ⓒ Ⓓ
2 Ⓐ Ⓑ Ⓒ Ⓓ	5 Ⓐ Ⓑ Ⓒ Ⓓ	8 Ⓐ Ⓑ Ⓒ Ⓓ	11 Ⓐ Ⓑ Ⓒ Ⓓ
3 Ⓐ Ⓑ Ⓒ Ⓓ	6 Ⓐ Ⓑ Ⓒ Ⓓ	9 Ⓐ Ⓑ Ⓒ Ⓓ	12 Ⓐ Ⓑ Ⓒ Ⓓ

Test 2

1 Ⓐ Ⓑ Ⓒ Ⓓ	5 Ⓐ Ⓑ Ⓒ Ⓓ	9 Ⓐ Ⓑ Ⓒ Ⓓ	13 Ⓐ Ⓑ Ⓒ Ⓓ
2 Ⓐ Ⓑ Ⓒ Ⓓ	6 Ⓐ Ⓑ Ⓒ Ⓓ	10 Ⓐ Ⓑ Ⓒ Ⓓ	14 Ⓐ Ⓑ Ⓒ Ⓓ
3 Ⓐ Ⓑ Ⓒ Ⓓ	7 Ⓐ Ⓑ Ⓒ Ⓓ	11 Ⓐ Ⓑ Ⓒ Ⓓ	15 Ⓐ Ⓑ Ⓒ Ⓓ
4 Ⓐ Ⓑ Ⓒ Ⓓ	8 Ⓐ Ⓑ Ⓒ Ⓓ	12 Ⓐ Ⓑ Ⓒ Ⓓ	

Test 3

1 Ⓐ Ⓑ Ⓒ Ⓓ	5 Ⓐ Ⓑ Ⓒ Ⓓ	9 Ⓐ Ⓑ Ⓒ Ⓓ	13 Ⓐ Ⓑ Ⓒ Ⓓ
2 Ⓐ Ⓑ Ⓒ Ⓓ	6 Ⓐ Ⓑ Ⓒ Ⓓ	10 Ⓐ Ⓑ Ⓒ Ⓓ	14 Ⓐ Ⓑ Ⓒ Ⓓ
3 Ⓐ Ⓑ Ⓒ Ⓓ	7 Ⓐ Ⓑ Ⓒ Ⓓ	11 Ⓐ Ⓑ Ⓒ Ⓓ	15 Ⓐ Ⓑ Ⓒ Ⓓ
4 Ⓐ Ⓑ Ⓒ Ⓓ	8 Ⓐ Ⓑ Ⓒ Ⓓ	12 Ⓐ Ⓑ Ⓒ Ⓓ	

Test 1

Time: 12 minutes. 12 questions.

DIRECTIONS: In each of the following groups of sentences, select the one sentence that is grammatically INCORRECT. Mark the answer sheet with the letter of that incorrect sentence.

1. (A) He would not accept of my hospitality.
   (B) He is a pleasant person until challenged.
   (C) We still don't know to whom to turn.
   (D) It is the shutters swinging in the wind.

2. (A) Why should he mind your having taken the stapler?
   (B) It has been functioning as a graduate school ever since.
   (C) He led his captors a merry chase.
   (D) All sorority members declined except she.

3. (A) Nothing is to be gained by further discussion.
   (B) No applicant has received a second chance.
   (C) He receives a gift when he takes home a good report card.
   (D) The noise of planes and bombers frightens children and adults.

4. (A) Today, fewer pedestrians are guilty of jaywalking.
   (B) You look well today, after this illness.
   (C) The terrain of New Mexico is quite like Arizona.
   (D) The amount of money in American banks is increasing.

5. (A) The professor finished the unit inside of a month.
   (B) After stealing the bread, he ran like a thief.
   (C) Swimming is more enjoyable than dancing.
   (D) The scouts walked a mile farther than they had intended.

6. (A) You ought to begin, oughtn't you?
   (B) When she graduates college she will be twenty-one.
   (C) The law prescribed when and to whom the tax should be paid.
   (D) We would rather die than surrender.

7. (A) He will continue his good work, being that we show appreciation.
   (B) I cannot drive somebody else's car.
   (C) He has but one aim, to succeed.
   (D) Everything would have turned out right if she had only waited.

8. (A) The meal was meant to be theirs.
   (B) We all prefer those other kinds of candy.
   (C) Has either of you a sharp pencil?
   (D) That was a great bunch of people.

9. (A) Amiable persons make amicable adjustments.
   (B) Being unable to hear the speaker, we fell asleep.
   (C) When Peter reached home, he found he lost his wallet.
   (D) It had lain there for many days.

10. (A) Everyone was present but him for whom the meeting was called.
    (B) The officer was wholly within his rights.
    (C) Not only did I eat too much, but I also drank to excess.
    (D) Let's meet around six o'clock.

11. (A) When I arrived, he was already there.
    (B) My diagnosis is worth more than a surgeon's.
    (C) I use all my pens without fear of them leaking.
    (D) When I arrived, they were all ready to go.

12. (A) I'll never agree to John changing his job.
    (B) He gained admittance to the ball park.
    (C) Please advise me what to do.
    (D) The wound was aggravated by rubbing.

Correct Answers

1. A	4. C	7. A	10. D
2. D	5. A	8. D	11. C
3. C	6. B	9. C	12. A

Explanatory Answers

1. **(A)** *Of* is unnecessary.

2. **(D)** *Except* is functioning as a preposition. The object of the preposition, in this case *her,* must be in the objective case.

3. **(C)** He *takes* the report card from school, but he *brings* it home.

4. **(C)** This is an incomplete comparison. The terrain of one state cannot be compared to the entirety of another state. This sentence should read: "The terrain of New Mexico is quite like *that* of Arizona."

5. **(A)** *Inside of a month* is unacceptable; the correct form is *in a month.*

6. **(B)** One must graduate *from* college.

7. **(A)** *Being that* is an unacceptable form.

8. **(D)** *Bunches* are for things; people congregate in *groups* or *crowds.*

9. **(C)** "When Peter reached home, he found he *had lost* his wallet." The past perfect tense is used to describe an activity begun and completed in the past before another past action.

10. **(D)** Use *about* to denote approximation of time, not *around.*

11. **(C)** "I use all my pens without fear of *their* leaking." *Leaking* is a gerund. The pronoun modifying a gerund must be in the possessive case.

12. **(A)** *Changing* is a gerund. "I'll never agree to *John's* changing his job."

Test 2

Time: 15 minutes. 15 questions.

DIRECTIONS: In each of the following groups of sentences, select the one sentence that is grammatically INCORRECT. *Mark the answer sheet with the letter of that incorrect sentence.*

1. (A) Everyone at camp must have his medical certificate on file before participating in competitive sports.
   (B) A crate of oranges were sent from Florida for all the children in cabin six.
   (C) John and Danny's room looks as if they were prepared for inspection.
   (D) Three miles is too far for a young child to walk.

2. (A) The game over, the spectators rushed out on the field and tore down the goalposts.
   (B) The situation was aggravated by disputes over the captaincy of the team.
   (C) Yesterday they lay their uniforms aside with the usual end-of-the-season regret.
   (D) It is sometimes thought that politics is not for the high-minded.

3. (A) The day is warm.
   (B) It should be called to his attention.
   (C) The girl was an unusually beautiful child.
   (D) He performed the job easy and quick.

4. (A) Being tired, I stretched out on a grassy knoll.
   (B) While we were rowing on the lake, a sudden squall almost capsized the boat.
   (C) Entering the room, a strange mark on the floor attracted my attention.
   (D) Mounting the curb, the empty car crossed the sidewalk and came to rest against a building.

5. (A) The text makes the process of developing and sustaining a successful home zoo appear to be a pleasant and profitable one.
   (B) The warmth and humor, the clear characterization of the Walmsey family, which includes three children, two dogs, and two cats, is such fun to read that this reviewer found herself reading it all over again.
   (C) You will be glad, I am sure, to give the book to whoever among your young friends has displayed an interest in animals.
   (D) The consensus among critics of children's literature is that the book is well worth the purchase price.

6. (A) Not one in a thousand readers take the matter seriously.
   (B) He was partially able to accomplish his purpose.
   (C) You are not as tall as he.
   (D) The people began to realize how much she had done.

7. (A) In the case of members who are absent, a special letter will be sent.
   (B) The visitors were all ready to see it.
   (C) I like Burns' poem, "To a Mountain Daisy."
   (D) John told William that he was sure he had seen it.

8. (A) B. Nelson & Co. has a sale of sport shirts today.
   (B) Venetian blinds—called that although they probably did not originate in Venice—are no longer used as extensively as they were at one time.
   (C) He determined to be guided by the opinion of whoever spoke first.
   (D) There was often disagreement as to whom was the better Shakespearean actor, Evans or Gielgud.

9. (A) The company published its new catalogue last week.
   (B) The man who he introduced was Mr. Carey.
   (C) The Rolls-Royce is the fastest car in England.
   (D) He finished the job satisfactorily.

10. (A) She saw the letter laying here this morning.
    (B) They gave the poor man some food when he knocked on the door.
    (C) The plans were drawn before the fight started.
    (D) He was here when the messenger brought the news.

11. (A) I regret the loss caused by the error.
    (B) The students will have a new teacher.
    (C) We shall go irregardless.
    (D) They swore to bring out all the facts.

12. (A) If my trip is a success, I should be back on Thursday.
    (B) We will send a copy of the article to you if you wish it.
    (C) They will have gone before the notice is sent to their office.
    (D) Can I borrow your bicycle tomorrow?

13. (A) He likes these kind of pencils better than those kind.
    (B) That Jackson will be elected is evident.
    (C) He does not approve of my dictating that letter.
    (D) Jack should make some progress in his work each day.

14. (A) The company has moved into its new building.
    (B) They will approve him going to the concert.
    (C) That business is good appears to be true.
    (D) It was he who won the prize.

15. (A) It must be here somewhere.
    (B) The reason is that there is no gasoline.
    (C) I will try and attend one meeting.
    (D) He walked up the hill.

Correct Answers

1. B	4. C	7. D	10. A	13. A
2. C	5. B	8. D	11. C	14. B
3. D	6. A	9. B	12. D	15. C

Explanatory Answers

1. **(B)** The subject of the sentence is a *crate,* which is singular; the verb therefore must take the singular form, *was sent.*

2. **(C)** The past tense of the verb *to lay* is *laid.* The verb *to lay* is correctly used since it means *placed.*

3. **(D)** He performed the job *easily* and *quickly.* Adverbs modify the verb; they tell how he performed the job.

4. **(C)** As written, the sentence states that a *strange mark* entered the room. The sentence should read: "As I entered the room, a strange mark on the floor attracted my attention."

5. **(B)** This sentence neglects to say what it is that the reviewer was reading. The pronoun *it* must refer to a noun—book, story, article, poem, etc.

6. **(A)** The singular subject, *one,* requires a singular verb, *takes.*

7. **(D)** This sentence is ambiguous. To whom does the second *he* refer?

8. **(D)** *Who* is the subject of the subordinate clause introduced by the conjunction *as to.*

9. **(B)** *Whom* is the object of the introduction. "He introduced *whom?* Mr. Carey."

10. **(A)** The correct verb is *to lie.* "She saw the letter *lying* here this morning."

11. **(C)** *Irregardless* is unacceptable; *regardless* is correct.

12. **(D)** When asking permission, use *may.*

13. **(A)** The demonstrative adjective must agree in number with the noun it modifies: *this kind* or *those kinds.*

14. **(B)** The pronoun modifying a gerund must be in the possessive case. "They will approve *his* going to the concert."

15. **(C)** Proper idiomatic form demands *try to attend.*

Test 3

Time: 15 minutes. 15 questions.

DIRECTIONS: In each of the following groups of sentences, select the one sentence that is grammatically INCORRECT. *Mark the answer sheet with the letter of that incorrect sentence.*

1. (A) The general regarded whomever the colonel honored with disdain.
   (B) Everyone who reads this book will think themselves knights errant on missions of heroism.
   (C) The reason the new leader was so unsuccessful was that he had fewer responsibilities.
   (D) All of the new mechanical devices we have today have made our daily living a great deal simpler, it is said.

2. (A) The town consists of three distinct sections, of which the western one is by far the larger.
   (B) Of London and Paris, the former is the wealthier.
   (C) Chicago is larger than any other city in Illinois.
   (D) America is the greatest nation, and of all other nations England is the greatest.

3. (A) I can but do my best.
   (B) I cannot help comparing him with his predecessor.
   (C) I wish that I was in Florida now.
   (D) I like this kind of grape better than any other.

4. (A) Neither Tom nor John was present for the rehearsal.
   (B) The happiness or misery of men's lives depends on their early training.
   (C) Honor as well as profit are to be gained by these studies.
   (D) The egg business is only incidental to the regular business of the general store.

5. (A) It was superior in every way to the book previously used.
   (B) His testimony today is different from that of yesterday.
   (C) If you would have studied the problem carefully, you would have found the solution more quickly.
   (D) The flowers smelled so sweet that the whole house was perfumed.

6. (A) When either or both habits become fixed, the student improves.
   (B) Neither his words nor his action was justifiable.
   (C) A calm almost always comes before a storm.
   (D) The gallery with all its pictures were destroyed.

7. (A) The convicted spy was hung at dawn.
   (B) His speech is so precise as to seem affected.
   (C) Besides the captain, there were six people on the boat.
   (D) We read each other's letters.

8. (A) A box of choice figs was sent him for Christmas.
   (B) Neither Charles nor his brother finished his assignment.
   (C) There goes the last piece of cake and the last spoonful of ice cream.
   (D) Diamonds are more desired than any other precious stones.

9. (A) As long as you are ready, you may as well start promptly.
  (B) My younger brother insists that he is as tall as me.
  (C) We walked as long as there was any light to guide us.
  (D) Realizing I had forgotten my gloves, I returned to the theater.

10. (A) Everyone can have a wonderful time in New York if they will just not try to see the entire city in one week.
  (B) Being a stranger in town myself, I know how you feel.
  (C) New York is a city of man-made wonders as awe-inspiring as those found in nature.
  (D) He felt deep despair (as who has not!) at the evidence of man's inhumanity to man.

11. (A) Consider that the person which is always idle can never be happy.
  (B) Because a man understands a woman does not mean they are necessarily compatible.
  (C) He said that accuracy and speed are both essential.
  (D) Can it be said that the better of the two books is less expensive?

12. (A) Neither the critics nor the author were right about the reaction of the public.
  (B) The senator depended upon whoever was willing to assist him.
  (C) I don't recall any time when Edgar has broken his word.
  (D) Every one of the campers but John and me is going on the hike.

13. (A) Never before have I seen anyone who has the skill John has when he repairs engines.
  (B) If anyone can be wholly just in his decisions, it is he.
  (C) Because of his friendliness, the new neighbor was immediately accepted by the community.
  (D) Imagine our embarrassment when us girls saw Miss Maltinge sitting with her beau in the front row.

14. (A) I wondered why it was that the mayor objected to the governor's reference to the new tax law.
  (B) I have never read *Les Miserables,* but I plan to do so this summer.
  (C) After much talk and haranguing, the workers received an increase in wages.
  (D) The author and myself were the only cheerful ones at the macabre gathering.

15. (A) There are very good grounds for such a decision.
  (B) Due to bad weather, the game was postponed.
  (C) The door opens, and in walk John and Mary.
  (D) Where but in America is there greater prosperity?

Correct Answers

1. B   4. C   7. A   10. A   13. D
2. A   5. C   8. C   11. A   14. D
3. C   6. D   9. B   12. A   15. B

Explanatory Answers

1. **(B)** *Everyone* is singular. The pronoun that refers to *everyone* must also be singular. The most common way to express this sentence is *"Everyone* who *reads this book will think himself* (or *herself*) a knight errant on missions of heroism."

2. **(A)** Since the comparison is between three sections, the comparative word must be *largest.*

3. **(C)** A wish or statement contrary to fact is stated in the subjunctive. "I wish that I *were* in Florida now."

4. **(C)** *As well as profit* is additional information, not part of the subject. The subject is the singular *honor,* and so the verb must be the singular *is.*

5. **(C)** Do not use *would have* in an *if* clause. "If you *had* studied the problem carefully, you would have found the solution more quickly."

6. **(D)** *Gallery* is the subject; *was destroyed* must be the predicate. *With all its pictures* is a prepositional phrase.

7. **(A)** A picture is *hung;* a *person* suspended by the neck until dead is *hanged.*

8. **(C)** Turn the sentence around and you discover that the compound, and therefore plural, subject is *the last piece of cake and the last spoonful of ice cream.* Since the subject is plural, the sentence must begin *there go.*

9. **(B)** *As* is a conjunction, not a preposition, and so the pronoun following it must be in the nominative case. Prove this to yourself by completing the sentence "... as tall as *I am."*

10. **(A)** *Everyone* is singular. The pronoun referring to everyone may be *he, she,* or *he or she.*

11. **(A)** *Which* refers only to objects; *who* and *whom* refer to people. In this sentence *who* is correct.

12. **(A)** When the subject is a correlative (*either/or* or *neither/nor*), the verb agrees in number with the second noun. Since *author* is singular, the verb must be *was.*

13. **(D)** *We girls* is the subject of the clause and must be in the nominative case.

14. **(D)** *Myself* is used only in a reflexive sense as when something is reflecting back on me. In this sentence there is no need for a reflexive. The *author and I* is the compound subject of the sentence.

15. **(B)** Never begin a sentence with *due to;* use *because of.* You may think that choice (C) seems awkward, but since both verbs are in the present tense the sentence is correct.

CAPITALIZATION

The English language has relatively few rules regarding capitalization. Beyond these few rules, each writer has discretion as to the use of capital letters for emphasis. The following capitalization rules apply at all times.

Capitalization Rules

1. Capitalize the first word of a sentence.

2. Capitalize the first word of a direct quotation.

   Example: It was Alexander Pope who wrote, *"A* little learning is a dangerous thing."

   NOTE: Do NOT capitalize the first word within quotation marks if it does not begin a complete sentence, as when a directly quoted sentence is broken.

   Example: "I tore my stocking," she told us, *"because* the drawer was left open."

3. Capitalize the letter *I* when it stands alone.

4. Capitalize the first and all other important words in a title.

   Example: The Art of Salesmanship

5. Capitalize a title when it applies to a specific person, group, or document.

   Example: The President will give a press conference this afternoon.

   Example: Senators Goldwater and Tower are leading figures in the Conservative Party.

   Example: Our Constitution should be strictly interpreted.

   NOTE: Do NOT capitalize a title when it does not refer to a specific person, place, or thing.

   Example: Some congressmen are liberal; others are more conservative.

   Example: It would be useful for our club to write a constitution.

6. Capitalize days of the week, months of the year, and holidays.

   Example: The check was mailed on *Thursday,* the day before *Christmas.*

   NOTE: Do NOT capitalize the seasons.

   Example: In Florida, *winter* is mild.

7. Capitalize all proper names.

   Example: China, First National Bank, Dwight Gooden

8. Capitalize the points of the compass only when referring to a specific place or area.

Example: Many retired persons spend the winter in the *South.*

NOTE: Do NOT capitalize the points of the compass when referring to a direction.

Example: Many birds fly *south* in the winter.

9. Capitalize languages and specific place names used as modifiers. Do NOT capitalize any other school subjects.

Example: Next year I will study *French,* biology, *English* literature, mathematics, *European* history, and ancient philosophy.

10. Capitalize nouns that are not regularly capitalized when they are used as part of proper names.

Example: Yesterday I visited *Uncle Charles,* my favorite *uncle.*

Example: *Locust Street* is an exceptionally narrow *street.*

11. In a letter

(a) capitalize all titles in the address and closing.

Example: Mr. John Jones, President

Example: Mary Smith, Chairman of the Board

(b) capitalize the first and last words, titles, and proper names in the salutation.

Example: Dear Dr. Williams

Example: My dear Sir:

(c) capitalize only the first word in a complimentary closing.

Example: Very truly yours,

Capitalization Drill

DIRECTIONS: This is a practice exercise to help you prepare for the test. The sentences below are written entirely in lower case. A number of words in each sentence are underscored, and each underscore is numbered. You must decide whether or not to capitalize the first letter of each underscored word. Print the first letter of each word, capitalized or lower case, on the appropriately numbered line to the right. The correct answers that follow give the rules that apply in each instance.

the applicant asked, "when may i expect to
1   2   3
learn whether or not i have gotten the job?"
                      4
"the committee will meet on thursday, june 5,"
 5   6   7   8
the interviewer replied, "and will announce its
    9   10
decision before summer vacations begin."
                11
the new secretary was instructed to answer the
12   13
telephone by saying, "arco publishing."
                       14   15
for my birthday i am going to see the play
16   17   18
children of a lesser god.
19   20 21 22   23
when aunt frances called, she explained that she
24   25   26
had been visiting her sister in east st. louis.
                      27   28   29 30
the national honor society inducts new
31   32   33   34
members each spring.
35   36
the young man told us, "in high school i
37   38   39   40   41
concentrated on shorthand, typing, and english,
                42   43   44
neglecting mathematics, american history, and
           45   46   47
chemistry.
48
my niece began her condolence letter, "my
49 50   51
dearest aunt dorothy.
52   53   54
the letter of rejection ended, "sincerely yours,
55   56   57
george blank, personnel manager."
58   59   60   61

1	2	3	
4			
5	6	7	8
9	10		
11			
12	13		
14	15		
16	17	18	
19	20	21	22	23
24	25	26	
27	28	29	30
31	32	33	34
35	36		
37	38	39	40	41
42	43	44	
45	46	47	
48			
49	50	51	
52	53	54	
55	56	57	
58	59	60	61

Answers to Capitalization Drill

1. (T) rule 1
2. (W) rule 2
3. (I) rule 3
4. (I) rule 3
5. (T) rules 1 and 2
6. (c) rule 5, not a specific committee
7. (T) rule 6
8. (J) rule 6
9. (i) rule 5, not a specific interviewer
10. (a) rule 2, not the beginning of a sentence
11. (s) rule 6
12. (T) rule 1
13. (s) rule 5, not a specific secretary
14. (A) rule 7
15. (P) rule 7
16. (F) rule 1
17. (b) rule 6, not a recognized holiday
18. (I) rule 3
19. (C) rule 4
20. (o) rule 4, not an important word
21. (a) rule 4, not an important word
22. (L) rule 4
23. (G) rule 4
24. (W) rule 1
25. (A) rule 10
26. (F) rule 7
27. (s) rule 10, not part of a proper name
28. (E) rules 7 and 8
29. (S) rule 7
30. (L) rule 7
31. (T) rule 1

32. (N) rule 7
33. (H) rule 7
34. (S) rule 7
35. (m) rule 5, too general
36. (s) rule 6
37. (T) rule 1
38. (I) rule 2
39. (h) rule 7, not part of a proper name
40. (s) rule 7, not part of a proper name
41. (I) rule 3
42. (s) rule 9
43. (t) rule 9
44. (E) rule 9
45. (m) rule 9
46. (A) rule 9
47. (h) rule 9
48. (c) rule 9
49. (M) rule 1
50. (n) rule 10, not part of a proper name
51. (M) rule 11b
52. (d) rule 11b
53. (A) rules 11b and 10
54. (D) rules 11b and 7
55. (T) rule 1
56. (S) rule 11c
57. (y) rule 11c
58. (G) rule 7
59. (B) rule 7
60. (P) rules 5 and 11a
61. (M) rules 5 and 11a

PUNCTUATION

Unlike the rules applying to capitalization, which are relatively few and easy to understand, the rules applying to punctuation are many and quite complex. This chapter covers the punctuation rules that are most useful to test-takers. Following the rules is a drill with explanations keyed to the rules.

The Apostrophe

A-1. Use an apostrophe in a contraction in place of any omitted letters.

Examples:
haven't	= have not
we're	= we are
let's	= let us
o'clock	= of the clock
class of '85	= class of 1985

Note: Do NOT begin a paragraph with a contraction.

A-2. Use an apostrophe to indicate possession. Place the apostrophe according to this rule: The apostrophe, when used to indicate possession, means *belonging to everthing to the left of the apostrophe.*

Examples:
lady's	= belonging to the lady
ladies'	= belonging to the ladies
children's	= belonging to the children

Note: To test for correct placement of the apostrophe, read *of the.*

Example: childrens' = of the childrens (obviously incorrect)

The placement rule applies at all times, even for compound nouns separated by hyphens and entities made up to two or more names.

Example: father-in-law's = belonging to a father-in-law

Example: Lansdale, Jackson, and Roosevelt's law firm = the law firm belonging to Lansdale, Jackson, and Roosevelt

Example: Brown and Sons' delivery truck = the delivery truck of Brown and Sons

A-3. Use an apostrophe to form plurals of numbers, letters, and phrases referred to as words.

Example: The Japanese child pronounced his *l*'s as *r*'s.

Example: Solution of the puzzle involves crossing out all the *3*'s and *9*'s.

Example: His speech was studded with *you know*'s.

The Colon

CN-1. Use a colon after the salutation in a business letter.

Example: Dear Board Member:

CN-2. Use a colon (or a slash) to separate the initials of the dictator of a letter from the initials of the typist.

Example: RLT:pop

CN-3. Use a colon to separate hours from minutes.

Example: The eclipse occurred at 10:36 A.M.

CN-4. Use of a colon is optional in the following cases:

(a) to introduce a list, especially after an expression such as *as follows*

(b) to introduce a long quotation

(c) to introduce a question

Example: My question is this: Are you willing to punch a time clock?

The Comma

CA-1. Use a comma after the salutation of a personal letter.

Example: Dear Mary,

CA-2. Use a comma after the complimentary close of a letter.

Example: Cordially yours,

CA-3. Use a pair of commas to set off an appositive, a phrase that follows a noun or pronoun and means the same as that noun or pronoun.

Example: Mr. Burke, our lawyer, gave us some good advice.

CA-4. Use a comma or pair of commas to set off a noun of address.

Example: When you finish your homework, Jeff, please take out the garbage.

CA-5. Use a pair of commas to set off parenthetical expressions, words that interrupt the flow of the sentence, such as *however, though, for instance, by the way.*

Example: We could not, however, get him to agree.

Example: This book, I believe, is the best of its kind.

NOTE: Test for placement of commas in a parenthetical expression by reading aloud. If you would pause before and after such an expression, then it should be set off by commas.

CA-6. Use a comma between two or more adjectives that modify a noun equally.

Example: The jolly, fat, ruddy man stood at the top of the stairs.

NOTE: If you can add the word *and* between the adjectives without changing the sense of the sentence, then use commas.

CA-7. Use a comma after an introductory phrase of five or more words.

Example: Because the prisoner had a history of attempted jailbreaks, he was put under heavy guard.

CA-8. Use a comma after a short introductory phrase whenever the comma would aid clarity.

Example: As a child she was a tomboy. (comma unnecessary)

Example: To Dan, Phil was friend as well as brother. (comma clarifies)

Example: In 1978, 300 people lost their lives in one air disaster. (comma clarifies)

CA-9. A comma is not generally used before a subordinate clause that ends a sentence, though in long, unwieldy sentences like this one, use of such commas is optional.

CA-10. Use a comma before a coordinating conjunction unless the two clauses are very short.

Example: The boy wanted to borrow a book from the library, but the librarian would not allow him to take it until he had paid his fines.

Example: Roy washed the dishes and Helen dried.

CA-11. Use a comma to separate words, phrases, or clauses in a series. The use of a comma before *and* is optional. If the series ends in *etc.,* use a comma before *etc.* Do not use a comma after *etc.* in a series, even if the sentence continues.

Example: Coats, umbrellas, and boots should be placed in the closet at the end of the hall.

Example: Pencils, scissors, paper clips, etc. belong in your top desk drawer.

CA-12. Use a comma to separate a short direct quotation from the speaker.

Example: She said, "I must leave work on time today."

Example: "Tomorrow I begin my summer job," he told us.

CA-13. Use a comma to indicate that you have omitted a word or words, such as *of* or *of the.*

Example: President, XYZ Corporation

CA-14. Use a comma to separate a name from a title or personal-name suffix.

    Example: Paul Feiner, Chairman

    Example: Carl Andrew Pforzheimer, Jr.

CA-15. Use a comma when first and last names are reversed.

    Example: Bernbach, Linda

CA-16. Use a comma to separate parts of dates or addresses.

    Example: Please come to a party on Sunday, May 9, at "The Old Mill" on Drake Road, Cheswold, Delaware.

    Exception: Do not use a comma between the postal service state abbreviation and the zip code.

    Example: Scarsdale, NY 10583

CA-17. Use a comma to separate thousands, millions, and trillions.

    Example: 75,281,646

CA-18. Use a pair of commas to set off a nonrestrictive adjective phrase or clause. A nonrestrictive phrase or clause is one that can be omitted without essentially changing the meaning of the sentence.

    Example: Our new sailboat, which has bright orange sails, is very seaworthy.

A restrictive phrase or clause is vital to the meaning of a sentence and cannot be omitted. Do NOT set it off with commas.

    Example: A sailboat without sails is useless.

CA-19. Use a comma if the sentence might be subject to different interpretations without it.

    Example: The banks that closed yesterday are in serious financial difficulty.
                 (Some banks closed yesterday and those banks are in trouble.)
                 The banks, which closed yesterday, are in serious financial difficulty.
                 (All banks closed yesterday and all are in trouble.)

    Example: My brother Bill is getting married.
                 (The implication is that I have more than one brother.)
                 My brother, Bill, is getting married.
                 (Here *Bill* is an appositive. Presumably he is the only brother.)

CA-20. Use a comma if a pause would make the sentence clear and easier to read.

    Example: Inside the people were dancing. (confusing)
                 Inside, the people were dancing. (clearer)

Example: After all crime must be punished. (confusing)
After all, crime must be punished. (clearer)

The pause is not infallible, but it is your best resort when all other rules governing use of the comma fail you.

The Dash

D-1. Use a dash—or parentheses—for emphasis or to set off an explanatory group of words.

> *Example:* The tools of his trade—probe, mirror, cotton swabs—were neatly arranged on the dentist's tray.

> NOTE: Unless the set-off expression ends a sentence, dashes, like parentheses, must be used in pairs.

D-2. Use a dash to mark a sudden break in thought that leaves a sentence unfinished.

> *Example:* He opened the door a crack and saw—

The Exclamation Mark

E-1. Use an exclamation mark only to express strong feeling or emotion or to imply urgency.

> *Example:* Congratulations! You broke the record.

> *Example:* Rush! Perishable contents.

The Hyphen

H-1. Use a hyphen to divide a word at the end of a line. Always divide words between syllables.

H-2. Use a hyphen in numbers from *twenty-one* to *ninety-nine*.

H-3. Use a hyphen to join two words serving together as a single adjective before a noun.

> *Example:* We left the highway and proceeded on a well-paved road.

> *Example:* That baby-faced man is considerably older than he appears to be.

H-4. Use a hyphen with the prefixes *ex-, self-, all-,* and the suffix *-elect*.

    Examples: ex-Senator, self-appointed, all-state, Governor-elect

H-5. Use a hyphen to avoid ambiguity.

    Example: After the custodian recovered the use of his right arm, he re-covered the office chairs.

H-6. Use a hyphen to avoid an awkward union of letters.

    Example: semi-independent, shell-like

The Period

P-1. Use a period at the end of a sentence that makes a statement, gives a command, or makes a "polite request" in the form of a question that does not require an answer.

    Example: I am preparing for my exam.

    Example: Proofread everything you type.

    Example: Would you please hold the script so that I may see if I have memorized my lines.

P-2. Use a period after an abbreviation and after the initial in a person's name.

    Example: Gen. Robert E. Lee led the Confederate forces.

NOTE: Do NOT use a period after postal service state name abbreviations such as AZ (for Arizona) or MI (for Michigan).

P-3. Use a period as a decimal point in numbers.

    Example: A sales tax of 5.5% amounts to $7.47 on a $135.80 purchase.

The Question Mark

QS-1. Use a question after a direct question or after a request for information.

    Example: Why do you wish to return to office work?

    Example: At what time does the last bus leave?

QS-2. Do NOT use a question mark after an indirect question; use a period.

    Example: He asked if they wanted to accompany him.

QS-3. Use a question mark to end a direct question even if the question does not encompass the entire sentence.

    Example: "Daddy, are we there yet?" the child asked.

QS-4. Use a question mark (within parentheses) to indicate uncertainty as to the correctness of a fact.

Example: John Carver, first governor of Plymouth Colony, was born in 1575(?) and died in 1621.

Quotation Marks

QT-1. Use quotation marks to enclose all directly quoted material. Words not quoted must remain outside the quotation marks.

Example: "If it is hot on Sunday," she said, "we will go to the beach."

QT-2. Do NOT enclose an indirect quote in quotation marks.

Example: She said that we might go to the beach on Sunday.

QT-3. When a multiple-paragraph passage is quoted, each paragraph of the quotation must begin with quotation marks, but ending quotation marks are used only at the end of the last quoted paragraph.

QT-4. A period ALWAYS goes inside the quotation marks, whether the quotation marks are used to denote quoted material, to set off titles, or to isolate words used in a special sense.

Example: The principal said, "Cars parked in the fire lane will be ticketed."

Example: The first chapter of *The Andromeda Strain* is entitled "The Country of Lost Borders."

Example: Pornography is sold under the euphemism "adult books."

QT-5. A comma ALWAYS goes inside the quotation marks.

Example: "We really must go home," said the dinner guests.

Example: If your skills become "rusty," you must study before you take the exam.

Example: Three stories in Kurt Vonnegut's *Welcome to the Monkey House* are "Harrison Bergeron," "Next Door," and "Epicac."

QT-6. A question mark goes inside the quotation marks if it is part of the quotation. If the whole sentence containing the quotation is a question, the question mark goes outside the quotation marks.

Example: He asked, "Was tne airplane on time?"

Example: What did you really mean when you said "I do"?

QT-7. An exclamation mark goes inside the quotation marks if the quoted words are an exclamation, outside if the entire sentence including the quoted words is an exclamation, outside if the entire sentence including the quoted words is an exclamation.

> *Example:* The sentry shouted, "Drop your gun!"

> *Example:* Save us from our "friends"!

QT-8. A colon and a semicolon ALWAYS go outside the quotation marks.

> *Example:* He said, "War is destructive"; she added, "Peace is constructive."

QT-9. Use quotation marks around words used in an unusual way.

> *Example:* A surfer who "hangs ten" is performing a tricky maneuver on a surfboard, not staging a mass execution.

QT-10. Set apart a quotation within a quotation by using single quotes.

> *Example:* George said, "The philosophy 'I think, therefore I am' may be attributed to Descartes."

QT-11. Use quotation marks to enclose the title of a short story, essay, short poem, song, or article.

> *Example:* Robert Louis Stevenson wrote a plaintive poem called "Bed in Summer."

NOTE: Titles of books and plays are NOT enclosed in quotation marks. They are printed in italics. In handwritten or typed manuscript, underscore titles of books and plays.

> *Example:* The song "Tradition" is from *Fiddler on the Roof.*

The Semicolon

S-1. You may use a semicolon to join two short, related independent clauses.

> *Example:* Anne is working at the front desk on Monday; Ernie will take over on Tuesday.

NOTE: Two main clauses must be separated by a conjunction *or* by a semicolon *or* they must be written as two sentences. A semicolon never precedes a coordinating conjunction. The same two clauses may be written in any one of three ways:
> Autumn had come and the trees were almost bare.
> Autumn had come; the trees were almost bare.
> Autumn had come. The trees were almost bare.

S-2. You may use a semicolon to separate two independent clauses that are joined by an adverb such as *however, therefore, otherwise,* or *nevertheless.* The adverb must be followed by a comma.

> *Example:* You may use a semicolon to separate this clause from the next; however, you will not be incorrect if you choose to write two separate sentences.

NOTE: If you are uncertain about how to use the semicolon to connect independent clauses, write two sentences instead.

S-3. Use a semicolon to separate a series of phrases or clauses each of which contains commas.

Example: The old gentleman's heirs were Margaret Whitlock, his half-sister; James Bagley, the butler; William Frame, companion to his late cousin, Robert Bone; and his favorite charity, the Salvation Army.

S-4. Use a semicolon to avoid confusion with numbers.

Example: Add the following: $1.25; $7.50; and $12.89.

Punctuation Drill

DIRECTIONS: *This is a practice exercise to help you prepare for the test. Write the proper punctuation mark or marks directly on or above each numbered space. If no punctuation is called for, leave the space blank. At the end of the exercise, you will find the sentences with all punctuation filled in correctly. Explanations follow the correctly punctuated sentences.*

The lawyer __ s __ dictation was so interrupted with *um* __ s and *er* __ s that the secretary
       1 2   3   4
complained __ He __ s __ driving me crazy __
           5   6   7   8

A very large __ low __ yellow __ moon is called a "harvest __ moon __
          9   10   11   12   13

Dr __ Roberts __ do you collect the 5 __ 25% sales __ tax on your charge for office __
  14   15   16   17   18
visits __
  19

The test deals with four __ natural __ sciences __ astronomy __ biology __ chemistry
                         20   21   22   23   24
__ and physics __
25   26

__ Oh __ wow __ the little boy enthused __ I __ m going to have my picture taken with
27   28   29   30 31
Reggie Jackson __
         32

Although the railroad __ s __ spokesman announced __ that all trains were on or close
                 33 34   35
to schedule __ our train arrived at 5 __ 48 instead of at 5 __ o __ clock __
   36   37   38 39   40

Bill McDonald __ the staff __ photographer __ was slightly injured in the accident __
             41   42   43   44
however __ his injury was not serious __
  45   46

The gourmet served a variety of wines with the feast __ claret __ a light __ white __
                                   47   48   49   50
wine __ with the fish __ zinfandel __ a spicy __ red __ wine __ with the meat __ and
  51   52   53   54   55   56   57
cream sherry __ a sweet __ thick __ wine __ with dessert __
       58   59   60   61   62

Last night __ s __ *Daily Newsprint*—an offshoot of the radical __ *This Week* __ s __
      63 64   65   66 67
News __ blatantly suggests that it is unnecessary to ensure a strong army by using the
      68

draft __ It states __ Manpower requirements are being adequately met __
    69   70   71

I was asked to ask you if the party will be over before 11 __ 30 __
                                                72 73

__ Do __ n __ t you think we __ v __ e waited long enough __ the students __ said __
74 75 76   77 78   79   80   81

Would you please check bulky __ packages __ cameras __ umbrellas __ etc __ in the
                                82   83   84   85 86

lobby __ before entering the museum __
   87   88

On Wednesday __ April 15 __ 1981 __ the girl received a letter __ that read __
              89   90   91   92   93
Congratulations __ You have been selected as a member of the class of __ 85 __
          94   95 96

Soon __ the barrel __ chested __ square __ jawed __ loud __ voiced __ dictator
97   98   99   100   101   102   103
felt strong enough to do away with individual __ freedom and self __ government
                                          104   105
altogether __ He abolished all political __ parties __ except his own __ the Fascist
          106   107   108   109
__ Party __ From then on __ Italy __ s __ voters were presented __ as are the
110   111   112   113 114   115
Russian __ voter __ s __ with a single __ list of candidates for office __
     116   117 118   119   120

Correctly Pùnctuated Sentences

(Although the punctuation is correct, the spacing is not entirely accurate because of the need to insert numbered lines.)

The lawyer ' s dictation was so interrupted with um ' s and er ' s that the secretary
      1 2   3   4
complained ," He ' s driving me crazy ."
            5   6 7   8

A very large , low , yellow __ moon is called a "harvest __ moon ."
          9   10   11   12   13

Dr . Roberts , do you collect the 5 . 25% sales __ tax on your charge for office __
  14   15   16   17   18
visits ?
  19

The test deals with four __ natural __ sciences : astronomy , biology , chemistry
                20   21   22   23   24
, and physics .
25   26

"Oh __ wow !" the little boy enthused ," I ' m going to have my picture taken with
    28   29   30 31
Reggie Jackson ."
         32

Although the railroad ' s __ spokesman announced __ that all trains were on or close
              33 34   35
to schedule , our train arrived at 5 : 48 instead of at 5 __ o ' clock .
      36   37   38 39   40

Bill McDonald , the staff __ photographer , was slightly injured in the accident ;
           41   42   43   44
however , his injury was not serious .
     45   46

The gourmet served a variety of wines with the feast : claret , a light , white __
                               47   48   49   50
wine , with the fish ; zinfandel , a spicy , red __ wine , with the meat ; and
    51   52   53   54 55   56   57
cream sherry , a sweet , thick __ wine , with dessert .
       58   59   60   61   62

Last night ' s __ *Daily Newsprint*—an offshoot of the radical __ *This Week* ' s __
        63 64   65   66 67
News — blatantly suggests that it is unnecessary to ensure a strong army by using the
    68
draft . It states ," Manpower requirements are being adequately met ."
  69   70   71

I was asked to ask you if the party will be over before 11 $\underset{72}{:}$ 30 $\underset{73}{.}$

$\underset{74}{"}$ Do $\underset{75}{}$ n $\underset{76}{'}$ t you think we $\underset{77}{'}$ v $\underset{78}{}$ e waited long enough $\underset{79}{?"}$ the students $\underset{80}{}$ said $\underset{81}{.}$

Would you please check bulky $\underset{82}{}$ packages $\underset{83}{,}$ cameras $\underset{84}{,}$ umbrellas $\underset{85}{,}$ etc $\underset{86}{.}$ in the lobby $\underset{87}{}$ before entering the museum $\underset{88}{.}$

On Wednesday $\underset{89}{,}$ April 15 $\underset{90}{,}$ 1981 $\underset{91}{,}$ the girl received a letter $\underset{92}{}$ that read $\underset{93}{,"}$ Congratulations $\underset{94}{!}$ You have been selected as a member of the class of $\underset{95}{'}$ 85 $\underset{96}{."}$

Soon $\underset{97}{}$ the barrel $\underset{98}{-}$ chested $\underset{99}{,}$ square $\underset{100}{-}$ jawed $\underset{101}{,}$ loud $\underset{102}{-}$ voiced $\underset{103}{}$ dictator felt strong enough to do away with individual $\underset{104}{}$ freedom and self $\underset{105}{-}$ government altogether $\underset{106}{.}$ He abolished all political $\underset{107}{}$ parties $\underset{108}{}$ except his own $\underset{109}{,}$ the Fascist $\underset{110}{}$ Party $\underset{111}{.}$ From then on $\underset{112}{,}$ Italy $\underset{113}{'}$ s $\underset{114}{}$ voters were presented $\underset{115}{,}$ as are the Russian $\underset{116}{}$ voter $\underset{117}{}$ s $\underset{118}{,}$ with a single $\underset{119}{}$ list of candidates for office $\underset{120}{.}$

Explanatory Answers

1. A-2
2. A-2 Reread the rules to see how the same rule can explain both the presence and absence of a punctuation mark.
3. A-3
4. A-3
5. CA-12 and QT-1
6. A-1
7. A-1
8. P-1, QT-1, and QT-4
9. CA-6
10. CA-6
11. CA-6
12. No punctuation needed
13. P-1, QT-4, and QT-9
14. P-2
15. CA-4
16. P-3
17. No punctuation needed
18. No punctuation needed
19. QS-1
20. CA-6
21. CA-6
22. CN-4, a dash also acceptable
23. CA-11
24. CA-11
25. CA-11, comma optional
26. P-1
27. QT-1
28. No punctuation needed
29. E-1, QT-1, and QT-7
30. CA-12 and QT-1
31. A-1
32. P-1, QT-1, and QT-4
33. A-2
34. A-2
35. QT-2
36. CA-7
37. CN-3
38. No punctuation needed
39. A-1
40. P-1
41. CA-3
42. No punctuation needed
43. CA-3
44. S-2
45. S-2
46. P-1
47. CN-4, a dash also acceptable
48. CA-3
49. CA-6
50. No punctuation needed
51. CA-3
52. S-3
53. CA-3
54. CA-6
55. No punctuation needed
56. CA-3
57. S-3
58. CA-3
59. CA-6
60. No punctuation needed
61. CA-3
62. P-1
63. A-2
64. A-2
65. No punctuation needed
66. A-2
67. A-2
68. D-1
69. P-1 The length of the first independent clause dictates that two sentences be formed, rather than one sentence joined with a semicolon.
70. CA-12 and QT-1
71. P-1, QT-1, and QT-4
72. CN-3
73. P-1 and QS-2
74. QT-1
75. A-1
76. A-1
77. A-1
78. A-1
79. QS-1, QS-3, QT-1, and QT-6
80. No punctuation needed
81. P-1
82. No punctuation needed
83. CA-11
84. CA-11
85. CA-11
86. P-2 and CA-11
87. CA-9
88. P-1
89. CA-16
90. CA-16
91. CA-16 and CA-8
92. No punctuation needed
93. CA-12 and QT-1
94. E-1
95. A-1
96. P-1, QT-1 and QT-4
97. CA-8

98. H-3
99. CA-6
100. H-3
101. CA-6
102. H-3
103. No punctuation needed
104. No punctuation needed
105. H-4
106. P-1
107. No punctuation needed
108. CA-18 *Except his own* is a restrictive clause; it is vital to the meaning of the sentence.
109. CA-3

110. No punctuation needed
111. P-1
112. CA-8 and CA-20
113. A-2
114. A-2
115. CA-18 *As are the Russian voters* is a nonrestrictive clause. While the clause adds information, the sentence retains the same meaning if the clause is elminated.
116. No punctuation needed
117. No punctuation needed
118. CA-18
119. No punctuation needed
120. P-1

SPELLING RULES

We all must spell. Some fortunate individuals are "natural" spellers. They are able to picture a word and instinctively spell it correctly. Most of us must memorize rules and rely on a dictionary. It is NOT a sign of weakness to consult a dictionary whenever you are in doubt. In fact, whenever you are not sure of the spelling of a word, you MUST look it up. Constant use of the dictionary, however, does slow your work.

You can improve your spelling by learning the following rules. You can also improve your spelling by making a list of words that you spell incorrectly or that you must look up repeatedly. Write each word correctly a number of times. Your eye will become accustomed to seeing the word correctly spelled. Occasionally the spelling of a word is best remembered by use of a mnemonic* device. Do not be ashamed to develop private clues. No one is testing you on the orthodoxy of your methods; you are only expected to spell correctly. An example of a mnemonic device used to avoid ie/ei confusion is spelling the word *friend* in the sentence, "A fri*end* is true to the *end*."

The English language is not kind to spellers. Words have been adopted from many different languages, each with its own spelling rules and exceptions. Not only may the same sound be produced by any number of different combinations of letters, but the same combination of letters may also produce a number of different sounds. In fact, there are very few rules to help you cope with the spelling of the roots of words. These simply must be learned. Besides the ie/ei rule, nearly all spelling rules apply to the adding of suffixes and prefixes.

Following are the most useful rules and the most common exceptions to these rules. Memorize whatever rules you can, and keep these pages handy for ready reference whenever you write.

1. *i* before *e*
   Except after *c*
   Or when sounded like *ay*
   As in *neighbor* or *weigh*.

   Exception: Neither, leisure, foreigner, seize, weird, height.

   NOTE: This rule also does not apply when the *ie* combination is pronounced *eh* even when it immediately follows the letter *c*.

   Examples: ancient, conscience, deficient, efficient, proficient

2. If a word ends in *y* preceded by a vowel, keep the *y* when adding a suffix.

   Examples: day, days; attorney, attorneys; spray, sprayer

3. If a word ends in *y* preceded by a consonant, change the *y* to *i* before adding a suffix.
   Examples: try, tries, tried: lady, ladies; dainty, daintiest; steady, steadily; heavy, heavier; study, studious; ally, alliance; defy, defiant; beauty, beautiful; justify, justifiable

   Exception: dry, dryly, dryness; shy, shyly; sly, slyly, slyness; spry, spryly; wry, wryly

*If you do not know the meaning of any word used in this book, look it up. A rich vocabulary is vital to career growth.

NOTE: This rule does not apply before *-ing* and *-ish.* To avoid double *i,* retain the *y* before *-ing* and *-ish.*

Examples: fly, flying; baby, babyish; relay, relaying

4. Silent *e* at the end of a word is usually dropped before a suffix beginning with a vowel.

Examples: dine + ing = dining
locate + ion = location
use + able = usable
offense + ive = offensive
relieve + ed = relieved
admire + ation = admiration

Exception: Words ending in *ce* and *ge* retain *e* before *-able* and *-ous* in order to retain the soft sounds of *c* and *g.*

Examples: peace + able = peaceable
courage + ous = courageous

5. Silent *e* is usually kept before a suffix beginning with a consonant.

Examples: care + less = careless
late + ly = lately
one + ness = oneness
game + ster = gamester
manage + ment = management

6. Some exceptions must simply be memorized. Some exceptions to the last two rules are: truly, duly, awful, argument, wholly, ninth, mileage, dyeing, acreage, canoeing, judgment.

7. A word of one syllable that ends in a *single* consonant preceded by a *single* vowel doubles the final consonant before a suffix beginning with a vowel or *y.*

Examples: hit, hitting; drop, dropped; big, biggest; mud, muddy; quit, quitter; flat, flatten

But: Help, helping because *help* ends in *two* consonants; need, needing because the final consonant is preceded by *two* vowels.

8. A word of more than one syllable that accents the *last* syllable and that ends in a *single* consonant preceded by a *single* vowel doubles the final consonant when adding a suffix beginning with a vowel.

Examples: begin, beginner; admit, admitted; control, controlling; excel, excellence; recur, recurrent; admit, admittance; transmit, transmittal; forbid, forbidden; control, controllable

But: Enter, entered because the accent is *not* on the last syllable; divert, diverted because the word ends in *two* consonants; refrain, refraining because *two* vowels precede the final consonant; equip, equipment because the suffix begins with a consonant.

9. A word ending in *er* or *ur* doubles the *r* in the past tense if the word is accented on the last syllable.

   Examples: occur, occurred; prefer, preferred; transfer, transferred

10. A word ending in *er* does *not* double the *r* in the past tense if the accent falls on other than the last syllable.

    Example: answer, answered; offer, offered; differ, differed

11. When *-full* is added to the end of a noun to form an adjective, the final *l* is dropped.

    Example: cheerful, cupful, hopeful

12. All words beginning with *over* are one word.

    Examples: overcast, overcharge, overhear

13. All words with the prefix *self* are hyphenated.

    Examples: self-control, self-defense, self-evident

14. The letter *q* is always followed by *u.*

    Examples: quiz, bouquet, acquire

15. Numbers from twenty-one to ninety-nine are hyphenated.

16. *Percent* is *never* hyphenated. It may be written as one word *(percent)* or as two words *(per cent).*

17. *Welcome* is one word with one *l.*

18. *All right* is always two words. There is no such word as *alright.*

19. *Already* means *prior to some specified time.*
    All ready means *completely ready.*

    Example: By the time I was *all ready* to go to the play, he had *already* left.

20. *Altogether* means *entirely.*
    All together means *in sum* or *collectively.*

    Example: There are *altogether* too many people to seat in this room when we are *all together.*

21. *Their* is the possessive of *they.*
    They're is the contraction for *they are.*
    There is *that place.*

    Example: *They're* going to put *their* books over *there.*

22. *Your* is the possessive of *you.*
    You're is the contraction of *you are.*

    Example: *You're* planning to leave *your* muddy boots outside, aren't you?

23. *Whose* is the possessive of *who.*
Who's is the contraction for *who is.*

> *Example:* Do you know *who's* ringing the doorbell or *whose* car is in the street?

24. *Its* is the possessive of *it.*
It's is the contraction for *it is.*

> *Example:* *It's* I who put *its* file over there.

Needless to say, there are many more rules than these, but these few will see you through thousands of words and hundreds of perplexing situations.

One final hint: If you find certain words you simply must look up every time you use them, write a list of these words, correctly spelled, and paste it onto the inside of the front cover of your dictionary. You will save valuable time with such a list. Consult this list of your "personal spelling devils" the day before your exam. Chances are that the words that trouble you trouble others as well; they may appear on your exam.

Spelling Drill

This is a practice exercise. Test yourself now to see how well you apply the rules you have just learned. Write the correct spelling of each word on the line to the right of each question. If a word is correctly spelled, write the correct spelling on the line anyway. At the end of the drill, you will find the correct spelling of each word, along with the number of the rule that governs its spelling. Do not be distressed if you do poorly. The purpose of this drill is to pinpoint for you the rules you need to study.

1. sense + ation

2. alright

3. quack

4. the plural of fury

5. siege

6. grotesqe

7. wonder + full

8. most early

9. liesure

10. communicate + ion

11. <u>Whose</u> planning to go to the beach?

12. value + able

13. one who suffers

14. over + reach

15. 76

16. feign

17. nice + ly

18. per + cent

19. We are having dinner at <u>there</u> house.

20. mile + age

21. nest + ing

22. refer + ed

1. _____

2. _____

3. _____

4. _____

5. _____

6. _____

7. _____

8. _____

9. _____

10. _____

11. _____

12. _____

13. _____

14. _____

15. _____

16. _____

17. _____

18. _____

19. _____

20. _____

21. _____

22. _____

23. Today is <u>all together</u> too cold to swim.   23. _____

24. marry + ing   24. _____

25. commit + ed   25. _____

26. help + full   26. _____

27. receipt   27. _____

28. 32   28. _____

29. self + righteous   29. _____

30. The dog cannot remember where it buried <u>it's</u> bone.   30. _____

31. proffer + ed   31. _____

32. rib + ing   32. _____

33. sputter + er   33. _____

34. We have <u>already</u> missed the bus.   34. _____

35. self + possessed   35. _____

36. play + ing   36. _____

37. defer + ed   37. _____

38. Are you sure of <u>your</u> facts?   38. _____

39. over + grown   39. _____

40. seed + y   40. _____

41. alert + ed   41. _____

42. wellcome   42. _____

43. The class was <u>already</u> for the exam.   43. _____

44. faith + full   44. _____

45. tag + ed   45. _____

46. abet + or   46. _____

47. <u>Their</u> going to the movies tonight.   47. _____

48. conceivable   48. _____

49. lace + able   49. _____

50. <u>Who's</u> pen is this?

50. _____

51. disgrace + full

51. _____

52. ceremony + ous

52. _____

53. concur + ed

53. _____

54. per cent

54. _____

55. aweful

55. _____

56. mother + ed

56. _____

57. detain + ing

57. _____

58. freight

58. _____

59. 99

59. _____

60. What is <u>they're</u> reason for leaving so early?

60. _____

61. over-cautious

61. _____

62. advantage + ous

62. _____

63. parquet

63. _____

64. cook + er

64. _____

65. coyly

65. _____

66. selfsame

66. _____

67. The weatherman says that <u>its</u> going to rain tonight.

67. _____

68. seive

68. _____

69. multiply + ing

69. _____

70. dyeing

70. _____

71. blur + y

71. _____

72. quote + ation

72. _____

73. regret + ed

73. _____

74. well + come

74. _____

75. I think <u>your</u> going to be last on the list.

75. _____

76. subsist + ed

76. _____

77. proficient

77. _____

78. sad + ness

78. _____

79. appreciate + ive

79. _____

80. <u>Alright,</u> Boy Scouts, everyone stand at attention.

80. _____

81. more moody

81. _____

82. observe + able

82. _____

83. <u>Whose</u> fingerprints are on the gun?

83. _____

84. limit + ing

84. _____

85. past tense of bother

85. _____

86. The move starts in an hour; why are you here <u>all</u> <u>ready?</u>

86. _____

87. farm + ing

87. _____

88. glad + en

88. _____

89. forget + able

89. _____

90. arguement

90. _____

91. announce + ment

91. _____

92. percieve

92. _____

93. service + able

93. _____

94. It may be many years before we are <u>all</u> <u>together</u> again.

94. _____

95. tremble + ing

95. _____

96. disbar + ed

96. _____

97. <u>Who's</u> muffler is making that terrible noise?

97. _____

98. eightieth

98. _____

99. pity + full

99. _____

100. Now <u>its</u> all done.

100. _____

Answers to Spelling Drill

1. sensation—rule 4
2. all right—rule 18
3. quack—rule 14
4. furies—rule 3
5. siege—rule 1
6. grotesque—rule 14
7. wonderful—rule 11
8. earliest—rule 3
9. leisure—rule 1, exception
10. communication—rule 4
11. who's—rule 23
12. valuable—rule 4
13. sufferer—rule 10
14. overreach—rule 12
15. seventy-six—rule 15
16. feign—rule 1, sounded like *ay*
17. nicely—rule 5
18. percent *or* per cent—rule 16
19. their—rule 21
20. mileage—rule 6
21. nesting—rule 7, *nest* ends in two consonants
22. referred—rule 9
23. altogether—rule 20
24. marrying—rule 3, note
25. committed—rule 8
26. helpful—rule 11
27. receipt—rule 1
28. thirty-two—rule 15
29. self-righteous—rule 13
30. its—rule 24
31. proffered—rule 10
32. ribbing—rule 7
33. sputterer—rule 8, accent not on the last syllable
34. already—rule 19
35. self-possessed—rule 13
36. playing—rule 2
37. deferred—rule 9
38. your—rule 22
39. overgrown—rule 12
40. seedy—rule 7, final consonant preceded by two vowels
41. alerted—rule 8, *alert* ends in two consonants
42. welcome—rule 17
43. all ready—rule 19
44. faithful—rule 11
45. tagged—rule 7

46. abettor—rule 8
47. they're—rule 21
48. conceivable—rules 1 and 4
49. laceable—rule 4, exception
50. whose—rule 23
51. disgraceful—rules 5 and 11
52. ceremonious—rule 3
53. concurred—rule 9
54. percent *or* per cent—rule 16
55. awful—rules 6 and 11
56. mothered—rule 10
57. detaining—rule 8, there are two vowels before the final consonant
58. freight—rule 1, sounded like *ay*
59. ninety-nine—rules 5 and 15
60. their—rule 21, possessive of *they*
61. overcautious—rule 12
62. advantageous—rule 4, maintain soft *g*
63. parquet—rule 14
64. cooker—rule 7, two vowels precede the final consonant
65. coyly—rule 2
66. self-same—rule 13
67. it's—rule 24, it is
68. sieve—rule 1
69. multiplying—rule 3, avoid double *i*
70. dyeing—rule 6
71. blurry—rule 7
72. quotation—rule 4
73. regretted—rule 8
74. welcome—rule 17
75. you're—rule 22, *you are*
76. subsisted—rule 8, the word ends in two consonants
77. proficient—rule 1, sounds like *eh*
78. sadness—rule 7, suffix begins with a consonant
79. appreciative—rule 4
80. all right—rule 18
81. moodier—rule 3
82. observable—rule 4
83. whose—rule 23, possessive of *who*
84. limiting—rule 8, accent not on last syllable
85. bothered—rule 10
86. already—rule 19
87. farming—rule 7, word ends with two consonants
88. gladden—rule 7
89. forgettable—rule 8

90. argument—rule 6
91. announcement—rule 5
92. perceive—rule 1
93. serviceable—rule 4, maintain soft *c*
94. all together—rule 20
95. trembling—rule 4

96. disbarred—rule 8
97. whose—rule 23, possessive of *who*
98. eightieth—rule 1 applies in each case
99. pitiful—rules 3 and 11
100. it's—rule 24, *it is*

400 FREQUENTLY MISSPELLED WORDS

If you are following our advice, you have begun to compile a list of your "personal spelling devils." Most of your words probably appear on the following list. These are words that have proved troublesome for most test-takers and are words that frequently appear on spelling tests.

Ask a family member or friend to dictate this list to you, and write each word. Then compare your written list with the printed list. Place an X next to each word that you misspelled. Be honest with yourself. Place an X also before each word that you spelled correctly from sheer luck. Now make a list of all words preceded by an X. For each of these words:

1. LOOK at the word carefully.
2. PRONOUNCE each syllable clearly.
3. PICTURE the word in your mind.
4. WRITE the word correctly at least three times.

When you feel confident that you have mastered this list, have you friend dictate it again. Check to discover which words you still do not know how to spell. Repeat the study process. If you are still having trouble with words you are likely to use often, add them to your "personal spelling devils" list.

A

aberration
abscess
absence
abundance
accessible
accidental
accommodate
accumulation
accurately
achievement
acknowledgment
acquaint
address
adjunct
affectionate
aggravate
aisle
alleged
all right
amateur
amendment
American
ancestor
ancient
anecdote
annoyance
antarctic
anticipate
apparatus
apparently
arctic
argue
arraignment
arrange
ascertain
asparagus
assessment
assistance
attaché
audience
August
author
available
awkward

B

bankruptcy
barbarian
barren
basically
beautiful
because
beggar
begun
beleaguered
besiege
bewilder
bicycle
breathe
bulletin
bureau
burial

C

cabinet
cafeteria
caffeine
calendar
campaign
capital
capitol
career
ceiling
cemetery
changeable
character
charlatan

chauffeur
chief
chimney
choose
college
column
committal
committee
community
competitor
confectionery
conscience
conscious
consequence
conquer
consul
continuous
correlation
counsel
courageous
criticism
crucial
crystallized
culpable
currency
curtain
customer

D

dairy
deceit
December
decide
deferred
demur
derogatory
desecrated
desert
descendant
desperate
dessert
diary
dictatorship
difficulty
dilapidated
diphtheria
disappearance
disappoint
disastrous
disease
dismal
dissatisfied
distinguished

doubt
dying

E

ecstasy
eczema
eight
either
embarrass
eminent
emphasis
emphatically
ephemeral
equipment
essential
exaggerate
exceed
except
exercise
exhaust
exhibition
exhortation
existence
explain
extension
extraordinary

F

familiar
fascinated
February
feudal
fiend
fierce
financier
freight
Friday
friend
forehead
foreign
foreword
forfeit
forward
furniture
further

G

gaseous
gelatin
geography
ghost
gingham
glacier

glandular
gnash
gonorrhea
government
grammar
grain
grandeur
grievous
guarantee
guard
guess
guidance

H

hallelujah
harassed
hearth
heathen
heavily
height
heinous
heretic
heritage
heroes
hieroglyphic
hindrance
hippopotamus
horrify
humorous
hundredth
hygienic
hymn
hypocrisy

I

imaginary
immediate
imminent
impartiality
incongruous
incumbent
independent
indict
inimitable
instantaneous
integrity
intercede
interference
interruption
introduce
irreparably

J

January
jealous
jeopardy
jewelry
journal
judgment
judicial
justice
justification

K

kernel
kindergarten
kiln
kilometer
kilowatt
kitchen
knee
knot
knowledge

L

laboratory
labyrinth
lacquer
leisure
legible
length
lieutenant
lightning
liquidate
literature
loneliness
loose
lovable

M

maintenance
maneuver
marriage
masquerade
materialize
mathematics
matinee
mechanical
medallion
medicine
medieval
memoir

mischievous
misspell
muscle

N

naturally
necessary
negligible
neither
nickel
niece
ninth
noticeable
nucleus

O

oasis
obligatory
obsolescence
occasion
occurrence
official
omitted
ordinance
outrageous

P

pamphlet
panicky
parallel
paraphernalia
parliamentary
patient
peculiar
persuade
physician
picnicking
pneumonia
possession
precious
preferred
prejudice
presumptuous
privilege
propaganda
publicity
punctilious
pursuit

Q

quarrel
queue
quiescent

quiet
quite
quotient

R

receipt
recognize
reference
regrettable
rehearsal
relevant
religious
renascence
repetitious
requirement
reservoir
resilience
resources
restaurant
resurrection
rhetorical

S

sacrilegious
scenery
schedule
scissors
secretary
separate
siege
seizure
sophomore
source
sovereign
specialized
specifically
statute
staunch
subversive
succeed
sufficient
surgeon
surgical
surely
stationary
stationery
symmetrical
sympathetic

T

temperamental
temperature
tendency

thorough
through
tomorrow
tragedy
transferred
transient
truculent
Tuesday
typical

U-Z

umbrella
unctuous

undoubtedly
unique
unusual
usage
usual
vacillate
vacuum
valuable
variety
vegetable
veil
vengeance
villain
Wednesday

weight
weird
whether
wholesome
wholly
wield
wouldn't
written
Xerox
xylophone
yacht
yield
zombie

Answer Sheet for Spelling Practice Tests

Test 1

1 Ⓐ Ⓑ Ⓒ Ⓓ	31 Ⓐ Ⓑ Ⓒ Ⓓ	61 Ⓐ Ⓑ Ⓒ Ⓓ
2 Ⓐ Ⓑ Ⓒ Ⓓ	32 Ⓐ Ⓑ Ⓒ Ⓓ	62 Ⓐ Ⓑ Ⓒ Ⓓ
3 Ⓐ Ⓑ Ⓒ Ⓓ	33 Ⓐ Ⓑ Ⓒ Ⓓ	63 Ⓐ Ⓑ Ⓒ Ⓓ
4 Ⓐ Ⓑ Ⓒ Ⓓ	34 Ⓐ Ⓑ Ⓒ Ⓓ	64 Ⓐ Ⓑ Ⓒ Ⓓ
5 Ⓐ Ⓑ Ⓒ Ⓓ	35 Ⓐ Ⓑ Ⓒ Ⓓ	65 Ⓐ Ⓑ Ⓒ Ⓓ
6 Ⓐ Ⓑ Ⓒ Ⓓ	36 Ⓐ Ⓑ Ⓒ Ⓓ	66 Ⓐ Ⓑ Ⓒ Ⓓ
7 Ⓐ Ⓑ Ⓒ Ⓓ	37 Ⓐ Ⓑ Ⓒ Ⓓ	67 Ⓐ Ⓑ Ⓒ Ⓓ
8 Ⓐ Ⓑ Ⓒ Ⓓ	38 Ⓐ Ⓑ Ⓒ Ⓓ	68 Ⓐ Ⓑ Ⓒ Ⓓ
9 Ⓐ Ⓑ Ⓒ Ⓓ	39 Ⓐ Ⓑ Ⓒ Ⓓ	69 Ⓐ Ⓑ Ⓒ Ⓓ
10 Ⓐ Ⓑ Ⓒ Ⓓ	40 Ⓐ Ⓑ Ⓒ Ⓓ	70 Ⓐ Ⓑ Ⓒ Ⓓ
11 Ⓐ Ⓑ Ⓒ Ⓓ	41 Ⓐ Ⓑ Ⓒ Ⓓ	71 Ⓐ Ⓑ Ⓒ Ⓓ
12 Ⓐ Ⓑ Ⓒ Ⓓ	42 Ⓐ Ⓑ Ⓒ Ⓓ	72 Ⓐ Ⓑ Ⓒ Ⓓ
13 Ⓐ Ⓑ Ⓒ Ⓓ	43 Ⓐ Ⓑ Ⓒ Ⓓ	73 Ⓐ Ⓑ Ⓒ Ⓓ
14 Ⓐ Ⓑ Ⓒ Ⓓ	44 Ⓐ Ⓑ Ⓒ Ⓓ	74 Ⓐ Ⓑ Ⓒ Ⓓ
15 Ⓐ Ⓑ Ⓒ Ⓓ	45 Ⓐ Ⓑ Ⓒ Ⓓ	75 Ⓐ Ⓑ Ⓒ Ⓓ
16 Ⓐ Ⓑ Ⓒ Ⓓ	46 Ⓐ Ⓑ Ⓒ Ⓓ	76 Ⓐ Ⓑ Ⓒ Ⓓ
17 Ⓐ Ⓑ Ⓒ Ⓓ	47 Ⓐ Ⓑ Ⓒ Ⓓ	77 Ⓐ Ⓑ Ⓒ Ⓓ
18 Ⓐ Ⓑ Ⓒ Ⓓ	48 Ⓐ Ⓑ Ⓒ Ⓓ	78 Ⓐ Ⓑ Ⓒ Ⓓ
19 Ⓐ Ⓑ Ⓒ Ⓓ	49 Ⓐ Ⓑ Ⓒ Ⓓ	79 Ⓐ Ⓑ Ⓒ Ⓓ
20 Ⓐ Ⓑ Ⓒ Ⓓ	50 Ⓐ Ⓑ Ⓒ Ⓓ	80 Ⓐ Ⓑ Ⓒ Ⓓ
21 Ⓐ Ⓑ Ⓒ Ⓓ	51 Ⓐ Ⓑ Ⓒ Ⓓ	81 Ⓐ Ⓑ Ⓒ Ⓓ
22 Ⓐ Ⓑ Ⓒ Ⓓ	52 Ⓐ Ⓑ Ⓒ Ⓓ	82 Ⓐ Ⓑ Ⓒ Ⓓ
23 Ⓐ Ⓑ Ⓒ Ⓓ	53 Ⓐ Ⓑ Ⓒ Ⓓ	83 Ⓐ Ⓑ Ⓒ Ⓓ
24 Ⓐ Ⓑ Ⓒ Ⓓ	54 Ⓐ Ⓑ Ⓒ Ⓓ	84 Ⓐ Ⓑ Ⓒ Ⓓ
25 Ⓐ Ⓑ Ⓒ Ⓓ	55 Ⓐ Ⓑ Ⓒ Ⓓ	85 Ⓐ Ⓑ Ⓒ Ⓓ
26 Ⓐ Ⓑ Ⓒ Ⓓ	56 Ⓐ Ⓑ Ⓒ Ⓓ	86 Ⓐ Ⓑ Ⓒ Ⓓ
27 Ⓐ Ⓑ Ⓒ Ⓓ	57 Ⓐ Ⓑ Ⓒ Ⓓ	87 Ⓐ Ⓑ Ⓒ Ⓓ
28 Ⓐ Ⓑ Ⓒ Ⓓ	58 Ⓐ Ⓑ Ⓒ Ⓓ	88 Ⓐ Ⓑ Ⓒ Ⓓ
29 Ⓐ Ⓑ Ⓒ Ⓓ	59 Ⓐ Ⓑ Ⓒ Ⓓ	89 Ⓐ Ⓑ Ⓒ Ⓓ
30 Ⓐ Ⓑ Ⓒ Ⓓ	60 Ⓐ Ⓑ Ⓒ Ⓓ	

Test 2

1 Ⓐ Ⓑ Ⓒ Ⓓ	10 Ⓐ Ⓑ Ⓒ Ⓓ	19 Ⓐ Ⓑ Ⓒ Ⓓ	28 Ⓐ Ⓑ Ⓒ Ⓓ
2 Ⓐ Ⓑ Ⓒ Ⓓ	11 Ⓐ Ⓑ Ⓒ Ⓓ	20 Ⓐ Ⓑ Ⓒ Ⓓ	29 Ⓐ Ⓑ Ⓒ Ⓓ
3 Ⓐ Ⓑ Ⓒ Ⓓ	12 Ⓐ Ⓑ Ⓒ Ⓓ	21 Ⓐ Ⓑ Ⓒ Ⓓ	30 Ⓐ Ⓑ Ⓒ Ⓓ
4 Ⓐ Ⓑ Ⓒ Ⓓ	13 Ⓐ Ⓑ Ⓒ Ⓓ	22 Ⓐ Ⓑ Ⓒ Ⓓ	31 Ⓐ Ⓑ Ⓒ Ⓓ
5 Ⓐ Ⓑ Ⓒ Ⓓ	14 Ⓐ Ⓑ Ⓒ Ⓓ	23 Ⓐ Ⓑ Ⓒ Ⓓ	32 Ⓐ Ⓑ Ⓒ Ⓓ
6 Ⓐ Ⓑ Ⓒ Ⓓ	15 Ⓐ Ⓑ Ⓒ Ⓓ	24 Ⓐ Ⓑ Ⓒ Ⓓ	33 Ⓐ Ⓑ Ⓒ Ⓓ
7 Ⓐ Ⓑ Ⓒ Ⓓ	16 Ⓐ Ⓑ Ⓒ Ⓓ	25 Ⓐ Ⓑ Ⓒ Ⓓ	34 Ⓐ Ⓑ Ⓒ Ⓓ
8 Ⓐ Ⓑ Ⓒ Ⓓ	17 Ⓐ Ⓑ Ⓒ Ⓓ	26 Ⓐ Ⓑ Ⓒ Ⓓ	35 Ⓐ Ⓑ Ⓒ Ⓓ
9 Ⓐ Ⓑ Ⓒ Ⓓ	18 Ⓐ Ⓑ Ⓒ Ⓓ	27 Ⓐ Ⓑ Ⓒ Ⓓ	

Test 3

1 Ⓐ Ⓑ Ⓒ Ⓓ		10 Ⓐ Ⓑ Ⓒ Ⓓ		19 Ⓐ Ⓑ Ⓒ Ⓓ		28 Ⓐ Ⓑ Ⓒ Ⓓ
2 Ⓐ Ⓑ Ⓒ Ⓓ		11 Ⓐ Ⓑ Ⓒ Ⓓ		20 Ⓐ Ⓑ Ⓒ Ⓓ		29 Ⓐ Ⓑ Ⓒ Ⓓ
3 Ⓐ Ⓑ Ⓒ Ⓓ		12 Ⓐ Ⓑ Ⓒ Ⓓ		21 Ⓐ Ⓑ Ⓒ Ⓓ		30 Ⓐ Ⓑ Ⓒ Ⓓ
4 Ⓐ Ⓑ Ⓒ Ⓓ		13 Ⓐ Ⓑ Ⓒ Ⓓ		22 Ⓐ Ⓑ Ⓒ Ⓓ		31 Ⓐ Ⓑ Ⓒ Ⓓ
5 Ⓐ Ⓑ Ⓒ Ⓓ		14 Ⓐ Ⓑ Ⓒ Ⓓ		23 Ⓐ Ⓑ Ⓒ Ⓓ		32 Ⓐ Ⓑ Ⓒ Ⓓ
6 Ⓐ Ⓑ Ⓒ Ⓓ		15 Ⓐ Ⓑ Ⓒ Ⓓ		24 Ⓐ Ⓑ Ⓒ Ⓓ		33 Ⓐ Ⓑ Ⓒ Ⓓ
7 Ⓐ Ⓑ Ⓒ Ⓓ		16 Ⓐ Ⓑ Ⓒ Ⓓ		25 Ⓐ Ⓑ Ⓒ Ⓓ		34 Ⓐ Ⓑ Ⓒ Ⓓ
8 Ⓐ Ⓑ Ⓒ Ⓓ		17 Ⓐ Ⓑ Ⓒ Ⓓ		26 Ⓐ Ⓑ Ⓒ Ⓓ		
9 Ⓐ Ⓑ Ⓒ Ⓓ		18 Ⓐ Ⓑ Ⓒ Ⓓ		27 Ⓐ Ⓑ Ⓒ Ⓓ		

Test 4

1 Ⓐ Ⓑ Ⓒ Ⓓ	7 Ⓐ Ⓑ Ⓒ Ⓓ	13 Ⓐ Ⓑ Ⓒ Ⓓ
2 Ⓐ Ⓑ Ⓒ Ⓓ	8 Ⓐ Ⓑ Ⓒ Ⓓ	14 Ⓐ Ⓑ Ⓒ Ⓓ
3 Ⓐ Ⓑ Ⓒ Ⓓ	9 Ⓐ Ⓑ Ⓒ Ⓓ	15 Ⓐ Ⓑ Ⓒ Ⓓ
4 Ⓐ Ⓑ Ⓒ Ⓓ	10 Ⓐ Ⓑ Ⓒ Ⓓ	16 Ⓐ Ⓑ Ⓒ Ⓓ
5 Ⓐ Ⓑ Ⓒ Ⓓ	11 Ⓐ Ⓑ Ⓒ Ⓓ	17 Ⓐ Ⓑ Ⓒ Ⓓ
6 Ⓐ Ⓑ Ⓒ Ⓓ	12 Ⓐ Ⓑ Ⓒ Ⓓ	18 Ⓐ Ⓑ Ⓒ Ⓓ

Test 5

1 Ⓐ Ⓑ Ⓒ Ⓓ	5 Ⓐ Ⓑ Ⓒ Ⓓ	9 Ⓐ Ⓑ Ⓒ Ⓓ	13 Ⓐ Ⓑ Ⓒ Ⓓ
2 Ⓐ Ⓑ Ⓒ Ⓓ	6 Ⓐ Ⓑ Ⓒ Ⓓ	10 Ⓐ Ⓑ Ⓒ Ⓓ	14 Ⓐ Ⓑ Ⓒ Ⓓ
3 Ⓐ Ⓑ Ⓒ Ⓓ	7 Ⓐ Ⓑ Ⓒ Ⓓ	11 Ⓐ Ⓑ Ⓒ Ⓓ	15 Ⓐ Ⓑ Ⓒ Ⓓ
4 Ⓐ Ⓑ Ⓒ Ⓓ	8 Ⓐ Ⓑ Ⓒ Ⓓ	12 Ⓐ Ⓑ Ⓒ Ⓓ	16 Ⓐ Ⓑ Ⓒ Ⓓ

Test 6

1 Ⓐ Ⓑ Ⓒ Ⓓ	11 Ⓐ Ⓑ Ⓒ Ⓓ	21 Ⓐ Ⓑ Ⓒ Ⓓ	31 Ⓐ Ⓑ Ⓒ Ⓓ
2 Ⓐ Ⓑ Ⓒ Ⓓ	12 Ⓐ Ⓑ Ⓒ Ⓓ	22 Ⓐ Ⓑ Ⓒ Ⓓ	32 Ⓐ Ⓑ Ⓒ Ⓓ
3 Ⓐ Ⓑ Ⓒ Ⓓ	13 Ⓐ Ⓑ Ⓒ Ⓓ	23 Ⓐ Ⓑ Ⓒ Ⓓ	33 Ⓐ Ⓑ Ⓒ Ⓓ
4 Ⓐ Ⓑ Ⓒ Ⓓ	14 Ⓐ Ⓑ Ⓒ Ⓓ	24 Ⓐ Ⓑ Ⓒ Ⓓ	34 Ⓐ Ⓑ Ⓒ Ⓓ
5 Ⓐ Ⓑ Ⓒ Ⓓ	15 Ⓐ Ⓑ Ⓒ Ⓓ	25 Ⓐ Ⓑ Ⓒ Ⓓ	35 Ⓐ Ⓑ Ⓒ Ⓓ
6 Ⓐ Ⓑ Ⓒ Ⓓ	16 Ⓐ Ⓑ Ⓒ Ⓓ	26 Ⓐ Ⓑ Ⓒ Ⓓ	36 Ⓐ Ⓑ Ⓒ Ⓓ
7 Ⓐ Ⓑ Ⓒ Ⓓ	17 Ⓐ Ⓑ Ⓒ Ⓓ	27 Ⓐ Ⓑ Ⓒ Ⓓ	37 Ⓐ Ⓑ Ⓒ Ⓓ
8 Ⓐ Ⓑ Ⓒ Ⓓ	18 Ⓐ Ⓑ Ⓒ Ⓓ	28 Ⓐ Ⓑ Ⓒ Ⓓ	38 Ⓐ Ⓑ Ⓒ Ⓓ
9 Ⓐ Ⓑ Ⓒ Ⓓ	19 Ⓐ Ⓑ Ⓒ Ⓓ	29 Ⓐ Ⓑ Ⓒ Ⓓ	39 Ⓐ Ⓑ Ⓒ Ⓓ
10 Ⓐ Ⓑ Ⓒ Ⓓ	20 Ⓐ Ⓑ Ⓒ Ⓓ	30 Ⓐ Ⓑ Ⓒ Ⓓ	40 Ⓐ Ⓑ Ⓒ Ⓓ

Test 7

1. Ⓐ Ⓑ _____
2. Ⓐ Ⓑ _____
3. Ⓐ Ⓑ _____
4. Ⓐ Ⓑ _____
5. Ⓐ Ⓑ _____
6. Ⓐ Ⓑ _____
7. Ⓐ Ⓑ _____
8. Ⓐ Ⓑ _____
9. Ⓐ Ⓑ _____
10. Ⓐ Ⓑ _____
11. Ⓐ Ⓑ _____
12. Ⓐ Ⓑ _____
13. Ⓐ Ⓑ _____
14. Ⓐ Ⓑ _____
15. Ⓐ Ⓑ _____
16. Ⓐ Ⓑ _____
17. Ⓐ Ⓑ _____
18. Ⓐ Ⓑ _____
19. Ⓐ Ⓑ _____
20. Ⓐ Ⓑ _____
21. Ⓐ Ⓑ _____
22. Ⓐ Ⓑ _____
23. Ⓐ Ⓑ _____
24. Ⓐ Ⓑ _____
25. Ⓐ Ⓑ _____
26. Ⓐ Ⓑ _____
27. Ⓐ Ⓑ _____
28. Ⓐ Ⓑ _____
29. Ⓐ Ⓑ _____
30. Ⓐ Ⓑ _____
31. Ⓐ Ⓑ _____
32. Ⓐ Ⓑ _____
33. Ⓐ Ⓑ _____
34. Ⓐ Ⓑ _____
35. Ⓐ Ⓑ _____
36. Ⓐ Ⓑ _____
37. Ⓐ Ⓑ _____
38. Ⓐ Ⓑ _____
39. Ⓐ Ⓑ _____
40. Ⓐ Ⓑ _____
41. Ⓐ Ⓑ _____
42. Ⓐ Ⓑ _____
43. Ⓐ Ⓑ _____
44. Ⓐ Ⓑ _____
45. Ⓐ Ⓑ _____
46. Ⓐ Ⓑ _____
47. Ⓐ Ⓑ _____
48. Ⓐ Ⓑ _____
49. Ⓐ Ⓑ _____
50. Ⓐ Ⓑ _____

51. Ⓐ Ⓑ _____
52. Ⓐ Ⓑ _____
53. Ⓐ Ⓑ _____
54. Ⓐ Ⓑ _____
55. Ⓐ Ⓑ _____
56. Ⓐ Ⓑ _____
57. Ⓐ Ⓑ _____
58. Ⓐ Ⓑ _____
59. Ⓐ Ⓑ _____
60. Ⓐ Ⓑ _____
61. Ⓐ Ⓑ _____
62. Ⓐ Ⓑ _____
63. Ⓐ Ⓑ _____
64. Ⓐ Ⓑ _____
65. Ⓐ Ⓑ _____
66. Ⓐ Ⓑ _____
67. Ⓐ Ⓑ _____
68. Ⓐ Ⓑ _____
69. Ⓐ Ⓑ _____
70. Ⓐ Ⓑ _____
71. Ⓐ Ⓑ _____
72. Ⓐ Ⓑ _____
73. Ⓐ Ⓑ _____
74. Ⓐ Ⓑ _____
75. Ⓐ Ⓑ _____
76. Ⓐ Ⓑ _____
77. Ⓐ Ⓑ _____
78. Ⓐ Ⓑ _____
79. Ⓐ Ⓑ _____
80. Ⓐ Ⓑ _____
81. Ⓐ Ⓑ _____
82. Ⓐ Ⓑ _____
83. Ⓐ Ⓑ _____
84. Ⓐ Ⓑ _____
85. Ⓐ Ⓑ _____
86. Ⓐ Ⓑ _____
87. Ⓐ Ⓑ _____
88. Ⓐ Ⓑ _____
89. Ⓐ Ⓑ _____
90. Ⓐ Ⓑ _____
91. Ⓐ Ⓑ _____
92. Ⓐ Ⓑ _____
93. Ⓐ Ⓑ _____
94. Ⓐ Ⓑ _____
95. Ⓐ Ⓑ _____
96. Ⓐ Ⓑ _____
97. Ⓐ Ⓑ _____
98. Ⓐ Ⓑ _____
99. Ⓐ Ⓑ _____
100. Ⓐ Ⓑ _____

Test 1

Time: 60 minutes. 89 questions.

DIRECTIONS: This test gives four suggested spellings for each word listed. Choose the spelling you know to be correct and mark your answer accordingly.

1. (A) transeint   (B) transient   (C) transcient   (D) transent

2. (A) heratage   (B) heritage   (C) heiritage   (D) heretage

3. (A) exibition   (B) exhibition   (C) exabition   (D) exhebition

4. (A) intiative   (B) enitiative   (C) initative   (D) initiative

5. (A) similiar   (B) simmilar   (C) similar   (D) simuler

6. (A) sufficiantly   (B) sufisiently   (C) sufficiently   (D) suficeintly

7. (A) anticipate   (B) antisipate   (C) anticapate   (D) antisapate

8. (A) intelligence   (B) inteligence   (C) intellegence   (D) intelegence

9. (A) referance   (B) referrence   (C) referense   (D) reference

10. (A) conscious   (B) consious   (C) conscius   (D) consceous

11. (A) paralell   (B) parellel   (C) parellell   (D) parallel

12. (A) abundence   (B) abundance   (C) abundants   (D) abundents

13. (A) spesifically   (B) specificaly   (C) specifically   (D) specefically

14. (A) elemanate   (B) elimenate   (C) elliminate   (D) eliminate

15. (A) resonance   (B) resonnance   (C) resonence   (D) reasonance

16. (A) benaficial   (B) beneficial   (C) benefitial   (D) bennaficial

17. (A) retrievable   (B) retreivable   (C) retrievible   (D) retreavable

18. (A) collosal   (B) colossal   (C) colosal   (D) collossal

19. (A) inflameable   (B) inflamable   (C) enflamabel   (D) inflammable

20. (A) auxillary   (B) auxilliary   (C) auxilary   (D) auxiliary

21. (A) corregated   (B) corrigated   (C) corrugated   (D) coregated

22. (A) accumalation   (B) accumulation   (C) acumulation   (D) accumullation

23. (A) consumation (B) consummation (C) consumeation (D) consomation

24. (A) retorical (B) rhetorical (C) rhetorrical (D) retorrical

25. (A) inimitable (B) iminitable (C) innimitable (D) inimitible

26. (A) proletarian (B) prolletarian (C) prolatarian (D) proleterian

27. (A) appelate (B) apellate (C) appellate (D) apelate

28. (A) esential (B) essencial (C) essential (D) essantial

29. (A) assessment (B) assesment (C) asessment (D) assesmant

30. (A) ordinence (B) ordinnance (C) ordinanse (D) ordinance

31. (A) disapearance (B) disappearance (C) disappearense (D) disappearence

32. (A) attendence (B) attendanse (C) attendance (D) atendance

33. (A) acertain (B) assertain (C) ascertain (D) asertain

34. (A) specimen (B) speciman (C) spesimen (D) speceman

35. (A) relevant (B) relevent (C) rellevent (D) relavant

36. (A) anesthetic (B) aenesthetic (C) anestitic (D) annesthetic

37. (A) foriegn (B) foreign (C) forriegn (D) forreign

38. (A) interuption (B) interruption (C) interrupsion (D) interrupcion

39. (A) acquiesence (B) acquiescence (C) aquiescense (D) acquiesance

40. (A) exceed (B) exsede (C) exseed (D) excede

41. (A) maneuver (B) manuver (C) maneuvere (D) manneuver

42. (A) correlation (B) corrolation (C) corellation (D) corralation

43. (A) hinderence (B) hindranse (C) hindrance (D) hindrence

44. (A) existence (B) existance (C) existense (D) existince

45. (A) bankrupcy (B) bankruptcy (C) bankruptsy (D) bankrupsy

46. (A) receipts (B) receits (C) reciepts (D) recieps

47. (A) impromtu (B) inpromtu (C) impromptu (D) impromptue

48. (A) pronounciation (B) pronunciatun (C) pronunciation (D) pronounciatun

49. (A) entirly (B) entirely (C) entirley (D) entireley

50. (A) complecation   (B) complicasion   (C) complication   (D) complacation

51. (A) condem   (B) condemn   (C) condemm   (D) condenm

52. (A) ocassion   (B) occassion   (C) ocasion   (D) occasion

53. (A) contagious   (B) contageous   (C) contagous   (D) contagiose

54. (A) perminent   (B) permenant   (C) permanent   (D) permanant

55. (A) proceed   (B) procede   (C) prosede   (D) proseed

56. (A) embarassment   (B) embarrasment   (C) embarasment   (D) embarrassment

57. (A) cematery   (B) cemetary   (C) cemitery   (D) cemetery

58. (A) believable   (B) believeable   (C) believeable   (D) believible

59. (A) council   (B) counsil   (C) counsle   (D) councel

60. (A) achievement   (B) acheivment   (C) achievment   (D) acheivement

61. (A) Wendesday   (B) Wensday   (C) Wednesday   (D) Wendnesday

62. (A) classify   (B) classafy   (C) classefy   (D) classifey

63. (A) concensus   (B) concencus   (C) consencus   (D) consensus

64. (A) suffiscent   (B) sufficient   (C) sufficiant   (D) suffiscient

65. (A) responsable   (B) responseable   (C) responsibil   (D) responsible

66. (A) remittence   (B) remmittence   (C) remmittance   (D) remittance

67. (A) probible   (B) probable   (C) probbable   (D) probabil

68. (A) weigt   (B) wieght   (C) weight   (D) waight

69. (A) argument   (B) argumint   (C) argumant   (D) arguement

70. (A) priceing   (B) prising   (C) priseing   (D) pricing

71. (A) ballanced   (B) balanced   (C) balansed   (D) balanct

72. (A) operateing   (B) oparating   (C) oparrating   (D) operating

73. (A) privelege   (B) privilege   (C) privelige   (D) privilige

74. (A) expenses   (B) expences   (C) expensses   (D) expensces

75. (A) mispell   (B) misspell   (C) misspel   (D) mispel

76. (A) occurrance   (B) occurence   (C) occurrence   (D) ocurrence

77. (A) receit (B) receipt (C) reciept (D) reciet

78. (A) conscience (B) conscence (C) consciense (D) conscense

79. (A) deterent (B) deterrant (C) deterant (D) deterrent

80. (A) responsable (B) responsceable (C) responsible (D) responcible

81. (A) noticable (B) noticible (C) noticeable (D) noticeble

82. (A) passable (B) passible (C) passeble (D) passeable

83. (A) dissplaid (B) displayed (C) dissplayed (D) displaid

84. (A) tryeing (B) trieing (C) trying (D) triing

85. (A) imaterial (B) immaterial (C) imaterrial (D) imatterial

86. (A) balancing (B) balanceing (C) balansing (D) balanseing

87. (A) conceed (B) consede (C) concede (D) conseed

88. (A) innumerible (B) innumerable (C) inumerable (D) inumerible

89. (A) maintainance (B) maintenance (C) maintenence (D) maintanance

Test 2

Time: 30 minutes. 35 questions.

DIRECTIONS: Each of the following four word groups contains one word that is spelled correctly. Choose the correctly spelled word.

1. (A) authority   (B) similiar   (C) refering   (D) preferebly

2. (A) suficient   (B) wheather   (C) actueally   (D) minimum

3. (A) volentary   (B) syllabus   (C) embodyeing   (D) pertanent

4. (A) simplified   (B) comunity   (C) emfasis   (D) advant

5. (A) approppriate   (B) expedient   (C) adopshun   (D) satisfactarily

6. (A) unconsiously   (B) pamflet   (C) asess   (D) adjacent

7. (A) mortgages   (B) infalible   (C) eradecated   (D) sourse

8. (A) predescessor   (B) obsolete   (C) unimpared   (D) sporadicaly

9. (A) impenitrable   (B) recognisable   (C) paresite   (D) vigilance

10. (A) emfatically   (B) manefold   (C) anxieties   (D) expence

11. (A) emfatically   (B) inculcate   (C) skilfel   (D) indigense

12. (A) indespensable   (B) encumbrance   (C) intolerible   (D) desicration

13. (A) exibit   (B) critisism   (C) recieved   (D) conspicuous

14. (A) biennial   (B) monatary   (C) beninant   (D) complacensy

15. (A) propriaty   (B) legalety   (C) acquiesce   (D) conversent

16. (A) ajusted   (B) porportionate   (C) inaugurated   (D) dubeous

17. (A) responsability   (B) soceity   (C) individuel   (D) increments

18. (A) subordonate   (B) transaction   (C) buisness   (D) effitiency

19. (A) condemnation   (B) exsees   (C) ordinerily   (D) capasity

20. (A) discuscion   (B) statistics   (C) producktion   (D) disguissed

21. (A) constrictive   (B) proposel   (C) partisipated   (D) desision

22. (A) comtroller   (B) inadequasy   (C) resolusion   (D) promotion

23. (A) progresive   (B) reciepts   (C) dependent   (D) secsion

24. (A) seperate   (B) speciallized   (C) funshions   (D) publicity

25. (A) instrament   (B) vicinity   (C) offical   (D) journale

26. (A) unecessary   (B) responsebility   (C) suprintendent   (D) recommendation

27. (A) resonable   (B) curency   (C) occur   (D) critisise

28. (A) apetite   (B) preliminary   (C) concilatory   (D) cruseal

29. (A) afilliation   (B) amendement   (C) ansient   (D) patient

30. (A) recipeint   (B) pretious   (C) uncertainty   (D) maritial

31. (A) illigetimate   (B) peciular   (C) addressee   (D) consintrated

32. (A) convalescent   (B) detramental   (C) elaberate   (D) accessable

33. (A) accomodate   (B) prejudise   (C) preveous   (D) exaggerate

34. (A) corroner   (B) inditment   (C) seized   (D) scissers

35. (A) araignment   (B) emolument   (C) faciletation   (D) ordanence

Test 3

Time: 30 minutes. 34 questions.

DIRECTIONS: In this test all words but one of each group are spelled correctly. Indicate the misspelled word in each group.

1. (A) extraordinary   (B) statesmen   (C) array   (D) financeer

2. (A) materialism   (B) indefatigible   (C) moribund   (D) rebellious

3. (A) queue   (B) equillibrium   (C) contemporary   (D) structure

4. (A) acquatic   (B) fascinated   (C) bogged   (D) accommodations

5. (A) embarrassment   (B) sosialization   (C) imposition   (D) incredulous

6. (A) politisians   (B) psychology   (C) susceptible   (D) antipathy

7. (A) convincing   (B) vicissetudes   (C) negligible   (D) foreign

8. (A) characters   (B) veracity   (C) testimony   (D) apolagetic

9. (A) shriek   (B) carelogue   (C) impeccable   (D) ruthless

10. (A) ocassions   (B) accomplishment   (C) assumed   (D) distinguished

11. (A) servicable   (B) preparation   (C) exceptional   (D) initiative

12. (A) primarely   (B) available   (C) paragraph   (D) routine

13. (A) ligament   (B) preseding   (C) mechanical   (D) anecdote

14. (A) judgment   (B) conclusion   (C) circumlocution   (D) breifly

15. (A) censor   (B) personel   (C) counterfeit   (D) advantageous

16. (A) liquified   (B) adage   (C) ancient   (D) imitation

17. (A) lapse   (B) questionnaire   (C) concieve   (D) staunch

18. (A) calendar   (B) typographical   (C) inexcusable   (D) sallient

19. (A) carreer   (B) eminently   (C) nevertheless   (D) fourth

20. (A) corperal   (B) sergeant   (C) lieutenant   (D) commandant

21. (A) partial   (B) business   (C) through   (D) comission

22. (A) accounts   (B) financial   (C) reciept   (D) answer

23. (A) except   (B) conection   (C) altogether   (D) credentials

24. (A) whose   (B) written   (C) strenth   (D) therefore

25. (A) catalogue   (B) familiar   (C) formerly   (D) secretery

26. (A) debtor   (B) shipment   (C) fileing   (D) correspond

27. (A) courtesy   (B) dictionery   (C) extremely   (D) exactly

28. (A) probaly   (B) directory   (C) acquired   (D) hurriedly

29. (A) hauled   (B) freight   (C) hankerchief   (D) millionaire

30. (A) goverment   (B) mileage   (C) scene   (D) ninety

31. (A) written   (B) permenent   (C) similar   (D) convenient

32. (A) cooperation (B) duplicate   (C) negotiable   (D) Febuary

33. (A) experience   (B) interupt   (C) cylinder   (D) campaign

34. (A) cordialy   (B) completely   (C) sandwich   (D) respectfully

Test 4

Time: 30 minutes. 18 questions.

DIRECTIONS: This probing test measures your ability to detect misspelled words in a text. In each of the following groups of four sentences, there is only one that does not contain a misspelled word. Choose the completely correct sentence in each group.

1. (A) In accordance with their usual custom, the employees presented a gift to the retiring president.
   (B) It is difficult not to critisize them under the circumstances.
   (C) The company has not paid a divedend to the owners of the preferred stock since the beginning of the depression.
   (D) At the time it was thought that any improvement on the invention was imposible.

2. (A) Whether the percentage of profit was as immence as has been charged is doubtful.
   (B) In the early years of the depression, transient and local homeless were sheltered together because of their common lack of funds to pay for domicile.
   (C) It is easier and wiser to suspend judgement until the facts are known.
   (D) The responsability for the situation was put squarely on those to whom it belonged.

3. (A) The recommendations of the committee were adopted by the convention.
   (B) It is usually considered unecessary to analyse the statistics under the present circumstances.
   (C) Hearafter, the company will refuse to sell hinges on credit.
   (D) The lieutenent to whom you referred in your last letter has been transferred to another post.

4. (A) It has been found impossible to adjust the requirements.
   (B) Advancement is slow because oppertunities for promotion are infrequent.
   (C) A carrear in the civil service is the ambition of the majority of young entrants.
   (D) Because he has been closly connected with the management of the enterprise for so long, he is well informed on the matter.

5. (A) The indictment supersedes the original document.
   (B) The responsibility of soceity to the individual is a matter of serious moment.
   (C) After the middle of the month, all salary incraments will be adjusted according to the new scheme of proportionate distribution.
   (D) He was given explisit directions to limit expenses as far as possible.

6. (A) They were somewhat dubious as to the propriety and quality of the procedure as contemplated.
   (B) It was certain that he would acquiese, once conversant with the full details.
   (C) Although only a bienial publication, its influence was far-reaching and its circulation extensive.
   (D) It was difficult to arouse him to any appreciation of the monatary aspects of the situation.

7. (A) His attitude throughout was one of benignant complacency, in spite of the derision of the multitude.
   (B) The exhibit deserved a more conspicious location and more favorable criticism than it received.
   (C) It should have been considered an incumbrance rather than an advantage, since it was not indespensable, and added greatly to the total load.
   (D) The situation has become intolerable and further desicration of the premises should be discouraged emphatically.

8. (A) To inculcate steadfast principals of economy and skillful administration is the task that confronts us.
   (B) The degree of indigence is relative, fluctuating with the rise and fall of the country's general prosperity.
   (C) The duties of the position are manefold, the anxieties, great, and the emoluments scarcely in keeping with the expense of energy demanded.
   (D) Though at first the gloom seemed impenitrable, shadows and, finally, objects became visible and later distinctly recognizable.

9. (A) Investigation into the nature of the paricites, which continually affect the vegetation, demands constant vigilance and unremitting care.
   (B) The example set by his predescessor enabled him to embark on his mission secure in the confidence of the majority of the citizens.
   (C) Customs that are obsolete in most communities are found sporadically in all their primitive vigor, unimpaired by the passage of time.
   (D) Formerly, guaranteed morgages were considered to be infallible investments, even by the most conservative.

10. (A) The signature of every recipiant must be secured before the list of donations is turned over to the organization.
    (B) The tendency to deviate from the proper scientific point of view in these matters should be eradecated at its source.
    (C) The authorship of the pamphlet was recently acknowledged, and an explanation of its appearance offered.
    (D) Income tax payers provided 46 per cent of all internal revenue reciepts during the last fiscal year.

11. (A) International peace is attainable, dependant only on the acceptance and application of certain principles.
    (B) What is expected to become a struggle between the radical and conservative sections was precipitated today.
    (C) He said that his action to stop further payments accorded with the request of the comptroler.
    (D) He regarded State legislation alone as inadiquate to deal with the issue.

12. (A) The sponsors of the resolution, in a joint statement, defended their proposel as a constructive step toward the promotion of world peace.
    (B) A large number of persons participated in the conference.
    (C) The most dramatic, and doubtless the most important, ruling was the desision of the court reversing its own previous opinion on the question of State Minimum Wage Laws.
    (D) Included in the report to be presented to the delegates as a basis for discuscion are statistics covering production in the various countries.

13. (A) He held fast to his original opinion that much of present research was disguissed promotion material.
(B) The tranquillity in which the session of the House of Representatives was ending was shattered by the bombshell of disagreement.
(C) His decision to assess adjacent property was widely condemmed.
(D) The majority of the approppriation acts and resolutions were special in nature.

14. (A) Is it expedient to amend the constitution by the adoption of the subjoined?
(B) It was the general opinion that this system had not functioned satisfactorily and that it needed to be simplefied.
(C) In the early days, protection against fire was provided by volentary fire departments.
(D) If you would oppose home rule for Illinois cities, draft a provision embodyeing your ideas as to the constitutional relationship which should exist between a state and a municipality.

15. (A) An attempt has been made to give the pertinent facts in sufficient detail so that the student may determine whether the decision actually made was sound.
(B) Should they also have been given authorety to review local bond issues under a plan similar to that adopted in Indiana?
(C) A corperal ranks below either a sergeant or a lieutenant.
(D) A carreer system is eminently desirable for the proper administration of civil service.

16. (A) I believe that I have never seen a typographical error in a calender.
(B) A lapse of memory is not inexcusable.
(C) A questionaire often contains the silliest questions a man can conceive.
(D) I advise you to be staunch and not to yeild, for he is wrong.

17. (A) The duties you will perform are similar to the duties of a patrollman.
(B) Officers must be constantly alert to sieze the initiative.
(C) Officers in this organization are not entitled to special privileges.
(D) Any changes in procedure wll be announced publically.

18. (A) It will be to your advantage to keep your firearm in good working condition.
(B) There are approximately fourty men on sick leave.
(C) Your first duty will be to pursuade the person to obey the law.
(D) Fires often begin in flameable material kept in lockers.

Test 5

Time: 15 minutes. 16 questions.

DIRECTIONS: In each of the following groups, either one word is misspelled, or all five words are correctly spelled. Next to each question write the letter corresponding to the correction that should be made.

1. picnicing, remittance, scintilla, niece, wholly

   (A) add a letter
   (B) change a letter
   (C) interchange two adjacent letters
   (D) omit a letter

2. coolly, eligable, ingenuous, singeing, shoeing

   (A) change "a" to "i"
   (B) change "u" to "i"
   (C) omit an "e"
   (D) add an "e"

3. diphtheria, dichotomy, hypocricy, outrageous, personnel

   (A) change a consonant
   (B) change a vowel
   (C) make no change
   (D) omit a consonant

4. despoliation, ecstasy, foliage, harrassed, supersede

   (A) add a letter
   (B) change a letter
   (C) interchange two letters
   (D) omit a letter

5. beneficent, deriliction, feasible, pantomime, sacrilegious

   (A) change wrong letter to a, b, c, d, f, g
   (B) change wrong letter to e, h, j, k, l, m
   (C) change wrong letter to i, n, p, q, r, s, t
   (D) change wrong letter to o, u, v, w, x, y, z

6. artillery, dispatch, occasionally, potsherd, similiar

   (A) change a letter
   (B) change the placement of a letter
   (C) omit a consonant
   (D) omit a vowel

7. indispensable, lief, minerology, occurring, seize

   (A) change a vowel to "a"
   (B) change a vowel to "i"

(C) interchange two adjacent vowels
(D) omit a letter

8. existence, gaseous, maintenance, sergeant, vengance

   (A) add "e"
   (B) change "a" to "e"
   (C) change "e" to "a"
   (D) omit "e"

9. changeable, echoes, geneology, mileage, nineteenth

   (A) change "eo" to "ea"
   (B) change "ea" to "i"
   (C) make no change
   (D) omit an "e"

10. apparel, embarrass, erroneous, parallel, quizzes

   (A) change a vowel
   (B) double a consonant
   (C) make no change
   (D) omit a consonant

11. cemetery, definitely, esculator, medicine, toboggan

   (A) change "e" to "a"
   (B) change "i" to "a"
   (C) change "o" to "a"
   (D) change "u" to "a"

12. innoculate, prejudice, privilege, rarefy, tragedy

   (A) add a consonant
   (B) change a vowel
   (C) make no change
   (D) omit a letter

13. affiliate, appetite, descendant, gelatin, maneuver

   (A) change a letter
   (B) double a letter
   (C) make no change
   (D) omit a letter

14. accessible, achievement, acknowledgment, iridescent, questionnaire

   (A) add a letter
   (B) change a letter
   (C) make no change
   (D) omit a letter

15. accommodate, aplomb, bronichal, surgeon, vacillation

   (A) add a letter
   (B) change the placement of a letter

(C) make no change
(D) omit a letter

16. bankruptcy, correspondance, pinning, impresario, rococo

    (A) add a letter
    (B) change a letter
    (C) make no change
    (D) omit a letter

Test 6

Time: 30 minutes. 40 questions.

DIRECTIONS: In this test all words but one of each group are spelled correctly. Indicate the misspelled word in each group.

1. (A) proscenium   (B) resillient   (C) biennial   (D) connoisseur

2. (A) queue   (B) equable   (C) ecstacy   (D) obsequious

3. (A) quizes   (B) frolicking   (C) maelstrom   (D) homonym

4. (A) pseudonym   (B) annihilate   (C) questionaire   (D) irascible

5. (A) diptheria   (B) annular   (C) acolyte   (D) descendant

6. (A) truculant   (B) rescind   (C) dilettante   (D) innuendo

7. (A) prevalence   (B) discrete   (C) efrontery   (D) admissible

8. (A) igneous   (B) annullment   (C) dissipate   (D) abattoir

9. (A) quiescent   (B) apologue   (C) myrrh   (D) inocuous

10. (A) propoganda   (B) gaseous   (C) iridescent   (D) similar

11. (A) supercede   (B) tyranny   (C) beauteous   (D) victuals

12. (A) geneology   (B) tragedy   (C) soliloquy   (D) prejudice

13. (A) remittance   (B) shoeing   (C) category   (D) gutteral

14. (A) catarrh   (B) parlamentary   (C) villain   (D) omitted

15. (A) vengeance   (B) parallel   (C) nineth   (D) mayoralty

16. (A) changeable   (B) therefor   (C) incidently   (D) dissatisfy

17. (A) orifice   (B) deferrment   (C) harass   (D) accommodate

18. (A) picnicking   (B) proceedure   (C) hypocrisy   (D) seize

19. (A) vilify   (B) efflorescence   (C) sarcophagus   (D) sacreligious

20. (A) paraphenalia   (B) apothecaries   (C) occurrence   (D) plagiarize

21. (A) irreparably   (B) comparitively   (C) lovable   (D) audible

22. (A) nullify   (B) siderial   (C) salability   (D) irrelevant

23. (A) asinine   (B) dissonent   (C) opossum   (D) indispensable

24. (A) discomfit   (B) sapient   (C) exascerbate   (D) sarsaparilla

25. (A) valleys   (B) maintainance   (C) abridgment   (D) reticence

26. (A) tolerance   (B) circumferance   (C) insurance   (D) dominance

27. (A) diameter   (B) tangent   (C) paralell   (D) perimeter

28. (A) providential   (B) personal   (C) accidental   (D) diagonel

29. (A) development   (B) retarded   (C) homogenious   (D) intelligence

30. (A) noticeable   (B) forceible   (C) practical   (D) erasable

31. (A) heroes   (B) folios   (C) sopranos   (D) usuel

32. (A) typical   (B) descend   (C) summarize   (D) continuel

33. (A) courageous   (B) recomend   (C) omission   (D) eliminate

34. (A) compliment   (B) illuminate   (C) auxilary   (D) installation

35. (A) preliminary   (B) acquainted   (C) syllable   (D) analysis

36. (A) accustomed   (B) negligible   (C) interupted   (D) bulletin

37. (A) summoned   (B) managment   (C) mechanism   (D) sequence

38. (A) comittee   (B) surprise   (C) noticeable   (D) emphasize

39. (A) occurrance   (B) likely   (C) accumulate   (D) grievance

40. (A) obstacle   (B) particuliar   (C) baggage   (D) fascinating

Test 7

Time: 60 minutes. 100 questions.

DIRECTIONS: In the following list, some words are spelled correctly, some misspelled. On your practice sheet, mark A for those words properly spelled; mark B and spell out the word correctly for those misspelled.

1. unparalleled
2. gastliness
3. mediocrity
4. exibition
5. posessing
6. lucritive
7. corresspondence
8. accellerated
9. labirynth
10. duplisity
11. repitious
12. jepardy
13. impartiallity
14. sobriquet
15. accesable
16. incredible
17. connoisseurs
18. fallibility
19. litagation
20. piquansy
21. fuedal
22. predetory
23. desparado
24. incongruity
25. delibarate
26. competetive
27. beleaguered
28. leiutenant
29. equinoxial
30. derogatory
31. denuncietory
32. panickey
33. calendar
34. belligerents

35. abolition
36. predjudice
37. propoganda
38. adolesents
39. irresistible
40. exortation
41. renascence
42. counsil
43. bullitin
44. aberation
45. integraty
46. cristallized
47. irrepairably
48. punctillious
49. catagory
50. parlament
51. medalion
52. bountious
53. aggrevate
54. midgit
55. wierd
56. elliminate
57. murmering
58. hystrionic
59. goverment
60. clamerous
61. garantee
62. presumptious
63. comemmerate
64. indispensible
65. bookeeping
66. disatisfied
67. tremendious
68. interseed

69. inaugerate
70. rehersel
71. nucleous
72. benefiting
73. wholy
74. discription
75. alright
76. representitive
77. mischievious
78. ingenuous
79. accidently
80. exilerate
81. pronounciation
82. fourty
83. mackeral
84. rescind
85. kleptomania
86. summerize
87. resillience
88. regretable
89. questionaire
90. privelege
91. judgment
92. plagiarism
93. vengence
94. subpoena
95. rythm
96. derth
97. impromtue
98. incumbant
99. forfiet
100. maintainance

Answer Key for Spelling Practice Tests

Test 1

1. B	13. C	24. B	35. A	46. A	57. D	68. C	79. D
2. B	14. D	25. A	36. A	47. C	58. A	69. A	80. C
3. B	15. A	26. A	37. B	48. C	59. A	70. D	81. C
4. D	16. B	27. C	38. B	49. B	60. A	71. B	82. A
5. C	17. A	28. C	39. B	50. C	61. C	72. D	83. B
6. C	18. B	29. A	40. A	51. B	62. A	73. B	84. C
7. A	19. D	30. D	41. A	52. D	63. D	74. A	85. B
8. A	20. D	31. B	42. A	53. A	64. B	75. B	86. A
9. D	21. C	32. C	43. C	54. C	65. D	76. C	87. C
10. A	22. B	33. C	44. A	55. A	66. D	77. B	88. B
11. D	23. B	34. A	45. B	56. D	67. B	78. A	89. B
12. B							

Test 2

1. A	8. B	15. C	22. D	29. D
2. D	9. D	16. C	23. C	30. C
3. B	10. C	17. D	24. D	31. C
4. A	11. B	18. B	25. B	32. A
5. B	12. B	19. A	26. D	33. D
6. D	13. D	20. B	27. C	34. C
7. A	14. A	21. A	28. B	35. B

Test 3

1. D	10. A	18. D	26. C
2. B	11. A	19. A	27. B
3. B	12. A	20. A	28. A
4. A	13. B	21. D	29. C
5. B	14. D	22. C	30. A
6. A	15. B	23. B	31. B
7. B	16. A	24. C	32. D
8. D	17. C	25. D	33. B
9. B			34. A

Test 4

1. A	7. A	13. B
2. B	8. B	14. A
3. A	9. C	15. A
4. A	10. C	16. B
5. A	11. B	17. C
6. A	12. B	18. A

Test 5

1. A	7. A	12. D
2. A	8. A	13. C
3. A	9. A	14. C
4. D	10. C	15. B
5. B	11. D	16. B
6. D		

Test 6

1. B	11. A	21. B	31. D
2. C	12. A	22. B	32. D
3. A	13. D	23. B	33. B
4. C	14. B	24. C	34. C
5. A	15. C	25. B	35. B
6. A	16. C	26. B	36. C
7. C	17. B	27. C	37. B
8. B	18. B	28. D	38. A
9. D	19. D	29. C	39. A
10. A	20. A	30. B	40. B

Test 7

1. A	27. A	
2. B ghastliness	28. B lieutenant	
3. A	29. B equinoctial	
4. B exhibition	30. A	
5. B possessing	31. B denunciatory	
6. B lucrative	32. B panicky	
7. B correspondence	33. A	
8. B accelerated	34. A	
9. B labyrinth	35. A	
10. B duplicity	36. B prejudice	
11. B repetitious	37. B propaganda	
12. B jeopardy	38. B adolescents	
13. B impartiality	39. A	
14. A	40. B exhortation	
15. B accessible	41. A	
16. A	42. B counsel	
17. A	43. B bulletin	
18. A	44. B aberration	
19. B litigation	45. B integrity	
20. B piquancy	46. B crystallized	
21. B feudal	47. B irreparably	
22. B predatory	48. B punctilious	
23. B desperado	49. B category	
24. A	50. B parliament	
25. B deliberate	51. B medallion	
26. B competitive	52. B bounteous	

53. B aggravate
54. B midget
55. B weird
56. B eliminate
57. B murmuring
58. B histrionic
59. B government
60. B clamorous
61. B guarantee
62. B presumptuous
63. B commemorate
64. B indispensable
65. B bookkeeping
66. B dissatisfied
67. B tremendous
68. B intercede
69. B inaugurate
70. B rehearsal
71. B nucleus
72. A
73. B wholly
74. B description
75. B all right
76. B representative

77. B mischievous
78. A
79. B accidentally
80. B exhilarate
81. B pronunciation
82. B forty
83. B mackerel
84. A
85. A
86. B summarize
87. B resilience
88. B regrettable
89. B questionnaire
90. B privilege
91. A
92. A
93. B vengeance
94. A
95. B rhythm
96. B dearth
97. B impromptu
98. B incumbent
99. B forfeit
100. B maintenance

VOCABULARY BUILDING

This section serves a double purpose. It will help you build a better vocabulary by providing hundreds of useful words and their meanings. It will also serve as a handy guide to good English usage by making clear-cut distinctions between words that are frequently misused. Don't try to take it all in at once. Study a page or two a day, and you will be surprised at the ease with which you can pick up a lot of valuable information.

A Dictionary of Commonly Misused Words

abbreviate—means *to shorten by omitting*.
abridge—means *to shorten by condensing*.
New York is *abbreviated* to N.Y., Tennesee to Tenn.
In order to save time in the reading, the report was *abridged*.

ability—means a *developed, actual* power.
capacity—means an *undeveloped, potential* power.
He now has fair writing *ability*, but additional courses will develop his *capacity* beyond the average level.

above—Avoid *above* except in business forms, where it may be used in reference to a preceding part of the text. In normal writing use *foregoing* or *preceding*, instead of *above*.
Unacceptable: The *above* books are available in the library.
Acceptable: The *above* prices are subject to change without notice.

accept—means *to take when offered*.
except—means *excluding*. (preposition)
except—means *to leave out*. (verb)
Since it is raining, we *accept* your offer of a ride to the store.
Everyone *except* Mary was ready on time.
The city council voted to *except* senior citizens from the tax increase.

access—means *availability*.

excess—means *too much*.
The lawyer was given *access* to the grand jury records.
The expenditures this month are far in *excess* of income.

accidently—No such word. The word is *accidentally* (adverb). Pronounce it ak-si-DENT-ally.

in accord with—means *in agreement with a person*.
I am *in accord with* you about this.

in accordance with—means *in agreement with a thing*.
The police officer acted in *accordance with* the law.

adapt—means *to adjust or change*.
adopt—means *to take as one's own*.
adept—means *skillful*.
Children *adapt* to change more easily than adults do.
The war orphan was *adopted* by the general and his wife.
It takes years of practice to become *adept* at figure skating.
Note: adapt *to*, adopt *by*, adept *in* or *at*.

adapted to—implies *original or natural suitability*.
The gills of the fish are *adapted* to underwater breathing.

adapted for—implies *created suitability*.
Atomic energy is constantly being *adapted for* new uses.

adapted from—implies *changed to be made suitable*.
The television mini-series was *adapted from* a best-selling novel.

addicted to—means *accustomed to by strong habit*.

subject to—means *exposed to* or *liable to*.
People *addicted to* drugs or alcohol need constant medical care.
The coast of Wales is *subject to* extremely heavy fogs.

addition—means *the act or process of adding*.

edition—means *a printing of a publication*.
In *addition* to a dictionary, he always used a thesaurus.
The first *edition* of Shakespeare's plays appeared in 1623.

admit—means to grant the existence of error, *without* original intent.

confess—means to grant the existence of error, *with* original intent.
I *admit* that I was mistaken in my calculations.
I *confess* that I am guilty of tax evasion.

admittance—means *permission to enter*.

admission—means *permission to enter, with certain privileges*.
No *admittance* to the laboratory was permitted.
You must show your identification badge to gain *admission* to the exhibit.

advantage—means *a superior position*.

benefit—means *a favor conferred* or *earned* (as a profit).
His great height gave him an *advantage* over his opponent.
The rules were changed for his *benefit*.
Note: To *take* advantage *of*, to *have* an advantage *over*.

adverse—means *unfavorable*. (pronounced AD-verse)

averse—means *disliking*. (pronounced a-VERSE)
He took the *adverse* decision in poor taste.
Many students are *averse* to criticism by their classmates.

advise—best means *to give advice*. *Advise* is losing favor as a synonym for *notify*.
Acceptable: The teacher will *advise* the student in habits of study.
Unacceptable: We are *advising* you of a delivery under separate cover. (Say *notifying*)

affect—means *to influence*. (a verb)

effect—means *an influence*. (a noun)

effect—means *to bring about*. (a verb)
Your education must *affect* your future.
The *effect* of the last war is still being felt.
A diploma *effected* a tremendous change in his attitude.
Note: *affect* also has a meaning of *pretend*.
She had an *affected* manner.

affection—means *feeling*.

affectation—means *pose*.
Alumni often show a strong *affection* for their former school.
The *affectation* of a Harvard accent is no guarantee of success.

affinity—means an *attraction to a person or thing*.

infinity—means an *unlimited time, space* or *quantity*.
She has an *affinity* for men who own sporty cars.
That the universe has *infinity* is questionable.

after—is unnecessary with the *past* participle.
Say: *After* checking the timetable, I left for the station.
DON'T say: *After having checked* (omit *after*) the timetable, I left for the station.

aggravate—means *to make worse*.

exasperate—means *to irritate* or *annoy*.
Scratching will only *aggravate* a skin rash.
He was *exasperated* by her inability to come to a decision.

agree—means *to be in general accord*.

concur—means *to be in specific agreement*.
They *agreed* to meet again the following week.
The directors *concurred* in the decision to sell stock in the company.

ain't—is an *unacceptable* contraction for *am not, are not,* or *is not*.

aisle—is *a passageway* between seats.
isle—is *a small island.* (both words rhyme with *pile*)

alibi—is an explanation on the basis of being *in another place.*
excuse—is an *explanation* on *any basis.*
His *alibi* offered at the trial was that he was out of the state at the time the crime was committed.
His *excuse* for failing on the test was that he was sick.

alimentary—refers to the process of *nutrition.*
elementary—means *primary.*
The *alimentary* canal includes the stomach and the intestines.
Elementary education is the foundation of all human development.

all ready—means *everybody* or *everything ready.*
already—means *previously.*
They were *all ready* to write when the teacher arrived.
They had *already* begun writing when the teacher arrived.

alright—is *unacceptable.*
all right—is *acceptable.*

all-round—means *versatile* or *general.*
all around—means *all over a given area.*
Only an *all-round* athlete can compete in the decathlon.
The police were lined up for miles *all around.*

all together—means *everybody* or *everything together.*
altogether—means *completely.*
The boys and girls sang *all together.*
The outburst was *altogether* strange for a person who is usually so easygoing.

all ways—means *in every possible way.*
always—means *at all times.*
He was in *all ways* acceptable to the voters.
His reputation had *always* been spotless.

allege—means *to state without proof* (same as *assert* or *maintain*)
claim—means *to state ownership by proof,* NOT *to assert* or *maintain.*
The newspaper report *alleges* the politician's guilt.

The informant *claimed* the reward for having helped catch the thief.

allow—does NOT mean *to suppose;* it means *to give permission.*
Acceptable: The teacher *allows* adequate time for study in class.
Unacceptable: I *allow* I haven't seen anything like this.

allude—means *to make a reference to.*
elude—means *to escape from.*
The report *alludes* to earlier studies of teenage eating habits.
The thief tried to *elude* the police by darting into a crowded store.

allusion—means *a reference.*
illusion—means *a deception of the eye or mind.*
The aging actress made *allusions* to her past successes.
As he approached the glistening pond, the thirsty traveler realized it was merely an *illusion.*

alongside of—means *side by side with.*
Bill stood *alongside of* Henry.
alongside—means *parallel to the side.*
Park the car *alongside* the curb.

alot—is *unacceptable.* It should always be written as two words: *a lot.*
allot—means *to apportion.*
We bought *a lot* of land on which to build a small house.
In order to finish the test, you must *allot* your time wisely.
Note: *A lot* should never be used in formal English to signify *very much* or *a large quantity.*
Unacceptable: I like spinach *a lot.* (say *very much*)

altar—means *a platform.*
alter—means *to change.*
The bride and groom approached the *altar.*
The tailor *altered* the old-fashioned suit.

alternate—(the noun) means *a substitute* or *second choice.*
alternative—means *a statement or offer of two things, both equally preferable, but only one of which may be accepted.*
He served as an *alternate* to the delegate selected.

Since there was no *alternative,* I had to accept the position.

alumnus—means *a male graduate.*
alumna—means *a female graduate.*
With the granting of the diploma, he became an *alumnus* of the school.
Note: The masculine plural form of *alumnus* is *alumni (ni* rhymes with *high)*
She is an *alumna* of Hunter College.
Note: The feminine plural form is *alumnae (ae* rhymes with *key)*

among—is used with *more than two persons or things.*
Note: *Amongst* should be avoided.
between—is used with *two persons or things.*
The inheritance was equally divided *among* the four children.
The business, however, was divided *between* the oldest and the youngest one.

amount—applies to quantities *that cannot be counted one by one.*
number—applies to quantities *that can be counted one by one.*
A large *amount* of grain was delivered to the storehouse.
A large *number* of bags of grain was delivered.

and—should NOT be used before *etc.*
etc.—is the Latin expression *et cetera* meaning *and other things, and so forth.* Since the *et* means *and,* a combination of the two would have to be translated "and and so forth."
Acceptable: Oranges, peaches, cherries, *etc.* are healthful.
Unacceptable: Pickles, pizza, frankfurters, *and etc.* should be eaten sparingly.

angel—is *a heavenly creature.*
angle—is *a point at which two sides meet,* also *a corner.*
Lucifer was the most famous of the fallen *angels.*
A line perpendicular to another line forms a right *angle.*

angry at—means *annoyed by a thing.*
angry with—means *annoyed by a person.*
We were *angry at* the gross carelessness of the attendant.
We were *angry with* the careless attendant.

annual—means *yearly.*
biannual—means *twice a year,* or *semiannual.*
biennial—means *once in two years* or *every two years.*
The office Christmas party is an *annual* event.
Most schools issue *biannual* report cards, in January and June.
The *biennial* election of congressmen is held in the even-numbered years.

ante—is a prefix meaning *before.*
anti—is a prefix meaning *against.*
The *ante*chamber is the room just before the main room.
An *anti*-fascist is one who is opposed to fascists.

anxious—means *worried.*
eager—means *keenly desirous.*
We were *anxious* about our first airplane flight.
We are *eager* to fly again.

any—should not be used for *at all.*
Say: I haven't rested *at all* (NOT *any*) during this Easter vacation.
Note: When a comparison is indicated, say *any other*—NOT *any.*
Acceptable: He likes France better than *any other* country.

anywheres—is *unacceptable.*
anywhere—is *acceptable.*
Say: We can't find it *anywhere.*
Also say: *nowhere* (NOT *nowheres*); *somewhere* (NOT *somewheres*).

apprehend—means *to catch the meaning of something.*
comprehend—means *to understand a thing completely.*
It is fairly simple to *apprehend* the stupidity of war.
It is far more difficult to *comprehend* geometric theorems.
Note: *Apprehend* may also mean *to take into custody.*
The police officer succeeded in *apprehending* the purse-snatcher.

apt—suggests *habitual behavior.*
likely—suggests *probable behavior.*
liable—suggests an exposure to something *harmful.*

Teenagers are *apt* to be rather lazy in the morning.
A cat, if annoyed, is *likely* to scratch.
Cheating on a test may make one *liable* to expulsion from school.

aren't I—is colloquial. Its use is to be discouraged.
Say: *Am I not* entitled to an explanation? (preferred to *Aren't I . . .*)

argue—means *to prove something by logical methods.*
quarrel—means *to dispute without reason or logic.*
The opposing lawyers *argued* before the judge.
The lawyers became emotional and *quarreled.*

around—meaning *about* or *near* is a poor colloquialism.
It's *about* ten o'clock. (NOT *around*)
We'll be *near* the house. (NOT *around*)

as—(used as a conjunction) is followed by a verb.
like—(used as a preposition) is NOT followed by a verb.
Do *as* I do, not *as* I say.
Try not to behave *like* a child.
Unacceptable: He acts *like* I do.

as far as—expresses *distance.*
so far as—indicates *a limitation.*
We hiked *as far as* the next guest house.
So far as we know, the barn was adequate for a night's stay.

as good as—should be used *for comparisons only.*
This motel is *as good as* the next one.
Note: *As good as* does NOT mean *practically.*
Unacceptable: They *as good as* promised us a place in the hall.
Acceptable: They *practically* promised us a place in the hall.

as if—is correctly used in the expression, "He talked *as if* his jaw hurt him."
Unacceptable: "He talked *like* his jaw hurt him."

as much—is *unacceptable* for *so* or *this.*
He thought *so.*
They admitted *this* freely.
NOT: He thought *as much,* or they admitted *as much* freely.

as regards to—is *unacceptable.* So is *in regards to.*
Say *in regard to* or *as regards.*
The teacher would say nothing *in regard to* the student's marks.

as to whether—is *unacceptable. Whether* includes the unnecessary words *as to.*
Acceptable: I don't know *whether* it is going to rain.

ascent—is *the act of rising.*
assent—means *approval.*
The *ascent* to the top of the mountain was perilous.
Congress gave its *assent* to the President's emergency directive.

astonish—means *to strike with sudden wonder.*
surprise—means *to catch unaware.*
The extreme violence of the hurricane *astonished* everybody.
A heat wave in April would *surprise* us.

at—should be avoided where it does not contribute to the meaning.
Say: Where shall I meet you? (DON'T add the word *at*)

at about—should not be used for *about.*
The group will arrive *about* noon.

attend to—means to *take care of.*
tend to—means to *be inclined to.*
One of the clerk's will *attend to* mail in my absence.
Lazy people *tend to* gain weight.

audience—means *a group of listeners.*
spectators—refers to *a group of watchers.*
The orchestra performed for an *audience* of students and parents.
The slow baseball game bored the *spectators.*
Note: A group that both watches and listens is called an *audience.*

average—means *conforming to norms or standards.*
ordinary—means *usual, customary,* or *without distinction.*
A book of about 300 pages is of *average* length.
The contents of the book were rather *ordinary.*

avocation—means *a temporary interest or employment.*
vocation—means *one's regular employment.*
Fishing and swimming are two of my favorite *avocations.*
I am by *vocation* a civil engineer.

award—means *the result of a decision of many; a decision.*
reward—means *pay for good or evil done.*
The judge gave him an *award* of $100.00 in damages in the case.
Satisfactory marks are the *reward* for intensive study.

back—should NOT be used with such words as *refer* and *return* since the prefix *re* means *back.*
Unacceptable: Refer *back* to the text, if you have difficulty recalling the facts.

backward } Both are *acceptable* and may be
backwards } used interchangeably as an adverb.
We tried to run *backward.* (or *backwards*)
Backward as an adjective means *slow in learning.* (DON'T say *backwards* in this case)
A *backward* pupil should be given every encouragement.

balance—meaning *remainder* is *acceptable* only in commercial usage.
Use *remainder* or *rest* otherwise.
Even after the withdrawal, his bank *balance* was considerable.
Three of the students voted for John; the *rest* voted for Jim.

bazaar—is a *marketplace* or a *charity sale.*
bizarre—means *odd* or *strange.*
We are going to the *bazaar* to buy things.
He dresses in a *bizarre* manner.

being that—is *unacceptable* for *since* or *because.*
Say: *Since* (or *Because*) you have come a long way, why not remain here for the night?

berth—is *a resting place.*
birth—means *the beginning of life.*
The new liner was given a wide *berth* in the harbor.
He was a fortunate man from *birth.*

beside—means *close to.*
besides—refers to *something that has been added.*
He lived *beside* the stream.
He found wild flowers and weeds *besides.*

better—means *recovering.*
well—means *completely recovered.*
He is *better* now than he was a week ago.
In a few more weeks, he will be *well.*

better part of—implies *quality.*
greater part of—implies *quantity.*
The better part of his performance came in the first act of the play.
Fortunately for the audience, the first act took *the greater part of* the time.

blame on—is *unacceptable* for *blame* or *blame for.*
Blame the person who is responsible for the error.
Don't *blame* me for it.
Unacceptable: Why do you put the *blame on* me?

born—means *brought into existence.*
borne—means *carried.*
All men are *born* free.
We have *borne* our burdens with patience.

both—means *two considered together.*
each—means *one of two or more.*
Both of the applicants qualified for the position.
Each applicant was given a generous reference.
Note: Avoid using such expressions as the following:
Both girls had a new typewriter. (Use *each girl* instead.)
Both girls tried to outdo the other. (Use *each girl* instead.)
They are *both* alike. (Omit *both.*)

breath—means *an intake of air.*
breathe—means *to draw air in and give it out.*
breadth—means *width.*
> Before you dive in, take a very deep *breath.*
> It is difficult to *breathe* under water.
> In a square, the *breadth* should be equal to the length.

bring—means *to carry toward the person who is speaking.*
take—means *to carry away from the speaker.*
> *Bring* the books here.
> *Take* your raincoat with you when you go out.

broke—is the past tense of *break. It is unacceptable* for *without money.*
> He *broke* his arm.

bunch—refers to *things.*
group—refers to *persons* or *things.*
> This looks like a delicious *bunch* of bananas.
> What a well-behaved *group* of children!
> **Note:** The colloquial use of bunch applied to *persons* is to be discouraged.
> A bunch of the boys were whooping it up. (group is preferable)

burst—is *acceptable* for *broke.*
bust—is *unacceptable* for *broke* (or *broken*).
> *Acceptable:* The balloon *burst.*
> *Unacceptable:* My pen is *busted.*
> *Acceptable:* That is a *bust* of Wagner.

business—is sometimes incorrectly used for *work.*
> *Unacceptable:* I went to *business* very late today. (Say *work.*)
> *Acceptable:* He owns a thriving *business.*

but—should NOT be used after the expression *cannot help.*
> *Acceptable:* One *cannot help noticing* the errors he makes in English.
> *Unacceptable:* One *cannot help but* notice . . .

calculate—means *to determine mathematically.*
> It does NOT mean *to think.*
> Some Chinese still know how to *calculate* on an abacus.
> *Unacceptable:* I *calculate* it's going to rain.

calendar—is *a system of time.*
colander—is *a kind of sieve.*
> In this part of the world, most people prefer the twelve-month *calendar.*
> Garden-picked vegetables should be washed in a *colander* before cooking.

can—means *physically able.*
may—implies *permission.*
> I *can* lift this chair over my head.
> You *may* leave after you finish your work.

cannon—is a *gun* for heavy firing.
canon—is a *rule* or *law* of the church.
> *Cannon* fire helped to hold back the enemy troops.
> Churchgoers are expected to observe the *canons.*

cannot help—must be followed by an *ing* form.
> We cannot help *feeling* (NOT *feel*) distressed about this.
> **Note:** cannot help *but* is *unacceptable.*

can't hardly—is a *double negative.* It is *unacceptable.*
> Say: The child *can hardly* walk in those shoes.

capital—is *the city.*
capitol—is *the building.*
> Paris is the *capital* of France.
> The *Capitol* in Washington is occupied by the Congress. (The Washington *Capitol* is capitalized).
> **Note:** *capital* also means wealth.

cease—means *to end.*
seize—means *to take hold of.*
> Will you please *cease* making those sounds?
> *Seize* him by the collar as he comes around the corner.

celery—is *a vegetable.*
salary—means *payment.* (generally a fixed amount, as opposed to wages).
> *Celery* grows in stalks.
> Your starting *salary* may appear low, but bonuses will make up for it.

censor—means *to examine for the purpose of judging moral aspects.*
censure—means *to find fault with.*

The government *censors* films in some countries.

She *censured* her son for coming home late.

cent—means *a coin*.
scent—means *an odor*.
sent—is the past tense of *send*.
His wit was a *complement* to her beauty.
The one-*cent* postal card is a thing of the past.
The *scent* of roses is pleasing.
We were *sent* to the rear of the balcony.

center around—is *unacceptable*. Use *center in* or *center on*.
The maximum power was *centered in* the nuclear reactor.
All attention was *centered on* the launching pad.

certainly—(and *surely*) is an *adverb*.
sure—is an *adjective*.
He was *certainly* learning fast.
Unacceptable: He *sure* was learning fast.

childish—means *silly, immature*.
childlike—means *innocent, unspoiled*.
Pouting appears *childish* in an adult.
His *childlike* appreciation of art gave him great pleasure.

choice—means *a selection*.
choose—means *to select*.
chose—means *have selected*.
My *choice* for a career is teaching.
We may *choose* our own leader.
I finally *chose* teaching for a career.

cite—means *to quote*.
sight—means *seeing*.
site—means *a place for a building*.
He was fond of *citing* from the Bible.
The *sight* of the wreck was appalling.
The Board of Education is seeking a *site* for the new school.

climate—is the average weather *over a period of many years*.
weather—is the *hour-by-hour or day-by-day* condition of the atmosphere.
He likes the *climate* of California better than that of Illinois.
The *weather* is sometimes hard to predict.

coarse—means *vulgar* or *harsh*.
course—means a *path* or a *study*.

He was shunned because of his *coarse* behavior.
The ship took its usual *course*.
Which *course* in English are you taking?

come to be—should NOT be replaced with the expression *become to be*, since *become* means *come to be*.
True freedom will *come to be* when all tyrants have been overthrown.

comic—means *intentionally funny*.
comical—means *unintentionally funny*.
A clown is a *comic* figure.
The peculiar hat she wore gave her a *comical* appearance.

comma—is *a mark of punctuation*.
coma—means *a period of prolonged unconsciousness*. (rhymes with *aroma*)
A *comma* can never separate two complete sentences.
The accident put him into a *coma* lasting three days.

common—means *shared equally by two or more*.
mutual—means *interchangeable*.
The town hall is the *common* pride of every citizen.
We can do business to our *mutual* profit and satisfaction.

compare to—means *to liken to something that has a different form*.
compare with—means *to compare persons or things with each other when they are of the same kind*.
contrast with—means *to show the difference between two things*.
A minister is sometimes *compared to* a shepherd.
Shakespeare's plays are often *compared with* those of Marlowe.
The writer *contrasted* the sensitivity of the dancer *with* the grossness of the pugilist.

complement—means *a completing part*.
compliment—is *an expression of admiration*.
His wit was a *complement* to her beauty.
He received many *compliments* on his valedictory speech.

comprehensible—means *understandable*.
comprehensive—means *including a great deal*.

Under the circumstances, your doubts were *comprehensible*.
Toynbee's *comprehensive* study of history covers many centuries.

comprise—means *to include*.
compose—means *to form the substance of*.
Toynbee's study of history *comprises* seven volumes.
Some modern symphonies are *composed* of as little as one movement.

concur in—must be followed by *an action*.
concur with—must be followed by *a person*.
I shall *concur in* the decision reached by the majority.
I cannot *concur with* the chairman, however much I respect his opinion.
Note: See **agree—concur.**

conform to—means *to adapt oneself to*.
conform with—means *to be in harmony with*.
Adolescents are inclined to *conform to* a group pattern.
They feel it dangerous not to *conform with* the rules of the group.

conscience—means *sense of right*.
conscientious—means *faithful*.
conscious—means *aware of oneself*.
Man's *conscience* prevents him from becoming completely selfish.
We all depend on him because he is *conscientious*.
The injured man was completely *conscious*.

considerable—is properly used *only as an adjective*, NOT as a noun.
Acceptable: The fraternal organization invested a *considerable amount* in government bonds.
Unacceptable: He lost *considerable* in the stock market.

consistently—means *in harmony*.
constantly—means *regularly, steadily*.
If you choose to give advice, act *consistently* with that advice.
Doctors *constantly* warn against overexertion after forty-five.

consul—means *a government representative*.
council—means *an assembly that meets for deliberation*.

counsel—means *advice*.
Americans abroad should keep in touch with their *consuls*.
The city *council* enacts local laws and regulations.
The defendant heeded the *counsel* of his lawyer.

contagious—means *catching*.
contiguous—means *adjacent* or *touching*.
Measles is a *contagious* disease.
The United States and Canada are *contiguous* countries.

contemptible—means *worthy of contempt*.
contemptuous—means *feeling contempt*.
His spying activities were *contemptible*.
It was plain to all that he was *contemptuous* of his co-workers.

continual—means *happening again and again at short intervals*.
continuous—means *without interruption*.
The teacher gave the class *continual* warnings.
Noah experienced *continuous* rain for forty days.

convenient to—should be followed by a *person*.
convenient for—should be followed by a *purpose*.
Will these plans be *convenient to* you?
You must agree that they are *convenient for* the occasion.

copy—is *an imitation of an original work* (not necessarily an exact imitation)
facsimile—is *an exact imitation of an original work*.
The counterfeiters made a crude *copy* of the hundred-dollar bill.
The official government engraver, however, prepared a *facsimile* of the bill.

core—means *the heart of something*.
corps—(pronounced like *core*) means an *organized military body*.
corpse—means *a dead body*.
The *core* of the apple was rotten.
The *corps* consisted of three full-sized armies.
The *corpse* was quietly slipped overboard after a brief service.

costumes—are *garments belonging to another period.*
customs—are *habitual practices.*
>The company played *Macbeth* in Elizabethan *costumes.*
>Every country has its own distinctive *customs.*

could of—is *unacceptable. (should of* is also *unacceptable)*
could have—is *acceptable. (should have* is *acceptable)*
>*Acceptable:* You *could have* done better with more care.
>*Unacceptable:* I *could of* won.
>AVOID ALSO: *must of, would of.*

couple—refers to *two things that are joined.*
pair—refers to *two things that are related, but not necessarily joined.*
>Four *couples* remained on the dance floor.
>The left shoe in this *pair* is a size seven: the right is a size nine.
>**Note:** *couple* refers to *two.* Do not use *couple* for more than two or for an undetermined number. The *couple* has just become engaged.
>Phone me in a *few* (NOT *couple of*) days.

credible—means *believable.*
creditable—means *worthy of receiving praise.*
credulous—means *believing too easily.*
>The pupil gave a *credible* explanation for his lateness.
>Considering all of the handicaps, he gave a *creditable* performance.
>Politicians prefer to address *credulous* people.

cute—is an abbreviated form of the word *acute.* It may mean *attractive* in colloquial usage. AVOID IT.

data—has *plural* meaning.
>The *data* for the report *are* (NOT *is*) ready.
>**Note 1:** The singular *(datum)* is seldom used.
>**Note 2:** *errata, strata, phenomena* are plural forms of *erratum, stratum, phenomenon.*

decease—means *death.*
disease—means *illness.*
>The court announced the *decease* of the crown prince.
>Leukemia is a deadly *disease.*

decent—means *suitable.*
descent—means *going down.*
dissent—means *disagreement.*
>The *decent* thing to do is to admit your guilt.
>The *descent* into the cave was treacherous.
>Two of the nine justices filed a *dissenting* opinion.

decided—means *unmistakable* when used of persons or things.
decisive—means *conclusive,* and is used of things only.
>He was a *decided* supporter of the left-wing candidate.
>The atom-bomb explosion over Hiroshima was the *decisive* act of World War II.

deference—means *respect.*
difference—means *unlikeness.*
>In *deference* to his memory, we did not play yesterday.
>The *difference* between the two boys is unmistakable.

definite—means *clear, with set limits.*
definitive—means *final, decisive.*
>We would prefer a *definite* answer to our *definite* question.
>The dictionary is the *definitive* authority for word meanings.

delusion—means *a wrong idea* that will probably influence action.
illusion—means *a wrong idea* that will probably *not* influence action.
>People were under the *delusion* that the earth was flat.
>It is just an *illusion* that the earth is flat.

deprecate—means *to disapprove of.*
depreciate—means *to lower the value.*
>His classmates *deprecated* his discourtesy.
>Property will *depreciate* rapidly unless kept in good repair.

desirable—means *that which is desired.*
desirous—means *desiring* or *wanting.*
>It was a most *desirable* position.
>He was *desirous* of obtaining it. (Note the preposition *of*)

despise—means *to look down upon.*
detest—means *to hate.*

Some wealthy persons *despise* the poor.
I *detest* cold weather. (NOT *despise*)

despite—means *notwithstanding, nevertheless.*
in spite of—is a synonym.
  Despite the weather, he went on the hike.
  Note: no preposition
  In spite of the weather, he went on the hike.

desert—(pronounced DEZZ-ert) means *an arid area.*
desert—(pronounced di-ZERT) means to *abandon;* also *a reward or punishment.*
dessert—(pronounced di-ZERT) means *the final course of a meal.*
  The Sahara is the world's most famous *desert.*
  She would never *desert* a friend in need.
  Execution was a just *desert* for his crime.
  We had plum pudding for *dessert.*

device—means *a way to do something.* (a noun)
devise—means *to find the way.* (a verb)
  A hook is a good fishing *device.*
  Some fishermen prefer to *devise* other ways for catching fish.

differ from—is used when there is a difference *in appearance.*
differ with—is used when there is a difference *in opinion.*
  A coat *differs from* a cape.
  You have the right to *differ with* me on public affairs.

different from—is *acceptable.*
different than—is *unacceptable.*
  Acceptable: Jack is *different from* his brother.
  Unacceptable: Florida climate is *different than* New York climate.

discover—means to *find something already in existence.*
invent—means to *create something that never existed before.*
  Pasteur *discovered* the germ theory of disease.
  Whitney *invented* the cotton gin.

discomfit—means to *upset.* (a verb)
discomfort—means *lack of ease.* (a noun)
  The general's plan was designed to *discomfit* the enemy.
  This collar causes *discomfort.*

discreet—means *cautious.*
discrete—means *separate.*
  The employee was *discreet* in her comments about her employer.
  Since these two questions are *discrete,* you must provide two separate answers.

disinterested—means *impartial.*
uninterested—means *not interested.*
  The judge must always be a *disinterested* party in a trial.
  As an *uninterested* observer, he was inclined to yawn at times.

divers—means *several.* (pronounced DIE-vurz)
diverse—means *different.* (pronounced di-VERSE)
  The store had *divers* foodstuffs for sale.
  Many of the items were completely *diverse* from staple foods.

doubt that—is *acceptable.*
doubt whether—is *unacceptable.*
  Acceptable: I *doubt that* you will pass this term.
  Unacceptable: We *doubt whether* you will succeed.

doubtless—is *acceptable.*
doubtlessly—is *unacceptable.*
  Acceptable: You *doubtless* know your work; why, then, don't you pass?
  Unacceptable: He *doubtlessly* thinks that you can do the job well.

due to—is *unacceptable* at the beginning of a sentence. Use *because of, on account of,* or some similar expression instead.
  Unacceptable: Due to the rain, the game was postponed.
  Acceptable: Because of the rain, the game was postponed.
  Acceptable: The postponement was *due to* the rain.

each other—refers to *two persons.*
one another—refers to *more than two persons.*
  The two girls have known *each other* for many years.
  Several of the girls have known *one another* for many years.

eats—is *unacceptable* as a synonym for *food.*
  We enjoyed the *food* (NOT *eats*) at the party.

economic—refers to *the subject of economics.*
economical—means *thrifty.*
>An *economic* discussion was held at the United Nations.
>A housewife should be *economical.*

either . . . or—is used when referring to choices.
neither . . . nor—is the *negative* form.
>*Either* you *or* I will win the election.
>*Neither* Bill *nor* Henry is expected to have a chance.

eligible—means *fit to be chosen.*
illegible—means *impossible to read.*
>Not all thirty-five-year-old persons are *eligible* to be President.
>His handwriting was *illegible.*

eliminate—means *to get rid of.*
illuminate—means *to supply with light.*
>Let us try to *eliminate* the unnecessary steps.
>Several lamps were needed to *illuminate* the room.

else—is superfluous in such expressions as the following:
>*Unacceptable:* We want *no one else* but you.
>*Acceptable:* We want *no one* but you.
>**Note:** The possessive form of *else* is *else's.*

emerge—means *to rise out of.*
immerge—means *to sink into.* (also *immerse*)
>The swimmer *emerged* from the pool.
>She *immerged* the soiled dress in the sudsy water.

emigrate—means *to leave one's country for another.*
immigrate—means *to enter another country.*
>Many people *emigrated* from Norway in mid-1860.
>Many Norwegians *immigrated* to the Middle West.

endorse—means *to write on the back of.*
>*Acceptable:* He *endorsed* the check.
>*Unacceptable:* He *endorsed* the check *on the back.*

enormity—means *viciousness.*
enormousness—means *vastness.*
>The *enormity* of his crime was appalling.
>The *enormousness* of the Sahara exceeds that of any other desert.

enthused—should be avoided.
enthusiastic—is preferred.
>*Acceptable:* We were *enthusiastic* over the performance.
>*Unacceptable:* I am truly *enthused* about my coming vacation.

equally as good—is *unacceptable.*
just as good—is *acceptable.*
>*Acceptable:* This book is *just as good* as that.
>*Unacceptable:* Your marks are *equally as good* as mine.

everyone—is written as one word when it is a *pronoun.*
every one—(two words) is used when each individual is stressed.
>*Everyone* present voted for the proposal.
>*Every one* of the voters accepted the proposal.
>**Note:** *Everybody* is written as one word.

every bit—is *incorrectly* used for *just as.*
>*Acceptable:* You are *just as* clever as she is.
>*Unacceptable:* He is *every bit* as lazy as his father.

everywheres—is *unacceptable.*
everywhere—is *acceptable.*
>We searched *everywhere* for the missing book.
>**Note:** *Everyplace* (one word) is likewise *unacceptable.*

every which way—meaning *in all directions* is *unacceptable.*
every way—is *acceptable.*
>He tried to solve the problem in *every* (OMIT *which*) way.

exceed—means *going beyond the limit.*
excel—refers to *superior quality.*
>You have *exceeded* the time allotted to you.
>All-round athletes are expected to *excel* in many sports.

except—is *acceptable.*
excepting—is *unacceptable.*
>*Acceptable:* All *except* Joe are going.
>*Unacceptable:* All cities, *excepting* Washington, are in a state.
>**Note:** Don't use *except* for *unless.*
>*Unacceptable:* He won't consent *except* you give him the money. (Say *unless*)

exceptional—means *extraordinary*.
exceptionable—means *objectionable*.
   Exceptional children learn to read before the age of five.
   The behavior of exceptional children is sometimes *exceptionable*.

excessively—means *beyond acceptable limits*.
exceedingly—means *to a very great degree*.
   In view of our recent feud, he was *excessively* friendly.
   The weather in July was *exceedingly* hot.

expand—means *to spread out*.
expend—means *to use up*.
   As the staff increases, we shall have to *expand* our office space.
   Don't *expend* all of your energy on one project.

expect—means *to look forward to*.
suspect—means *to imagine to be bad*.
   We *expect* that the family will all be together for the holidays.
   They *suspect* that we have a plan to attack them.

faint—means *to lose consciousness*.
feint—means *to make a pretended attack*.
   The lack of fresh air caused her to *faint*.
   His *feint* toward the left drew his opponent out of position, and he was able to win the point.

fair—means *light in color, reasonable, pretty*.
fare—means *a set price*.
   Your attitude is not a *fair* one.
   Children may ride the bus for half-*fare*.

farther—is used to describe *concrete distance*.
further—is used to describe *abstract ideas*.
   Chicago is *farther* from New York than Cincinnati is.
   I'll explain my point of view *further*.

faze—meaning *to worry* or *disturb* may be used colloquially.
phase—means *an aspect*.
   Don't let his angry look *faze* you.
   A crescent is a *phase* of the moon.

feel bad—means *to feel ill*.
feel badly—means *to have a poor sense of touch*.
   I *feel bad* about the accident I saw.

The numbness in his limbs caused him to *feel badly*.

feel good—means *to be happy*.
feel well—means *to be in good health*.
   I *feel very good* about my recent promotion.
   Spring weather always made him *feel well*.

fellow—means *man* or *person* in the *colloquial* sense only.

fever—refers to an *undue rise of temperature*.
temperature—refers to the *degree of heat*, which may be normal.
   We had better call the doctor—he has a *fever*.
   The *temperature* is 80 degrees.

fewer—refers to *persons or things that can be counted*.
less—refers to *something considered as a mass*.
   We have *fewer* customers this week than last week.
   I have *less* money in my pocket than you have.

financial—refers to *money matters in a general sense*.
fiscal—refers to the *public treasury*.
   Scholars are usually not *financial* successes.
   The government's *fiscal* year begins July 1 and ends June 30.

fix—means *to fasten in place*. There are certain senses in which *fix* should *NOT* be used.
   Acceptable: He *fixed* the leg to the table.
   Unacceptable: The mechanic *fixed* the car. (Say *repaired*)
   Unacceptable: How did I ever get into this *fix*? (Say *predicament*)

flout—means *to insult*.
flaunt—means *to make a display of*.
   He *flouted* the authority of the principal.
   She *flaunted* her expensive new jewelry for all to see!

flowed—is the past participle of *flow*.
flown—is the past participle of *fly*.
   The flood waters had *flowed* over the levee before nightfall.
   He had *flown* for 500 hours before he crashed.

folk—means *people in the sense of a group*. It is no longer used alone, but in combination with other words.

folks—is *unacceptable* for *friends, relatives, etc.*
Unacceptable: I'm going to see my *folks* on Sunday.
Acceptable: Anthropologists study *folk*ways, *folk*lore, and *folk*songs.

forbear—means *to refrain from doing something.* (accent on second syllable)

forebear—means *ancestor.* (accent on first syllable)
Forbear seeking vengeance.
Most of our *forebears* came from England.

formally—means *in a formal way.*
formerly—means *at an earlier time.*
The letter of reference was *formally* written.
He was *formerly* a delegate to the convention.

former—means *the first of two.*
latter—means *the second of two.*
The *former* half of the book was in prose.
The *latter* half of the book was in poetry.

fort—means *a fortified place.*
forte—means *a strong point.*
A small garrison was able to hold the *fort.*
Portrait painting was her *forte.*
Note: *forte* (pronounced FOR-tay) is a musical term meaning *loudly.*

forth—means *forward.*
fourth—*comes after third.*
They went *forth* like warriors of old.
The *Fourth* of July is our Independence Day.

funny—means *humorous* or *laughable.*
That clown is truly *funny.*
Note: *Funny* meaning *odd* or *strange* is a colloquial use that should be avoided.
Say: I have a *queer* feeling in my stomach. (NOT *funny*)

genius—means *extraordinary natural ability* or *one so gifted.*
genus—means *class* or *kind.*
Mozart showed his *genius* for music at a very early age.
The rose-of-Sharon flower probably does not belong to the *genus* of roses.

Note: A particular member of a genus is called a *species.*

get—is a verb that strictly means *to obtain.*
Please *get* my bag.
There are many slang forms of *get* that should be avoided:
AVOID: Do you *get* me? (Say: Do you *understand* me?)
You can't *get away* with it. (Say: You won't *avoid* punishment if you do it.)
Get wise to yourself. (Say: *Use* common sense.)
We didn't *get* to go. (Say: We didn't *manage* to go.)

get-up—meaning *dress* or *costume* should be *avoided.*

gibe ⎤ (pronounced alike)—both mean
jibe ⎦ to *scoff.*
We are inclined to *gibe* at awkward speakers.
Jibe also means *to agree.*
The two stories are now beginning to *jibe.*

got—means *obtained.*
He *got* the tickets yesterday.
AVOID: You've *got* to do it. (Say: You *have* to do it.)
We *have got* no sympathy for them. (Say: We *have* no sympathy for them.)
They *have got* a great deal of property. (Say: They *have* a great deal of property.)

graduated—is followed by the preposition *from.*
He *graduated* (or *was graduated*) from high school in 1981.
Unacceptable: He *graduated* college.
Note: A *graduated* test tube is one that has markings on it to indicate volume or capacity.

guess—is *unacceptable* for *think* or *suppose.*
I *think* I'll go downtown. (NOT I *guess*)
guessed—is the past tense of *guess.*
guest—means *one who is entertained.*
Because I had no time to figure it out, I *guessed* at the answer to the question.
Our *guest* arrived in time for dinner.

habit—means *an individual tendency to repeat a thing.*
custom—means *group habit.*

He had a *habit* of breaking glasses before each ball game.
The *custom* of the country was to betroth girls at the age of ten.

had ought—is *unacceptable.*
Say: You *ought* not to eat fish if you are allergic to it.

hanged—is used in reference to a *person.*
hung—is used in reference to a *thing.*
The prisoner was *hanged* at dawn.
The picture was *hung* above the fireplace.

healthy—means *having health.*
healthful—means *giving health.*
The man is *healthy.*
Fruit is *healthful.*

heap—means *a pile.*
heaps—is *unacceptable* in the sense of *very much.*
She threw her clothes in a *heap* on the floor.
Unacceptable: Thanks *heaps* for the gift.
Note: *Lots* is also *unacceptable* for very much.

help—meaning employees is *unacceptable.*
Unacceptable: Some of the *help* are sick.
(Say *employees*)

here—means *in this place.*
hear—means *to perceive with the ear.*
Here are our seats.
Can you *hear* what the actors are saying?

holy—means *sacred.*
holey—means *with holes.*
wholly—means *completely or altogether.*
Easter Week is a *holy* time in many lands.
Socks tend to become *holey* after a while.
We are *wholly* in agreement with your decision.

however—means *nevertheless.*
how ever—means *in what possible way.*
We are certain, *however,* that you will like this class.
We are certain that, *how ever* you decide to study, you will succeed.

identical with—means *agreeing exactly in every respect.*

similar to—means *having a general likeness or resemblance.*
By coincidence, his plan was *identical with* mine.
He had used methods *similar to* mine.

idle—means *unemployed* or *unoccupied.*
idol—means *image* or *object of worship.*
Idle men, like *idle* machines, are inclined to lose their sharpness.
Some dictators prefer to be looked upon as *idols* by the masses.

if—introduces a *condition.*
whether—introduces a *choice.*
I shall go to Europe *if* I win the prize.
He asked me *whether* I intended to go to Europe. (not *if*)

if it was—implies that *something might have been true in the past.*
if it were—implies *doubt,* or indicates something that is *contrary to fact.*
If your book was there last night, it is there now.
If it were summer now, we would all go swimming.

immunity—implies *resistance to a disease.*
impunity—means *freedom from punishment.*
The Salk vaccine helps develop an *immunity* to poliomyelitis.
Because he was an only child, he frequently misbehaved with *impunity.*

imply—means *to suggest or hint at.* (The speaker *implies*)
infer—means to *deduce or conclude.* (The listener *infers*)
Are you *implying* that I have disobeyed orders?
From your carefree attitude, what else are we to *infer?*

in—usually refers to *a state of being.* (no motion)
into—is used for *motion from one place to another.*
The records are *in* that drawer.
I put the records *into* that drawer.
Note: "We were walking in the room" is correct even though there is motion. The motion is *not* from one place to another.

in back of—means *behind*.
in the back of—(or *at the back of*) means *in the rear of*.
> The shovel is *in back of* (that is, *behind*) the barn.
> John is sitting *in the back of* the theatre.

infect—means *to contaminate with germs*.
infest—means *to be present in large numbers* (in a *bad sense*)
> The quick application of an antiseptic can prevent *infection*.
> The abandoned barn was *infested* with field mice.

ingenious—means *skillful, imaginative*.
ingenuous—means *naive, frank, candid*
> The *ingenious* boy created his own rocket.
> One must be *ingenuous* to accept the Communist definition of freedom.

inside
inside of} When referring to time, use *within*.
> She is arriving *within* two hours. (NOT *inside* or *inside of*)

invite—is *unacceptable* for *inviation*.
> Say: We received an *invitation* to the party.

irregardless—is *unacceptable*.
regardless—is *acceptable*.
> *Unacceptable: Irregardless* of the weather, I am going to the game.
> *Acceptable: Regardless* of his ability, he is not likely to win.

irresponsible—means *having no sense of responsibility*.
not responsible for—means *not accountable for something*.
> *Irresponsible* people are frequently late for appointments.
> Since you came late, we are *not responsible* for your having missed the first act.

its—means *belonging to it*.
it's—means *it is*.
> The house lost *its* roof.
> *It's* an exposed house now.

join together—is incorrect for *connect*. Omit *together*.
> *Acceptable:* I want to *join* these pieces of wood.
> *Unacceptable:* All of us should *join together* to fight intolerance.

judicial—means *pertaining to courts* or *to the law*.
judicious—means *wise*.
> The problem required the *judicial* consideration of an expert.
> We were certainly in no position to make a *judicious* decision.

jump at—means *to accept eagerly*.
jump to—means *to spring to*.
> We would be foolish not to *jump at* such an opportunity.
> At the sound of the bell, they all *jumped to* attention.

kind of
sort of} are *unacceptable* for *rather*.
> Say: We are *rather* disappointed in you.

knew—is the past tense of *know*.
new—means *not old*.
> He *knew* he had to be home before dark.
> She bought a *new* red sweater for her mother.

last—refers to *the final member in a series*.
latest—refers to *the most recent in time*.
latter—refers to *the second of two*.
> This is the *last* bulletin. There won't be any other bulletins.
> This is the *latest* bulletin. There will be other bulletins.
> Of the two most recent bulletins, the *latter* is more encouraging.

later on—is *unacceptable* for *later*.
> Say: *Later* we shall give your request full attention.

lay—means *to place*. (transitive verb)
lie—means *to recline*. (intransitive verb)

Note the forms of each verb:

TENSE	LAY (PLACE)	LIE (RECLINE)
Present	The chicken is *laying* an egg.	The child *is lying* down.
Past	The chicken *laid* an egg.	The child *lay* down.
Pres. Perf.	The chicken *has laid* an egg.	The child *has lain* down.

learn—means *to acquire knowledge.*
teach—means *to give knowledge.*
> We can *learn* many things just by observing carefully.
> In technical matters it is better to get someone to *teach* you.

least—means *the smallest.*
less—means *the smaller of two.*
> This was the *least* desirable of all the locations we have seen.
> This is the *less* violent of the two movies playing.

leave—means *to go away from.* (A verb is NOT used with *leave*)
let—means *to permit.* (A verb is used with *let*)
> *Leave* this house at once.
> *Let* me *remain* in peace in my own house. (*remain* is the verb used with *let*)

legible—means *able to be read.*
readable—means *able to be read with pleasure.*
> Your themes have become increasingly more *legible.*
> In fact, I now find most of them extremely *readable.*

lengthened—means *made longer.*
lengthy—means *annoyingly long.*
> The essay, now *lengthened,* is more readable.
> However, try to avoid writing *lengthy* explanations of obvious facts.

libel—is *a written and published statement injurious to a person's character.*
slander—is *a spoken statement of the same sort.*
> The unfavorable references to me in your book are *libelous.*
> When you say these vicious things about me, you are committing *slander.*

lightening—is the present participle of *to lighten.*

lightning—means *the flashes of light accompanied by thunder.*
> Leaving the extra food behind resulted in *lightening* the pack.
> Summer thunderstorms produce startling *lightning* bolts.

line—meaning occupation is *unacceptable.*
> He is in the engineering *profession.*
> *Unacceptable:* What *line* are you in? (Say: *occupation*)

loan—is a *noun.*
lend—is a *verb.*
> The bank was willing to grant him a *loan* of $500.00.
> The bank was willing to *lend* him $500.00.

lonely—means *longing for companionship.*
solitary—means *isolated.*
> Some people are forced to live *lonely* lives.
> Sometimes *solitary* surroundings are conducive to deep thought.

lots—(or *a lot, a whole lot*) meaning a *great deal, much,* is *unacceptable.*
> *Unacceptable:* He has *lots* of friends. (Say *many*)
> *Unacceptable:* I have a *lot* of trouble. (Say *a great deal of*).

luxuriant—means *abundant growth.*
luxurious—implies *wealth.*
> One expects to see *luxuriant* plants in the tropics.
> The *luxurious* surroundings indicated both wealth and good taste.

many—refers to *a number.*
much—refers to *a quantity in bulk.*
> How *many* inches of rain fell last night?
> I don't know; but I would say *much* rain fell last night.

may—is used in the *present tense.*
might—is used in the *past tense.*

We are hoping that he *may* come today.
He *might* have done it if you had encouraged him.

it's I—is always *acceptable.*
it's me—is *acceptable* only in *colloquial* speech or writing.

It's him
This is her } always *unacceptable*
It was them

It's he
This is she } always *acceptable*
It was they

measles—is plural in form, singular in meaning.
Say: *Measles is* now a minor childhood disease.
Note also, *mumps, shingles, chills,* etc. *is* . . .

memorandum—is *a reminder.* The plural is *memoranda.*
Send me a short *memorandum* of his meeting with you.
The *memoranda* will help me reconstruct the story of the meeting.
Note: *addendum–addenda; bacterium –bacteria; datum–data; dictum–dicta; erratum–errata; medium–media; stratum –strata.*

metal—is *the common chemical element.*
mettle—means *spirit.*
Lead is one of the more familiar *metals.*
One had to admire his *mettle* in the face of a crisis.

might—means *powerful* or *bulky.* Do NOT use it to mean *very.*
Samson was a *mighty* warrior.
The Philistines were all *very* (NOT *mighty*) unhappy to meet him.

miss out on—is *unacceptable* for *miss.*
We almost *missed* (not *missed out on*) seeing the game because of the traffic tieup.

moment—is a *brief, indefinite space of time.*
minute—means *the sixtieth part of an hour.*
The lightning flared for a *moment.*
The thunder followed one *minute* afterwards—or so it seemed.
Unacceptable: I'll be there in a *minute.*
(Say *moment* if you mean *briefly.*)

moneys—is *the plural of money.*
We shall vote on the disposition of the various *moneys* in the treasury.
Note: *alley–alleys; monkey–monkeys; valley–valleys.*

moral—means *good or ethical;* also, *an ethical lesson to be drawn.*
morale—(pronounced more-AL) means *spirit.*
The *moral* of the story is that it pays to be honest.
The *morale* of the troops rose after the general's inspiring speech.

more than—is correct. Do not add *rather* to this construction.
Say: I depend *more* on you *than* (NOT *rather than*) on him.
But: I depend on you *rather than* on him.

most—is an adjective in the *superlative degree.*
almost—is an adverb, meaning *nearly.*
He is the *most* courteous boy in the class.
It's *almost* time to go to school.

myself—is *unacceptable* for *I* or *me.*
My son and *I* will play.
He is a better player than *I.*
They gave my son and *me* some berries.
Note: *Myself* may be used if the subject of the verb is *I.*
Since I know *myself* better, let me try it my way.

nauseous—means *causing sickness.* (NAWSH-us)
nauseated—means *being sick.* (NAW-she-ate-id)
The odor is *nauseous.*
I feel *nauseated.* (NOT *nauseous*)

near—is an adjective meaning *close.*
nearly—is an adverb meaning *almost.*
Before 1933, only *near* beer was available.
Unacceptable: It is *near* a week since you called. (Say *nearly*)

needless to say—Avoid this expression—it doesn't mean anything.
Unacceptable: Needless to say, I refused to go. (omit *needless to say*)

neither—means *not either of two,* and should NOT be used for *none* or *not one.*
Neither of his two books was very popular.

Of the many plays he has written, *not one* (or *none*) was very popular.

never—means *at no time.* Do NOT use it for *not.*
Shakespeare was *never* in Italy.
Shakespeare was *not* very fond of France.

nevertheless—means *notwithstanding.*
nonetheless—means *not any the less* and is always followed by an adjective.
I have often warned you; *nevertheless,* you have persisted in doing the wrong thing.
I am *nonetheless* willing to give you a second chance.

nice—means *precise* or *exact.*
Your argument makes a *nice,* logical distinction.
Some use *nice* for anything and everything that is *pleasing.*
Try to be more exact in your descriptive word.*
AVOID: This is *nice* weather. (Say *sunny* or whatever you really mean)
He is such a *nice* person. (Say *kind* or whatever you really mean.)
*Other trite "blanket" expressions to avoid are: *fine, elegant, grand, lovely, splendid, terrific, swell, wonderful*—also, *rotten, lousy, miserable, terrible, awful.*
Note: *Nicely* is *unacceptable* for *well.*
Considering the seriousness of his illness, he is now doing *well.* (NOT *nicely*)

no-account—(and *no-good* and *no-use*) is *unacceptable* for *worthless.*
of no account—meaning *useless* is *acceptable.*
He is a *worthless* (NOT *no-account*) painter.
He will always be a painter *of no account.*

no better—(or **no worse**) is *acceptable* in colloquial use.
He is *no better* than this record.
Note: *No different* is *unacceptable.*
Your proposal is *not different* from mine.

noplace—as a solid word, is *unacceptable* for *no place* or *nowhere.*
Acceptable: You now have *nowhere* to go.

nohow—is *unacceptable* for *regardless.*
Unacceptable: I can't do this *nohow.*

no sooner . . . than—(NOT *no sooner . . . when*) is the *acceptable* expression.
No sooner did the rain start *than* (not *when*) the game was called off.

nowhere near—is *unacceptable* for *not nearly.*
The work was *not nearly* finished by nightfall.

nowheres—is *unacceptable.*
nowhere—is *acceptable.*
The child was *nowhere* (NOT *nowheres*) to be found.

notable—means *remarkable.*
notorious—means *of bad reputation.*
December 7, 1941, was a *notable* day.
At that time, the *notorious* Tojo commanded the Japanese forces.

nothing more or less—is *unacceptable* for *nothing more nor less.*
Correct English is *nothing more nor less* than a matter of careful practice.

number—is singular *when the total is intended.*
The *number* (of pages in the book) is 500.
number—is plural *when the individual units are referred to.*
A *number* of pages (in the book) were printed in italic type.

observance—means the *act of complying.*
observation—means the *act of noting.*
In *observance* of the new regulation, we shall omit further tests.
His scientific *observations* became the basis for a new rocket theory.

occupancy—refers to *the mere act of occupying,* usually legally.
occupation—means *the forceful act of occupying.*
According to the lease, the tenant still had *occupancy* of the apartment for another month.
The *occupation* by the enemy worried the townspeople.

of any—(and *of anyone*) is *unacceptable* for *of all.*
His was the highest mark *of all.*
(NOT *of any* or *of anyone*)

off of—is *unacceptable*.
>He took the book *off* (NOT *off of*) the table.

oftentimes—is *unacceptable* for *often*.
>He *often* went back to the scenes of his childhood.

O.K.—is *acceptable* for *all right* or *approved* in informal business and informal social usage.
>AVOID the use of *O.K.* in formal situations.
>*Acceptable:* This retyped letter is *O.K.*

on account of—is *unacceptable* for *because*.
>We could not meet you *because* (NOT *on account of*) we did not receive your message in time.

one and the same—is repetitious. Omit *one and*.
>Your plan and mine are *the same*.

one . . . one—is the *acceptable* construction in such expressions as:
>The more *one* listens to his speeches, the more *one* (NOT *he*) wonders how a young man can be so wise.

oral—means *spoken*.
verbal—means *expressed in words*, either spoken or written.
>In international intrigue, *oral* messages are less risky than written ones.
>Shorthand must usually be transcribed into *verbal* form.

other . . . than—is *acceptable; other . . . but* (or *other . . . except*) is *unacceptable*.
>We have no *other* motive *than* friendship in asking you.

other—is an adjective and means *different*.
otherwise—is an adverb and means *in a different way*.
>What you did was *other* (NOT *otherwise*) than what you had promised.
>I cannot look *otherwise* (NOT *other*) than with delight at the improvement in your work.
>All students, *except* (NOT *other than*) those exempted, should take the examination.
>All students, *unless* they have been exempted (NOT *otherwise*), will take the examination.

out loud—is *unacceptable* for *aloud*.
>He read *aloud* (NOT *out loud*) to his family every evening.

outdoor—(and *out-of-doors*) is an adjective.
outdoors—is an adverb.
>We spent most of the summer at an *outdoor* music camp.
>Most of the time we played string quartets *outdoors*.
>**Note:** *Out-of-doors* is *acceptable* in either case.

over—is *unacceptable* for *at*.
>We shall be *at* (NOT *over*) your house tonight.

overly—is *unacceptable* for *over*.
>We were *over-anxious* (not *overly anxious*) about the train's delay.

over with—is *unacceptable* for *completed*.
>Thank goodness, that job is now *over!*

packed—means *full*.
pact—means *a treaty*.
>The crate is *packed* with mixed fruits.
>The peace *pact* between the former enemy nations was signed today.

part—means *a fraction of a whole*.
portion—means *an allotted or designated part*.
>We had time to read just a *part* of the story.
>Tomorrow, each of us will be responsible for reading a *portion* of the story.

part from—a *person*.
part with—a *thing*.
>It was difficult for him to *part from* his classmates.
>It will be difficult for him to *part with* his memories as well.

partial to—is *unacceptable* for *fond of*.
>I am *fond of* (or *prefer*) bamboo fishing rods. (NOT *partial to*)

party—refers to a *group*, NOT an *individual*.
>A *party* of men went on a scouting mission.
>I told the woman (NOT *party*) that she had been using the phone too long.
>**Note:** *Party* may be used in a legal sense: The *party* of the second part.

passed—is the past tense of *to pass*.

past—means *just preceding*.
> The week *passed* very slowly.
> The *past* week was a very dull one.

patron—means *supporter*.
customer—is a *buyer*.
> She was well known as a *patron* of early American art.
> The rain kept the *customers* away.

pedal—means *a lever operated by foot*. (AVOID *foot* pedal)
peddle—means *to sell from door to door*.
> It is impossible to ride a bicycle without moving the *pedals*.
> The traveling salesman today seldom *peddles* from door to door.

people—comprise *a united or collective group of individuals*.
persons—are *individuals that are separate and unrelated*.
> Only five *persons* remained in the theater after the first act.
> The *people* of New York City have enthusiastically accepted "Shakespeare-in-the-Park" productions.

per—is Latin and is *chiefly commercial*.
> *per diem* (by the day); *per minute*, etc.
> AVOID *as per* your instruction (Say *according to*)

percent—(also **per cent**) expresses *rate of interest*.
percentage—means *a part or proportion of the whole*.
> The interest rate of some banks is 8 *percent*.
> The *percentage* of unmarried people in our community is small.

persecute—means *to make life miserable for someone*. (It's nonlegal)
prosecute—means *to conduct a criminal investigation*. (It's legal)
> Some racial groups insist on *persecuting* other groups.
> The district attorney is *prosecuting* the racketeers.

personal—refers to a *person*.
personnel—means *an organized body of individuals*.
> The general took a *personal* interest in every one of his men.
> He believed that this was necessary in order to maintain the morale of the *personnel* in his division.

plain—means *simple*, or *a prairie*.
plane—means *a flat surface*, or *a tool*.
> The Great *Plains* are to be found in Western America.
> In *plane* geometry, we are concerned with two dimensions: length and width.

plenty—is a noun; it means *abundance*.
> America is a land of *plenty*.
> There is *plenty of* (NOT *plenty*) room in the compact car for me.
> **Note:** *plenty* as an adverb is *unacceptable*.
> **Note:** *plenty* as an adjective is *unacceptable*.
> The compact car is *quite* (NOT *plenty*) large enough for me.

pole—means *a long stick*.
poll—means *vote*.
> We bought a new *pole* for the flag.
> The seniors took a *poll* to determine the graduate most likely to succeed.

poorly—meaning *in poor health* is *unacceptable*.
> Grandfather was feeling *in poor health* (NOT *poorly*) all last winter.

pour—is to send flowing *with direction and control*.
spill—is to send flowing *accidentally*.
> Please *pour* some cream into my cup of coffee.
> Careless people *spill* things.

posted—meaning *informed* is *unacceptable*.
> One can keep *well-informed* (NOT *well-posted*) by reading *The New York Times* daily.

practicable—means *useful, usable*, or *workable*, and is applied only to objects.
practical—means *realistic, having to do with action*. It applies to persons and things.
> There is as yet no *practicable* method for resisting atomic bomb attacks.
> *Practical* technicians, nevertheless, are attempting to translate the theories of the atomic scientists into some form of defense.

precede—means *to come before.*
proceed—means *to go ahead.* (*procedure* is the noun)
supersede—means *to replace.*
>What are the circumstances that *preceded* the attack?
>We can then *proceed* with our plan for resisting a second attack.
>It is then possible that Plan B will *supersede* Plan A.

predominately—is *unacceptable* for *predominantly,* meaning *powerfully* or *influentially.*
>The *predominantly* rich people in the area resisted all governmental attempts to create adequate power facilities.

prescribe—means *to lay down a course of action.*
proscribe—means *to outlaw or forbid.*
>The doctor *prescribed* plenty of rest and good food for the man.
>Theft is *proscribed* by law.

principal—means *chief* or *main* (as an adjective); *a leader* (as a noun).
principle—means *a fundamental truth or belief.*
>His *principal* supporters came from among the peasants.
>The *principal* of the school asked for cooperation from the staff.
>Humility was the guiding *principle* of Buddha's life.
>Note: *Principal* may also mean *a sum placed at interest.*
>Part of his monthly payment was applied as interest on the *principal.*

prodigy—means *a person endowed with extraordinary gifts or powers.*
protégé—means *someone under the protection of another.*
>Mozart was a musical *prodigy* at the age of three.
>The veteran ballplayer offered invaluable advice to his young *protégé.*

prophecy—(rhymes with *sea*) is the noun meaning *prediction.*
prophesy—(rhymes with *sigh*) is the verb meaning *to predict.*
>The *prophecy* of the three witches eventually misled Macbeth.
>The witches had *prophesied* that Macbeth would become king.

proposal—means *an offer.*
proposition—means *a statement.*
>Lincoln's *proposal* for freeing the slaves through government purchase was unacceptable to the South.
>The *proposition* that all men are created equal first appeared in the writings of the French Encyclopedists.

propose—means *to offer.*
purpose—means *to resolve* or *to intend.*
>Let the teacher *propose* the subject for our debate.
>The teacher *purposed* to announce the subject of the debate next week.

put across—meaning *to get something accepted* is *unacceptable.*
>A good teacher may be defined as one who *succeeds in her purpose.* (NOT *puts it across*)

put in—meaning *to spend, make* or *devote* is *unacceptable.*
>Every good student should *spend* (NOT *put in*) at least four hours a day in studying.
>Be sure to *make* (NOT *put in*) an appearance at the council meeting.

rain—means *water from the clouds.*
reign—means *rule.*
rein—means *a strap for guiding a horse.*
>The *rain* in Spain falls mainly on the plain.
>A queen now *reigns* over England.
>When the *reins* were pulled too tightly, the horse reared.

raise—means to *lift, erect.*
raze—(pronounced like *raise*) means to *tear down.*
>The neighbors helped him *raise* a new barn.
>The tornado *razed* his barn.
>AVOID *raise* in connection with rearing children.
>She *brought up* three lovely girls. (NOT *raised*)

rarely or ever—is *unacceptable.*
>Say *rarely ever, rarely if ever, rarely or never.*
>One *rarely if ever* (NOT *rarely or ever*) sees a trolley car today.
>Students today *seldom if ever* (NOT *seldom or ever*) read Thackeray's novels.

real—meaning *very* or *extremely* is *unacceptable*.
>He is a *very* (NOT *real*) handsome young man.
>He is *really* handsome.

reason is because—is *unacceptable* for *the reason is that*.
>The *reason* young people do not read Trollope today *is that* his sentences are too involved.
>**Note:** Avoid *due to* after *reason is*.
>*The reason* he refused *was that he was proud* (NOT *due to his pride*).

rebellion—means *open, armed organized resistance to authority*.
revolt—means *similar resistance on a smaller scale*.
revolution—means *the overthrowing of one government and the setting up of another*.
>Bootlegging has sometimes been referred to as a *rebellion* against high whiskey taxes.
>An increase in the grain tax caused a peasants' *revolt* against the landowners.
>The American *Revolution* resulted in the recognition of the United States as an independent nation.

reckon—meaning *suppose* or *think* is *unacceptable*.
>I *think* it may rain this afternoon.

recollect—means *to bring back to memory*.
remember—means *to keep in memory*.
>Now I can *recollect* your returning the money to me.
>I *remember* the occasion well.

reconciled to—means *resigned to* or *adjusted to*.
reconciled with—means *to become friendly again with someone;* also, *to bring one set of facts into harmony with another one*.
>I am now *reconciled to* this chronic ache in my back.
>The boy was *reconciled with* his parents after he had promised not to run away from home again.
>How does one *reconcile* the politician's shabby accomplishments *with* the same politician's noble promises?

regular—meaning *real* or *true* is *unacceptable*.
>He was a *real* (NOT *regular*) tyrant.

respectably—means *in a manner deserving respect*.
respectfully—means *with respect and decency*.
respectively—means *as relating to each, in the order given*.
>Young people should dress *respectably* for a job interview.
>The students listened *respectfully* to the principal.
>John and Bill are the sons *respectively* of Mr. Smith and Mr. Brown.

restive—means *fretting under restraint*.
restless—means *fidgety*.
>As the principal continued talking, the students became *restive*.
>Spring always makes me feel *restless*.

retaliate—means *to return evil for evil*.
reciprocate—means *to return in kind—usually a favor for a favor*.
>The boxer *retaliated* with a stunning blow to his opponent's jaw.
>She *reciprocated* the kindness of the two young men who helped her change her tire by inviting them to her home for dinner.

right along—is *unacceptable* for *continuously*.
>His contemporaries were *continuously* (NOT *right along*) in opposition to Shakespeare.
>**Note:** *Right away* and *right off* are *unacceptable* for *at once*.
>Other of Shakespeare's contemporaries, especially Ben Jonson, *immediately* (NOT *right off* or *right away*) recognized his genius.

rob—one *robs a person*.
steal—one *steals a thing*.
>They *robbed* the blind man of his money.
>He *stole* my wallet.
>**Note:** "They *robbed* the First National Bank" is correct because they actually robbed the persons working in the bank.

rout—(rhymes with *stout*) means *a defeat*.
route—(rhymes with *boot*) means *a way of travel*.
>The *rout* of the army was near.
>The postman follows the same *route* each day.

same as—is *unacceptable* for *in the same way* and *just as*.

The owner's son was treated *in the same way as* any other worker. (NOT *the same as*)

AVOID *same* as a pronoun, except in *legal* usage.

If the books are available, please send *them* (NOT *same*) by parcel post.

saw—is the past tense of *see.*
seen—is the past participle of *see.*
We *saw* a play yesterday. (NOT *seen*)
I have never *seen* a live play before. (NOT *saw*)

scan—means *to examine carefully.* It can also mean to *examine hastily* or *superficially.*
You must *scan* a book on nuclear physics in order to understand it thoroughly.
When I am in a hurry, I *scan* the headlines.

seem—as used in the expression *I couldn't seem to* and *I don't seem to* is *unacceptable.*
We *can't find* (NOT We *can't seem to find*) the address.

self-confessed—is *unacceptable for confessed.*
Omit *self.*
He was a *confessed* slayer.

sensible of—means *aware of.*
sensitive to—means *affected by.*
I am very *sensible of* my shortcomings in written English.
He is *sensitive* to criticism.

sensual—means *pleasure-loving.*
sensuous—means *influenced through the senses, esthetic.*
The *sensual* man cares little about the salvation of his soul.
A *sensuous* person usually appreciates art and music.

settle—meaning *to pay* is *unacceptable.*
We *paid* all our former bills. (NOT *settled*)
AVOID: We'll *settle* you, We'll *settle* your dinner, etc.

shape—meaning *state* or *condition* is *unacceptable.*
The refugees were in a serious *condition* (NOT *shape*) when they arrived here.

show up—meaning *to make an appearance* is *unacceptable.*

We were all disappointed in the star's failure to *appear* (NOT *to show up*).
Note: *Show up* meaning *to expose* is *unacceptable.*
It is my firm intention to *expose* (NOT *show up*) your hypocrisy.

sign up—meaning *to enlist* or *enroll* is *unacceptable.*
Many students sought to *enroll in* (NOT *sign up*) the course after hearing the professor speak.

simple reason—is *unacceptable* for *reason.* Omit the word *simple* in similar expressions: *simple truth, simple purpose,* etc.
Unacceptable: I refuse to do it for the *simple reason* that I don't like your attitude.
Acceptable: The *truth* (omit *simple*) is that I feel tired.

simply—meaning *absolutely* is *unacceptable.*
The performance was *absolutely* (NOT *simply*) thrilling.

sit—means *take a seat.* (intransitive verb)
set—means *place.* (transitive verb)
Note the forms of each verb:

TENSE	SIT (TAKE A SEAT)
Present	He *is sitting* on a chair
Past	He *sat* on the chair.
Pres. Perf.	He *has sat* on the chair.

TENSE	SET (PLACE)
Present	He *is setting* the lamp on the table.
Past	He *set* the lamp on the table.
Pres. Perf.	He *has set* the lamp on the table.

size up—meaning *to estimate* is *unacceptable.*
The detectives were able *to estimate* (NOT *size up*) the fugitive's remaining ammunition supply from his careless shooting.

so—should be avoided for *very, great,* etc.
She is *very* (NOT *so*) beautiful!
So should not be used for *so that* to express purpose.

Unacceptable: He gave up his seat *so that* (NOT *so*) the old lady could sit down.

sociable—means *friendly.*
social—means *relating to people in general.*
Sociable individuals prefer to have plenty of people around them.
The President's *social* program included old age insurance, housing, education, etc.

sole—means *all alone.*
soul—means *human spirit.*
He was the *sole* owner of the business.
Man's *soul* is unconquerable.

some—meaning *somewhat* is *unacceptable.*
She is *somewhat* (NOT *some*) better today.
Note: *Some* is *unacceptable* in such expressions as the following:
We had a *very* (NOT *some*) strong scare this morning.

some time—means *a portion of time.*
sometime—means *at an indefinite time in the future.*
sometimes—means *occasionally.*
I'll need *some time* to make a decision.
Let us meet *sometime* after twelve noon.
Sometimes it is better to hesitate before signing a contract.

somewheres—is *unacceptable.*
somewhere—is *acceptable.*

specie—means *money as coins.* (*Specie* is singular only.)
species—means *a class of related things.* (*Species* is singular and plural.)
He preferred to be paid in *specie*, rather than in bank notes.
The human *species* is relatively young. (singular)
Several animal *species* existed before man. (plural)

stand—meaning *to tolerate* is *unacceptable.*
I refuse *to tolerate* (NOT *to stand for*) your nonsense.

start in—is *unacceptable* for *start.*
We shall *start* (NOT *start in*) to read the story in a few minutes.

state—means *to declare formally.*
say—means *to speak generally.*

Our ambassador *stated* the terms for a cease-fire agreement.
We *said* (NOT *stated*) that we would not attend the meeting.

stationary—means *standing still.*
stationery—means *writing materials.*
In ancient times people thought the earth was *stationary.*
We bought writing paper at the *stationery* store.

statue—means *a piece of sculpture.*
stature—means *height.*
statute—is *a law.*
The *Statue* of Liberty stands in New York Harbor.
The athlete was a man of great *stature.*
Compulsory education was established by *statute.*

stay—means *to remain.*
stop—means *to cease.*
We *stayed* (NOT *stopped*) at the hotel for three days.
The power failure caused the clock to stop.
Note: *To stop off, to stop over,* and *to stay put* are *unacceptable.*

stayed—means *remained.*
stood—means *remained upright* or *erect.*
Because of the bad weather, we *stayed* in the house all day.
The soldiers *stood* at attention for one hour.

summons—is singular; *summonses* is the plural.
We received a *summons* to appear in court.
This was the first of three *summonses* we were to receive that week.
Note: *Summons* is also a verb.
We were *summonsed* to appear in court. (also *summoned*)

sure—for *surely* is *unacceptable.*
You *surely* (NOT *sure*) are not going to write that!

surround—means *to enclose on all sides.* Do NOT add *on all sides* to it.
The camp was *surrounded* by heavy woods.

suspicioned—is *unacceptable* for *suspected.*
We *suspected* (NOT *suspicioned*) that he was ready to betray us.

take in—is *unacceptable* in the sense of *deceive* or *attend.*
We were *deceived* (NOT *taken in*) by his oily manner.
We should like to *attend* (NOT *take in*) a few plays during our vacation.

take stock in—is *unacceptable* for *rely on.*
We rarely *rely on* (NOT *take stock in*) the advice of inexperienced employees.

tasteful—means *having good taste.*
tasty—means *pleasing to the taste.*
The home of our host was decorated in a *tasteful* manner.
Our host also served us very *tasty* meals.

tenants—are *occupants.*
tenets—are *principles.*
Several *tenants* occupied that apartment during the first month.
His religious *tenets* led him to perform many good deeds.

tender—means *to offer officially* or *formally.*
give—means *to donate* or *surrender something willingly.*
The discredited official decided to *tender* his resignation.
He *gave* testimony readily before the grand jury.

testimony—means *information given orally only.*
evidence—means *information given orally or in writing.*
He gave *testimony* readily to the grand jury.
The defendant presented written *evidence* to prove he was not at the scene of the crime.

that there
this here } are *unacceptable.* Omit *there, here.*
That (NOT *that there*) person is taller than *this* (NOT *this here*) one.

their—means *belonging to them.*
there—means *in that place.*
they're—means *they are.*
We took *their* books home with us.
You will find your books over *there* on the desk.

They're not as young as we expected them to be.

theirselves—is *unacceptable* for *themselves.*
Say: Most children of school age are able to care for *themselves* in many ways.

therefor—means *for that.*
therefore—means *because of that.*
One day's detention is the punishment *therefor.*
You will *therefore* have to remain in school after dismissal time.

these kind—is *unacceptable.*
this kind—is *acceptable.*
I am fond of *this kind* of apple.
Note: *These kinds of apples* would be also *acceptable.*

through—means *from one end to the other.*
thorough—means *exhaustive.*
We followed the path *through* the woods.
They conducted a *thorough* search for the missing child.

thusly—is *unacceptable* for *thus.*
Speak words *thus:* . . .

to my knowledge—implies *certain knowledge.*
to the best of my knowledge—implies *limited knowledge.*
He is, *to my knowledge,* the brightest boy in the class.
As for his character, he has never, *to the best of my knowledge,* been in trouble with the law.

track—means *a path* or *road.*
tract—means *a brief but serious piece of writing; a piece of land.*
The horses raced around the fairgrounds *track.*
John Locke wrote a famous *tract* on education.
The heavily wooded *tract* was sold to a lumber company.

treat—means *to deal with.*
treat of—means *to give an explanation of.*
treat with—means *to negotiate with.*
I shall *treat* that subject in our next lesson.
The lesson itself will *treat of* Shakespeare's humor.

I shall *treat with* the delinquent students at some other time.

try to—is *acceptable.*
try and—is *unacceptable.*
> *Try to* come (NOT *try and* come).
> **Note:** *plan on going* is *unacceptable. plan to go* is *acceptable.*

two—is the *numeral 2.*
to—means *in the direction of.*
too—means *more than* or *also.*
> There are *two* sides to every story.
> Three *twos* (or 2's) equal six.
> We shall go *to* school.
> We shall go, *too.*
> The weather is *too* hot for school.

type man—(*type book, type game,* etc.) is *unacceptable* for *type of man, type of book, type of game,* etc.
> He is the right *type of man* for this position.

ugly—meaning *unpleasant* or *dangerous* is *unacceptable.*
> This is a very *dangerous* (NOT *ugly*) situation.

ulterior—means *hidden underneath.*
underlying—means *fundamental.*
> His noble words were contradicted by his *ulterior* motives.
> Shakespeare's *underlying* motive in *Hamlet* was to criticize the moral climate of his time.

unbeknownst to—is *unacceptable* for *without the knowledge of.*
> The young couple decided to get married *without the knowledge of* (NOT *unbeknownst to*) their parents.

unique—means *the only one of its kind* and therefore does not take *very, most, extremely* before it.
> The First Folio edition of Shakespeare's works is *unique* (NOT *very unique*).
> **Note:** The same rule applies to *perfect.*

upwards of—is *unacceptable* for *more than.*
> There are *more than* (NOT *upwards of*) one million people unemployed today.

valuable—means *of great worth.*
valued—means *held in high regard.*
invaluable—means *priceless.*
> This is a *valuable* manuscript.
> The expert gave him highly *valued* advice.
> A good name is an *invaluable* possession.

virtually—means *in effect.*
actually—means *in fact.*
> A tie in the final game was *virtually* a defeat for us.
> We had *actually* won more games than they at that time.

waive—means *to give up.*
wave—means *a swell or roll of water.*
> As a citizen, I refuse to *waive* my right of free speech.
> The *waves* reached to the top deck of the ship.

ways—is *unacceptable* for *way.*
> We climbed a little *way* (NOT *ways*) up the hill.

went and took—(*went and stole,* etc.) is *unacceptable.*
> They *stole* (NOT *went and stole*) our tools.

what—is *unacceptable* for *that.*
> Everything *that* (NOT *what*) you write displeases me.

when—(and *where*) should NOT be used to introduce a definition of a noun.
> A tornado *is a* twisting, high wind on land (NOT *is when a twisting, high wind is on land*).
> A pool *is a place for swimming.* (NOT *is where people swim*)

whereabouts—is *unacceptable* for *where.*
> *Where* (NOT *whereabouts*) do you live?
> **Note:** *Whereabouts* as a noun meaning a place is *acceptable.*
> Do you know his *whereabouts?*

whether—means *if it be the case that.*
weather—means *the condition of the atmosphere.*
> The extent of his injuries will determine *whether* he can play in the next game.
> The swimming meet was canceled because the *weather* turned so cold.

while—is *unacceptable* for *and* or *though*.

> The library is situated on the south side; (OMIT *while*) the laboratory is on the north side.
>
> *Though* (NOT *while*) I disagree with you, I shall not interfere with your right to express your opinion.
>
> *Though* (NOT *while*) I am in my office every day, you do not attempt to see me.

who
whom The following is a method (without going into grammar rules) for determining when to use *who* or *whom*.

> "Tell me (*who, whom*) you think should represent our company."
>
> **Step One**—Change the who–whom part of the sentence to its natural order.
>
> "You think (*who, whom*) should represent our company?"
>
> **Step Two**—Substitute HE for WHO, HIM for WHOM.
>
> "You think (he, him) should represent our company?"
>
> You would say *he* in this case.
>
> **Therefore**—"Tell me *who* you think should represent the company." is correct.

whose—means *of* or *relating to whom*.
who's—means *who is*.

> *Whose* notebook is this?
>
> *Who's* going to the concert with you?

win—you *win* a game.
beat—you *beat* another player.

> We *won* the contest.
>
> He *beat* me in tennis. (NOT *won* me)
>
> **Note:** Don't use *beat* for swindle. Say: The peddler *swindled* the customer out of five dollars. (NOT *beat*)

worst kind—(and *worst way*) is *unacceptable* for *very badly* or *extremely*.

> The school is *greatly in need of more teachers*. (NOT *needs teachers the worst way*).

would have—is *unacceptable* for *had*.

> I wish you *had* (NOT *would have*) called earlier.

your—is the possessive of *you*.
you're—is a contraction of *you are*.

> Are these *your* keys?
>
> If *you're* ready, we should leave now.

Answer Sheet for Vocabulary Building Practice Tests

Test 1

1. _____
2. _____
3. _____
4. _____
5. _____
6. _____
7. _____
8. _____
9. _____
10. _____

11. _____
12. _____
13. _____
14. _____
15. _____
16. _____
17. _____
18. _____
19. _____
20. _____

Test 2

1 Ⓐ Ⓑ Ⓒ Ⓓ   3 Ⓐ Ⓑ Ⓒ Ⓓ   5 Ⓐ Ⓑ Ⓒ Ⓓ   7 Ⓐ Ⓑ Ⓒ Ⓓ
2 Ⓐ Ⓑ Ⓒ Ⓓ   4 Ⓐ Ⓑ Ⓒ Ⓓ   6 Ⓐ Ⓑ Ⓒ Ⓓ   8 Ⓐ Ⓑ Ⓒ Ⓓ

Test 1

Time: 15 minutes. 20 questions.

DIRECTIONS: Choose the correct word or words to complete each of the sentences below.

1. I made a (conscience, conscious, concise) decision not to attend the party.

2. Their verbal (duel, dual) went on for some time, yet neither was able to best the other.

3. She is not (adverse, averse) to working evenings if the pay is good.

4. Hayfever season is here, and many people are finding it difficult to (breath, breathe, breadth).

5. There were very few suspects, since very few people had (excess, access) to the safe.

6. He published a (tract, track) on the subject of obedience.

7. (Illegible, Eligible) bachelors are harder and harder to find.

8. The motel I recommended was (further, farther) away but worth the extra drive.

9. Jeanne could not (allude, elude) to the subject without hurting my brother's feelings.

10. The (weather, whether) will not (effect, affect) our plans.

11. Everyone is coming (accept, except, excepting) Jill.

12. The game was (already, all ready) in progress when we arrived.

13. I think we can (proceed, precede) to the main business of the meeting now.

14. Once the salesperson had convinced the customer to (by, buy) the skirt, she suggested a blouse in a (complimentary, complementary) color.

15. You would not expect a man of his (statue, stature, statute) in public life to stoop to such behavior.

16. She said her business was (personnel, personal), and so I decided to see her in private.

17. (There, Their) car was stolen (sometime, sometimes, some time) during the week.

18. The (sole, soul) objection was raised by the owner of the (stationary, stationery) store.

19. Even after she left the room, the (sent, scent, cent) of her perfume hung in the air.

20. He found the perfect (cite, sight, site) for the house.

Test 2

Time: 15 minutes. 20 questions.

DIRECTIONS: Select the one sentence in each group that contains an error in word usage.

1. (A) At the library she found an abridged version of the lengthy novel.
   (B) Ten people have already accepted our invitation to brunch.
   (C) A new regulation gives all students access to their school records.
   (D) Be sure you have the latest addition of the textbook.

2. (A) There is nothing more aggravating than waiting for the phone to ring.
   (B) His refusal to comply with the rules was altogether unacceptable to the coach.
   (C) Magicians are masters of illusion.
   (D) If it rains, we'll have to alter our plans for a picnic.

3. (A) The missing ring was nowhere to be found.
   (B) He was eager to get home after the long, difficult drive.
   (C) We should arrive around two o'clock.
   (D) If you fall asleep on the beach, you are liable to wake up badly burned.

4. (A) Besides English, I am studying French and Spanish this term.
   (B) He walked like he was in pain.
   (C) Please take these books back to the library.
   (D) The telephone wire reaches as far as the kitchen, but no farther.

5. (A) Due to the icy roads, school will be closed today.
   (B) Homemade apple pie is my favorite dessert.
   (C) Deep in the woods, I came upon an old deserted house.
   (D) Joe is so different from Bill, it's hard to believe they are brothers.

6. (A) My guess is that we will have two guests for dinner.
   (B) The plane was delayed because of the thunder and lightning.
   (C) These boots are equally as good as the others.
   (D) Can you lend me five dollars until tomorrow?

7. (A) It was near a week before she replied to my letter.
   (B) No sooner did we leave than the rain started.
   (C) The prize was divided equally among the four winners.
   (D) During the last week of school, time passed very slowly for the students eagerly awaiting the start of summer vacation.

8. (A) Sometimes it's better to let your friends know exactly how you feel.
   (B) We stayed at my aunt's house for a week.
   (C) They're putting on their skates right now.
   (D) Although we waited in the cold for nearly two hours, the rock star never showed up.

Answer Key for Vocabulary Building Practice Tests

Test 1

1. conscious
2. duel
3. averse
4. breathe
5. access
6. tract
7. Eligible
8. farther
9. allude
10. weather, affect

11. except
12. already
13. proceed
14. buy, complementary
15. stature
16. personal
17. Their, some time
18. sole, stationery
19. scent
20. site

Test 2

1. **(D)** Be sure you have the latest *edition* of the textbook.
2. **(A)** There is nothing more *exasperating* (or *irritating*) than waiting for the phone to ring.
3. **(C)** We should arrive *about* two o'clock.
4. **(B)** He walked *as if* he was in pain.
5. **(A)** *Because* of the icy roads, school will be closed today.
6. **(C)** These boots are *just as good* as the others.
7. **(A)** It was *nearly* a week before she replied to my letter.
8. **(D)** Although we waited in the cold for nearly two hours, the rock star never *appeared*.

READING COMPREHENSION

Skill with reading interpretation questions is an important knack for master test-takers. This chapter provides plenty of practice with the kind of reading questions you are likely to face. Although the selections cover a variety of topics, you won't have to memorize any information to select the correct answer. Clear thinking is the key to success in interpreting each passage correctly. Practice now and profit later.

Concentration, speed, retentiveness, ability to associate the ideas you read . . . these are the hallmarks of the master test-taker. It doesn't matter what they give you to read, these capabilities will help you score high. That's why this chapter tests your reading in a variety of fields. It asks that you flex your mental muscles and acquire competence through flexibility.

These varied reading passages question you in several ways. Can you quickly grasp the main idea? Can you remember and associate specific details? Can you judge the truth or falsity of what you read? Can you make reasonable inferences from your reading?

If you bear in mind that a good piece of writing usually has a central thought and that each paragraph in that piece has its own important idea, the following suggestions should help you.

1. Read the paragraph through quickly to get the general sense.
2. Reread the paragraph, concentrating on the central idea, and try to picture it as a unit.
3. Examine the various choices carefully but rapidly, *eliminating immediately* those that are farfetched or irrelevant.
4. Be sure to consider only the facts given in the paragraph to which the choice refers.
5. Be especially careful of trick expressions or "catch-words," which sometimes destroy the validity of a seemingly true statement. These include the following expressions: "under all circumstances," "at all times," "never," "always," "under no conditions," "absolutely," "completely," and "entirely."
6. In this sort of question you may correctly infer an answer from the information given, even if it's not actually stated.

In questions that test your ability to single out details and facts, answer *solely* on the basis of the information given.

In questions that test your ability to judge truth or falsity, your answers should also be based *solely* on the information given. If you must make inferences, infer cautiously because these questions test your ability to spot precisely what *is* and what *is not* stated.

In most reading questions, a paragraph is followed by one or more statements based on the paragraph. Each statement is in turn followed by several choices that will complete the statement. You may never have seen the paragraph before, but you must now read it carefully so that you understand it.

Then read the statements and choices. Choose the one that is most correct. Try to pick the one that is most complete, most accurate, the one that is best supported by and necessarily flows from the paragraph. *Be sure* that it contains nothing false so far as the paragraph itself is concerned. When you've answered all of the questions, score yourself faithfully by checking with the answers that follow the last question. But please don't look at those answers until you've written your own. You just won't be helping yourself if you do that. Besides you'll have ample opportunity to do the questions again, and to check with the answers, in the event that your first try results in a low score.

Answer Sheet for Reading Comprehension Practice Test

1 Ⓐ Ⓑ Ⓒ Ⓓ Ⓔ   7 Ⓐ Ⓑ Ⓒ Ⓓ   13 Ⓐ Ⓑ Ⓒ Ⓓ Ⓔ

2 Ⓐ Ⓑ Ⓒ Ⓓ Ⓔ   8 Ⓐ Ⓑ Ⓒ Ⓓ   14 Ⓐ Ⓑ Ⓒ Ⓓ Ⓔ

3 Ⓐ Ⓑ Ⓒ Ⓓ Ⓔ   9 Ⓐ Ⓑ Ⓒ Ⓓ   15 Ⓐ Ⓑ Ⓒ Ⓓ

4 Ⓐ Ⓑ Ⓒ Ⓓ Ⓔ   10 Ⓐ Ⓑ Ⓒ Ⓓ Ⓔ   16 Ⓐ Ⓑ Ⓒ Ⓓ

5 Ⓐ Ⓑ Ⓒ Ⓓ Ⓔ   11 Ⓐ Ⓑ Ⓒ Ⓓ Ⓔ   17 Ⓐ Ⓑ Ⓒ Ⓓ

6 Ⓐ Ⓑ Ⓒ Ⓓ Ⓔ   12 Ⓐ Ⓑ Ⓒ Ⓓ Ⓔ

Reading Comprehension Test

Time: 25 minutes. 17 questions.

DIRECTIONS: Each selection is followed by a number of questions based upon the information given in the selection. Read the selection carefully; then read each question carefully before marking your answers. The answer key to these test questions will be found at the end of the test.

Selection For Question 1

Unfortunately, specialization in industry creates workers who lack versatility. When a laborer is trained to perform only one task, he or she is almost entirely dependent for employment on the demand for that particular skill. If anything happens to interrupt that demand, he or she is unemployed.

1. This paragraph indicates that

   (A) the unemployment problem is a direct result of specialization in industry
   (B) the demand for labor of a particular type is constantly changing
   (C) the average laborer is not capable of learning more than one task at a time
   (D) some cases of unemployment are due to laborers' lack of versatility
   (E) too much specialization is as dangerous as too little

Selection For Question 2

Good management is needed now more than ever. The essential characteristic of management is organization. An organization must be capable of handling responsibility and authority. It must also be able to maintain the balance and perspective necessary to make the weighty decisions thrust upon it today.

2. The preceding paragraph is a plea for

   (A) better business
   (B) adequately controlled responsibility
   (C) well regulated authority
   (D) better management through organization
   (E) less perspective and more balance

Selection For Question 3

The increasing size of business organizations has resulted in less personal contact between superior and subordinate. Consequently, business executives today depend more on records and reports to secure information and exercise control over the operations of various departments.

3. According to this paragraph, the increasing size of business organizations

   (A) has caused a complete cleavage between employer and employee
   (B) has resulted in less personal contact between superior and subordinate

(C) has tended toward class distinctions in large organizations

(D) has resulted in a more indirect means of controlling the operations of various departments

(E) has made evaluation of the work of the employee more objective

Selection For Question 4

Lacking a flair for positive administration, the mediocre executive attempts to ensure efficiency by implanting job anxiety in his or her subordinates. This safe, unimaginative method secures the barest minimum of efficiency.

4. Of the following, the most accurate statement according to this quotation is that

(A) implanting anxiety about job retention is a method usually employed by the mediocre executive to improve the efficiency of his or her organization

(B) an organization will operate with at least some efficiency if employees realize that unsatisfactory work performance may subject them to dismissal

(C) successful executives with a flair for positive administration relieve their subordinates of any concern for their job security

(D) the implantation of anxiety about job security in subordinates should not be used as a method of improving efficiency

(E) anxiety in executives tends to make them think that it is present in employees also

Selection For Question 5

In large organizations some standardized, simple, inexpensive method of giving employees information about company policies and rules, as well as specific instructions regarding their duties, is practically essential. This is the purpose of all office manuals of whatever type.

5. The above selection notes that office manuals

(A) are all about the same

(B) should be simple enough for the average employee to understand

(C) are necessary to large organizations

(D) act as constant reminders to the employee of his or her duties

(E) are the only means by which the executive of a large organization can reach his or her subordinates

Selection For Questions 6 to 8

The ability to do a particular job and performance on the job do not always go hand in hand. People with great potential abilities sometimes fall down on the job because of laziness or lack of interest, whereas people with mediocre talents achieve excellent results through industry and loyalty to the interests of their employers. The final test of any employee is his or her performance on the job.

6. The most accurate of the following statements, on the basis of the above paragraph is that

(A) employees who lack ability are usually not industrious

(B) an employee's attitudes are more important than his or her abilities

(C) mediocre employees who are interested in their work are preferable to employees who possess great ability

(D) superior capacity for performance should be supplemented with proper attitudes

7. On the basis of the above paragraph, the employee of most value to his or her employer is *not* necessarily the one who

(A) best understands the significance of his or her duties

(B) achieves excellent results

(C) possesses the greatest talents

(D) produces the greatest amount of work

8. According to the above paragraph, an employee's efficiency is best determined by an

(A) appraisal of the employee's interest in his or her work

(B) evaluation of the work performed by him or her

(C) appraisal of the employee's loyalty to his or her employer

(D) evaluation of the employee's potential ability to perform his or her work

Selection For Question 9

Interest is essentially an attitude of continuing attentiveness, found where activity is satisfactorily self-expressive. Whenever work is so circumscribed that the chance for self-expression or development is denied, monotony is present.

9. On the basis of this selection, it is most accurate to state that

(A) tasks that are repetitive in nature do not permit self-expression and therefore create monotony

(B) interest in one's work is increased by financial and nonfinancial incentives

(C) jobs that are monotonous can be made self-expressive by substituting satisfactory working conditions

(D) workers whose tasks afford them no opportunity for self-expression find such tasks to be monotonous

(E) work is monotonous unless there is activity that satisfies the worker

Selection For Question 10

During the past few years business has made rapid strides in applying to the field of office management the same fundamental principles of procedure and method that have been in successful use for years in production work. Present-day competition, resulting in smaller margins of profit, has made it essential to give careful attention to the efficient organization and management of internal administrative affairs so that individual productivity may be increased and unit costs reduced.

10. According to the above paragraph

(A) office management always lags behind production work

(B) present-day competition has increased individual productivity

(C) efficient office management seeks to reduce gross costs

(D) the margin of profits widens as individual productivity is increased

(E) similar principles have met with equal success in the fields of office management and production work

Selection For Question 11

Direct lighting is the least satisfactory lighting arrangement. The desk or ceiling light with a reflector that diffuses all the rays downward is sure to cause glare on the working surface.

11. The preceding paragraph indicates that direct lighting is least satisfactory as a method of lighting chiefly because

(A) the light is diffused, causing eye strain
(B) the shade on the individual desk lamp is not constructed along scientific lines
(C) the working surface is usually obscured by the glare
(D) the ordinary reflector causes the rays to fall perpendicularly
(E) direct lighting is injurious to the eyes

Selection For Question 12

The principal advantage of wood over steel office equipment lies, surprisingly, in the greater safety afforded papers in a fire. Although the wooden exterior of a file cabinet may burn somewhat, the papers will not be charred as quickly as they would in a steel cabinet. This is because wood burns slowly and does not transmit heat, whereas steel, although it does not burn, is a conductor of heat. So, under similar circumstances, papers would be charred more quickly in a steel cabinet.

12. Judging from this information alone, the principal advantage of wood over steel office equipment is

(A) in case of fire, papers will not be destroyed in a wooden cabinet
(B) wooden equipment is cheaper to replace
(C) steel does not resist fire as well as wood
(D) steel equipment is heavy and cannot be moved about very easily
(E) wood is a poor conductor of heat

Selection For Questions 13 and 14

Forms are printed sheets of paper on which information is to be entered. Although what is printed on the form is most important, the kind of paper used in making the form is also important. The kind of paper should be selected with regard to the use to which the form will be subjected. Printing a form on an unnecessarily expensive grade of paper is wasteful. On the other hand, using too cheap or flimsy a form can materially interfere with satisfactory performance of the work the form is planned to do. Thus, a form printed on both sides normally requires a heavier paper than a form printed on only one side. Forms to be used as permanent records or expected to have a very long life in files require a quality of paper that will not disintegrate or discolor with age. A form that will go through a great deal of handling requires a strong, tough paper, whereas thinness is a necessary qualification where the making of several carbon copies of a form will be required.

13. According to this paragraph, the type of paper used for making forms

   (A) should be chosen in accordance with the use to which the form will be put
   (B) should be chosen before the type of printing to be used has been decided on
   (C) is as important as the information that is printed on it
   (D) should be strong enough to be used for any purpose

14. According to this paragraph, forms that are

   (A) printed on both sides are usually economical and desirable
   (B) to be filed permanently should not deteriorate as time goes on
   (C) expected to last for a long time should be handled carefully
   (D) to be filed should not be printed on inexpensive paper

Selection For Questions 15 to 17

The equipment in a mail room may include a mail metering machine. This machine simultaneously stamps, postmarks, seals, and counts letters as fast as the operator can feed them. It can also print the proper postage directly on a gummed strip to be affixed to bulky items. It is equipped with a meter, which is removed from the machine and sent to the post office to be set for a given number of stampings of any denomination. The setting of the meter must be paid for in advance. One of the advantages of metered mail is that it bypasses the cancellation operation and thereby facilitates handling by the post office. Mail metering also makes the pilfering of stamps impossible but does not prevent the passage of personal mail in company envelopes through the meters unless there is established a rigid control or censorship over outgoing mail.

15. According to this selection, the post office

   (A) is responsible for training new clerks in the use of mail metering machines
   (B) usually recommends that both large and small firms adopt the use of mail metering machines
   (C) is responsible for setting the meter to print a fixed number of stampings
   (D) examines the mail metering machines to see that they are properly installed in the mail room

16. According to the above, the use of mail metering machines

   (A) requires the employment of more clerks in a mail room than does the use of postage stamps
   (B) interferes with the handling of large quantities of outgoing mail
   (C) does not prevent employees from sending their personal letters at company expense
   (D) usually involves smaller expenditures for mail room equipment than does the use of postage stamps

17. On the basis of this paragraph, it is more accurate to state that

   (A) mail metering machines are often used for opening envelopes
   (B) postage stamps are generally used when bulky packages are to be mailed
   (C) the use of metered mail tends to interfere with rapid mail handling by the post office
   (D) mail metering machines can seal and count letters at the same time

Answer Key for Reading Comprehension Practice Test

1. D	5. C	9. D	13. A
2. D	6. D	10. D	14. B
3. D	7. C	11. D	15. C
4. B	8. B	12. E	16. C
			17. D

Part Three

PRACTICE TESTS FOR CLERICAL ABILITY

APTITUDE TESTS FOR CLERICAL OFFICE WORK

Aptitude tests do not test you for what you know in a subject area but for certain aptitudes required in an occupation. Questions measuring aptitudes required for clerical office work are usually part of the exams given for office worker positions. Scores on aptitude tests indicate how well and how fast you can perform tasks regardless of what you learned in the past. In other words, these tests are designed to test your abilities useful in clerical work, such as powers of observation, attention to detail, speed, and ability to understand what a task is about.

Aptitude tests are based on the application of certain abilities to a task. How well you can apply your abilities can be improved significantly by practice. The practice tests provided will confront you with various tasks requiring the application of abilities useful in clerical work. The practice tests will familiarize you with various tasks found in questions on actual exams. By practicing on these tests you will increase your self-confidence; you will be able to recognize quickly what is required by the tasks and do them with increasing speed and accuracy.

Your score on aptitude tests will depend on the number of questions you can complete within the time limit set. Although you will be penalized for errors, it is important to concentrate on speed. By proceeding very carefully you can reduce your errors. However, if you complete only a small number of questions, your score will be low even if you have avoided all errors. Therefore, it is suggested that you should concentrate on completing as many questions as possible but should not neglect accuracy entirely.

The practice tests which follow consist of various types of test questions for clerical aptitude. Since it is unlikely that you can recall the correct answers to aptitude test questions, you can do these tests several times over again for practice.

Answer Sheet for Name and Number Comparison Practice Tests

Test 1

1 Ⓐ Ⓑ Ⓒ Ⓓ Ⓔ	6 Ⓐ Ⓑ Ⓒ Ⓓ Ⓔ	11 Ⓐ Ⓑ Ⓒ Ⓓ Ⓔ	16 Ⓐ Ⓑ Ⓒ Ⓓ Ⓔ
2 Ⓐ Ⓑ Ⓒ Ⓓ Ⓔ	7 Ⓐ Ⓑ Ⓒ Ⓓ Ⓔ	12 Ⓐ Ⓑ Ⓒ Ⓓ Ⓔ	17 Ⓐ Ⓑ Ⓒ Ⓓ Ⓔ
3 Ⓐ Ⓑ Ⓒ Ⓓ Ⓔ	8 Ⓐ Ⓑ Ⓒ Ⓓ Ⓔ	13 Ⓐ Ⓑ Ⓒ Ⓓ Ⓔ	18 Ⓐ Ⓑ Ⓒ Ⓓ Ⓔ
4 Ⓐ Ⓑ Ⓒ Ⓓ Ⓔ	9 Ⓐ Ⓑ Ⓒ Ⓓ Ⓔ	14 Ⓐ Ⓑ Ⓒ Ⓓ Ⓔ	19 Ⓐ Ⓑ Ⓒ Ⓓ Ⓔ
5 Ⓐ Ⓑ Ⓒ Ⓓ Ⓔ	10 Ⓐ Ⓑ Ⓒ Ⓓ Ⓔ	15 Ⓐ Ⓑ Ⓒ Ⓓ Ⓔ	20 Ⓐ Ⓑ Ⓒ Ⓓ Ⓔ

Test 2

1 Ⓐ Ⓑ Ⓒ Ⓓ Ⓔ	6 Ⓐ Ⓑ Ⓒ Ⓓ Ⓔ	11 Ⓐ Ⓑ Ⓒ Ⓓ Ⓔ	16 Ⓐ Ⓑ Ⓒ Ⓓ Ⓔ
2 Ⓐ Ⓑ Ⓒ Ⓓ Ⓔ	7 Ⓐ Ⓑ Ⓒ Ⓓ Ⓔ	12 Ⓐ Ⓑ Ⓒ Ⓓ Ⓔ	17 Ⓐ Ⓑ Ⓒ Ⓓ Ⓔ
3 Ⓐ Ⓑ Ⓒ Ⓓ Ⓔ	8 Ⓐ Ⓑ Ⓒ Ⓓ Ⓔ	13 Ⓐ Ⓑ Ⓒ Ⓓ Ⓔ	18 Ⓐ Ⓑ Ⓒ Ⓓ Ⓔ
4 Ⓐ Ⓑ Ⓒ Ⓓ Ⓔ	9 Ⓐ Ⓑ Ⓒ Ⓓ Ⓔ	14 Ⓐ Ⓑ Ⓒ Ⓓ Ⓔ	19 Ⓐ Ⓑ Ⓒ Ⓓ Ⓔ
5 Ⓐ Ⓑ Ⓒ Ⓓ Ⓔ	10 Ⓐ Ⓑ Ⓒ Ⓓ Ⓔ	15 Ⓐ Ⓑ Ⓒ Ⓓ Ⓔ	20 Ⓐ Ⓑ Ⓒ Ⓓ Ⓔ

Test 3

1 Ⓐ Ⓑ Ⓒ Ⓓ Ⓔ	5 Ⓐ Ⓑ Ⓒ Ⓓ Ⓔ	8 Ⓐ Ⓑ Ⓒ Ⓓ Ⓔ
2 Ⓐ Ⓑ Ⓒ Ⓓ Ⓔ	6 Ⓐ Ⓑ Ⓒ Ⓓ Ⓔ	9 Ⓐ Ⓑ Ⓒ Ⓓ Ⓔ
3 Ⓐ Ⓑ Ⓒ Ⓓ Ⓔ	7 Ⓐ Ⓑ Ⓒ Ⓓ Ⓔ	10 Ⓐ Ⓑ Ⓒ Ⓓ Ⓔ
4 Ⓐ Ⓑ Ⓒ Ⓓ Ⓔ		

Test 4

1 Ⓐ Ⓑ Ⓒ Ⓓ Ⓔ	6 Ⓐ Ⓑ Ⓒ Ⓓ Ⓔ	11 Ⓐ Ⓑ Ⓒ Ⓓ Ⓔ	16 Ⓐ Ⓑ Ⓒ Ⓓ Ⓔ
2 Ⓐ Ⓑ Ⓒ Ⓓ Ⓔ	7 Ⓐ Ⓑ Ⓒ Ⓓ Ⓔ	12 Ⓐ Ⓑ Ⓒ Ⓓ Ⓔ	17 Ⓐ Ⓑ Ⓒ Ⓓ Ⓔ
3 Ⓐ Ⓑ Ⓒ Ⓓ Ⓔ	8 Ⓐ Ⓑ Ⓒ Ⓓ Ⓔ	13 Ⓐ Ⓑ Ⓒ Ⓓ Ⓔ	18 Ⓐ Ⓑ Ⓒ Ⓓ Ⓔ
4 Ⓐ Ⓑ Ⓒ Ⓓ Ⓔ	9 Ⓐ Ⓑ Ⓒ Ⓓ Ⓔ	14 Ⓐ Ⓑ Ⓒ Ⓓ Ⓔ	19 Ⓐ Ⓑ Ⓒ Ⓓ Ⓔ
5 Ⓐ Ⓑ Ⓒ Ⓓ Ⓔ	10 Ⓐ Ⓑ Ⓒ Ⓓ Ⓔ	15 Ⓐ Ⓑ Ⓒ Ⓓ Ⓔ	20 Ⓐ Ⓑ Ⓒ Ⓓ Ⓔ

Test 5

1 Ⓐ Ⓑ Ⓒ Ⓓ Ⓔ	5 Ⓐ Ⓑ Ⓒ Ⓓ Ⓔ	9 Ⓐ Ⓑ Ⓒ Ⓓ Ⓔ	13 Ⓐ Ⓑ Ⓒ Ⓓ Ⓔ
2 Ⓐ Ⓑ Ⓒ Ⓓ Ⓔ	6 Ⓐ Ⓑ Ⓒ Ⓓ Ⓔ	10 Ⓐ Ⓑ Ⓒ Ⓓ Ⓔ	14 Ⓐ Ⓑ Ⓒ Ⓓ Ⓔ
3 Ⓐ Ⓑ Ⓒ Ⓓ Ⓔ	7 Ⓐ Ⓑ Ⓒ Ⓓ Ⓔ	11 Ⓐ Ⓑ Ⓒ Ⓓ Ⓔ	15 Ⓐ Ⓑ Ⓒ Ⓓ Ⓔ
4 Ⓐ Ⓑ Ⓒ Ⓓ Ⓔ	8 Ⓐ Ⓑ Ⓒ Ⓓ Ⓔ	12 Ⓐ Ⓑ Ⓒ Ⓓ Ⓔ	16 Ⓐ Ⓑ Ⓒ Ⓓ Ⓔ

Name and Number Comparison Practice Tests

Test 1

Time: 20 minutes. 20 questions.

DIRECTIONS: Each of the questions in this test consists of three similar names. For each question, compare the three names and decide which ones, if any, are exactly alike. Mark your Answer Sheet as follows:

Blacken A if all three are exactly alike
Blacken B if only the first and second are exactly alike
Blacken C if only the first and third are exactly alike
Blacken D if only the second and third are exactly alike
Blacken E if all three are different

1. Lee Berlin
   Lea Berlin
   Les Berlin

2. Webster Cayne
   Webster Cayne
   Wester Cain

3. Charles Danis
   Charles Donis
   Charles Danis

4. Frank Collyer
   Frank Collyer
   Frank Collyer

5. Sylvia Gross
   Sylvia Grohs
   Sylvia Grohs

6. Thomas O'Neill
   Thomas O'Neil
   Thomas O'Neal

7. Jess M. Olsen
   Jess N. Olson
   Jess M. Olsen

8. Irene Crawford
   Irene Crowford
   Irene Crawford

9. Charles Duggan
   Charles Duggan
   Charles Dugan

10. Frank Dudley
    Frank Dudlee
    Frank Dudley

11. John Finn
    John Fin
    John Finn

12. Ray Finkelstein
    Ray Finklestein
    Ray Finkelstien

13. Sam Freedman
    Sam Friedman
    Sam Freedman

14. Harold Friedberg
    Harold Friedberg
    Harold Freedberg

15. Trude Friedl
    Trude Freidl
    Trude Freidl

16. Frank Gershaw
    Frank Gershaw
    Frank Gerchaw

17. Nancy Gerlach
    Nancy Gerlach
    Nancy Gerlach

18. Dorothy Goldberg
    Dorothy Goldburg
    Dorothy Goldberg

19. Philip Green
    Philip Greene
    Philip Greene

20. George Hampton
    George Hamton
    George Hamptun

Test 2

Time: 20 minutes. 20 questions.

DIRECTIONS: Each of the questions in this test consists of three similar numbers. For each question, compare the three numbers and decide which ones, if any, are exactly alike. Mark your Answer Sheet as follows:

> *Blacken A if all three are exactly alike*
> *Blacken B if only the first and second are exactly alike*
> *Blacken C if only the first and third are exactly alike*
> *Blacken D if only the second and third are exactly alike*
> *Blacken E if all three are different*

1. 78541	5. 97338	9. 55149	13. 29522	17. 92889
78514	93378	55419	25922	92889
75814	98337	55419	25922	98289

2. 36395	6. 37050	10. 22037	14. 50090	18. 24892
36395	35070	22037	50090	24892
36395	37050	22037	50900	28492

3. 89612	7. 62324	11. 93476	15. 25816	19. 46648
86912	62324	94376	25816	44648
89621	62324	94376	25816	46648

4. 78111	8. 25622	12. 90731	16. 71555	20. 57048
71118	26522	90731	75111	57084
71118	22256	90731	75155	57084

Test 3

Time: 10 minutes. 10 questions.

DIRECTIONS: *Each of the questions in this test consists of three similar names or numbers. For each question, compare the three names or three numbers and decide which ones, if any, are exactly alike. Mark your Answer Sheet as follows:*

Blacken A *if all three are exactly alike*
Blacken B *if only the first and second are exactly alike*
Blacken C *if only the first and third are exactly alike*
Blacken D *if only the second and third are exactly alike*
Blacken E *if all three are different*

1. James McKiernan	James McKiernen	James McKiernan
2. Marya Mannes	Mayra Mannes	Marya Mannis
3. Henry Rauch	Henry Rauch	Henry Raush
4. Jeanne Sorrels	Jeanne Sorells	Jeanne Sorrells
5. John H. Griscom	John H. Griscom	John H. Griscom
6. 7314916	7314961	7314961
7. 4258701	4258071	4258701
8. 1869572	1869572	1896572
9. 6371485	6374185	6371845
10. 5926374	5926374	5926374

Test 4

Time: 20 minutes. 20 questions.

DIRECTIONS: Each of the questions in this test consists of three similar names or numbers. For each question, compare the three names or three numbers and decide which ones, if any, are exactly alike. Mark your Answer Sheet as follows:

> *Blacken A if all three are exactly alike*
> *Blacken B if only the first and second are exactly alike*
> *Blacken C if only the first and third are exactly alike*
> *Blacken D if only the second and third are exactly alike*
> *Blacken E if all three are different*

1. Vincent Imperial
   Vincent Impirial
   Vincent Imperail

2. Robert Innes
   Robert Innes
   Robert Innes

3. Patrick Keane
   Patrick Keene
   Patrick Keen

4. Dora Krigsmann
   Dora Krigsman
   Dora Krigsman

5. Albert Lentz
   Albert Lentz
   Albet Lents

6. Seymour Lindell
   Seymour Lindel
   Seymour Lindell

7. Hugh Lunny
   Hugh Luny
   Hugh Lunny

8. Mal Mallin
   Mal Mallin
   Mal Malin

9. May Marshall
   May Marshall
   May Marshall

10. Walter Mattson
    Walter Mattson
    Walter Matson

11. 63381
    63381
    63318

12. 81585
    85185
    85185

13. 90463
    90426
    90463

14. 22249
    22249
    22294

15. 57422
    52742
    57224

16. 36264
    36264
    36264

17. 20637
    26037
    26037

18. 56299
    52699
    52996

19. 22804
    22804
    22804

20. 33266
    33266
    36623

Test 5

Time: 16 minutes. 16 questions.

DIRECTIONS: Each of the questions in this test consists of three similar names or numbers. For each question, compare the three names or three numbers and decide which ones, if any, are exactly alike. Mark your Answer Sheet as follows:

> *Blacken A if all three are exactly alike*
> *Blacken B if only the first and second are exactly alike*
> *Blacken C if only the first and third are exactly alike*
> *Blacken D if only the second and third are exactly alike*
> *Blacken E if all three are different*

1.	Cornelius Detwiler	Cornelius Detwiler	Cornelius Detwiler
2.	6452054	6452654	6452054
3.	8501268	8501268	8501286
4.	Ella Burk Newham	Ella Burk Newnham	Elena Burk Newnham
5.	Jno. K. Ravencroft	Jno. H. Ravencroft	Jno. H. Ravencoft
6.	Martin Wills Pullen	Martin Wills Pulen	Martin Wills Pullen
7.	3457988	3457986	3457986
8.	4695682	4695862	4695682
9.	Stricklund Kanedy	Stricklund Kanedy	Stricklund Kanedy
10.	Joy Harlor Witner	Joy Harloe Witner	Joy Harloe Witner
11.	R. M. O. Uberroth	R. M. O. Uberroth	R. N. O. Uberroth
12.	1592514	1592574	1592574
13.	2010202	2010202	2010220
14.	6177396	6177936	6177396
15.	Drusilla S. Ridgeley	Drusilla S. Ridgeley	Drusilla S. Ridgeley
16.	Andrei I. Toumantzev	Andrei I. Tourmantzev	Andrei I. Toumantzov

Answer Key for Name and Number Comparison Practice Tests

Test 1

1. E	4. A	7. C	10. C	13. C	16. B	19. D
2. B	5. D	8. C	11. C	14. B	17. A	20. E
3. C	6. E	9. B	12. E	15. D	18. C	

Test 2

1. E	5. E	9. D	13. D	17. B
2. A	6. C	10. A	14. B	18. B
3. E	7. A	11. D	15. A	19. C
4. D	8. E	12. A	16. E	20. D

Test 3

1. C	3. B	5. A	7. C	9. E
2. E	4. E	6. D	8. B	10. A

Test 4

1. E	5. B	9. A	13. C	17 D
2. A	6. C	10. B	14. B	18. E
3. E	7. C	11. B	15. E	19. A
4. D	8. B	12. D	16. A	20. B

Test 5

1. A	5. E	9. A	13. B
2. C	6. C	10. D	14. C
3. B	7. D	11. B	15. A
4. E	8. C	12. D	16. E

Answer Sheet for Matching Letters and Numbers Practice Tests

Test 1

1 Ⓐ Ⓑ Ⓒ Ⓓ Ⓔ   6 Ⓐ Ⓑ Ⓒ Ⓓ Ⓔ   11 Ⓐ Ⓑ Ⓒ Ⓓ Ⓔ   16 Ⓐ Ⓑ Ⓒ Ⓓ Ⓔ
2 Ⓐ Ⓑ Ⓒ Ⓓ Ⓔ   7 Ⓐ Ⓑ Ⓒ Ⓓ Ⓔ   12 Ⓐ Ⓑ Ⓒ Ⓓ Ⓔ   17 Ⓐ Ⓑ Ⓒ Ⓓ Ⓔ
3 Ⓐ Ⓑ Ⓒ Ⓓ Ⓔ   8 Ⓐ Ⓑ Ⓒ Ⓓ Ⓔ   13 Ⓐ Ⓑ Ⓒ Ⓓ Ⓔ   18 Ⓐ Ⓑ Ⓒ Ⓓ Ⓔ
4 Ⓐ Ⓑ Ⓒ Ⓓ Ⓔ   9 Ⓐ Ⓑ Ⓒ Ⓓ Ⓔ   14 Ⓐ Ⓑ Ⓒ Ⓓ Ⓔ   19 Ⓐ Ⓑ Ⓒ Ⓓ Ⓔ
5 Ⓐ Ⓑ Ⓒ Ⓓ Ⓔ   10 Ⓐ Ⓑ Ⓒ Ⓓ Ⓔ   15 Ⓐ Ⓑ Ⓒ Ⓓ Ⓔ   20 Ⓐ Ⓑ Ⓒ Ⓓ Ⓔ

Test 2

1 Ⓐ Ⓑ Ⓒ Ⓓ Ⓔ   6 Ⓐ Ⓑ Ⓒ Ⓓ Ⓔ   11 Ⓐ Ⓑ Ⓒ Ⓓ Ⓔ   16 Ⓐ Ⓑ Ⓒ Ⓓ Ⓔ
2 Ⓐ Ⓑ Ⓒ Ⓓ Ⓔ   7 Ⓐ Ⓑ Ⓒ Ⓓ Ⓔ   12 Ⓐ Ⓑ Ⓒ Ⓓ Ⓔ   17 Ⓐ Ⓑ Ⓒ Ⓓ Ⓔ
3 Ⓐ Ⓑ Ⓒ Ⓓ Ⓔ   8 Ⓐ Ⓑ Ⓒ Ⓓ Ⓔ   13 Ⓐ Ⓑ Ⓒ Ⓓ Ⓔ   18 Ⓐ Ⓑ Ⓒ Ⓓ Ⓔ
4 Ⓐ Ⓑ Ⓒ Ⓓ Ⓔ   9 Ⓐ Ⓑ Ⓒ Ⓓ Ⓔ   14 Ⓐ Ⓑ Ⓒ Ⓓ Ⓔ   19 Ⓐ Ⓑ Ⓒ Ⓓ Ⓔ
5 Ⓐ Ⓑ Ⓒ Ⓓ Ⓔ   10 Ⓐ Ⓑ Ⓒ Ⓓ Ⓔ   15 Ⓐ Ⓑ Ⓒ Ⓓ Ⓔ   20 Ⓐ Ⓑ Ⓒ Ⓓ Ⓔ

Test 3

1 Ⓐ Ⓑ Ⓒ Ⓓ   5 Ⓐ Ⓑ Ⓒ Ⓓ   8 Ⓐ Ⓑ Ⓒ Ⓓ   11 Ⓐ Ⓑ Ⓒ Ⓓ
2 Ⓐ Ⓑ Ⓒ Ⓓ   6 Ⓐ Ⓑ Ⓒ Ⓓ   9 Ⓐ Ⓑ Ⓒ Ⓓ   12 Ⓐ Ⓑ Ⓒ Ⓓ
3 Ⓐ Ⓑ Ⓒ Ⓓ   7 Ⓐ Ⓑ Ⓒ Ⓓ   10 Ⓐ Ⓑ Ⓒ Ⓓ   13 Ⓐ Ⓑ Ⓒ Ⓓ
4 Ⓐ Ⓑ Ⓒ Ⓓ

Test 4

1 Ⓐ Ⓑ Ⓒ Ⓓ   4 Ⓐ Ⓑ Ⓒ Ⓓ   7 Ⓐ Ⓑ Ⓒ Ⓓ   10 Ⓐ Ⓑ Ⓒ Ⓓ
2 Ⓐ Ⓑ Ⓒ Ⓓ   5 Ⓐ Ⓑ Ⓒ Ⓓ   8 Ⓐ Ⓑ Ⓒ Ⓓ   11 Ⓐ Ⓑ Ⓒ Ⓓ
3 Ⓐ Ⓑ Ⓒ Ⓓ   6 Ⓐ Ⓑ Ⓒ Ⓓ   9 Ⓐ Ⓑ Ⓒ Ⓓ   12 Ⓐ Ⓑ Ⓒ Ⓓ

Test 5

1 Ⓐ Ⓑ Ⓒ Ⓓ   5 Ⓐ Ⓑ Ⓒ Ⓓ   8 Ⓐ Ⓑ Ⓒ Ⓓ
2 Ⓐ Ⓑ Ⓒ Ⓓ   6 Ⓐ Ⓑ Ⓒ Ⓓ   9 Ⓐ Ⓑ Ⓒ Ⓓ
3 Ⓐ Ⓑ Ⓒ Ⓓ   7 Ⓐ Ⓑ Ⓒ Ⓓ   10 Ⓐ Ⓑ Ⓒ Ⓓ
4 Ⓐ Ⓑ Ⓒ Ⓓ

Test 6

1 Ⓐ Ⓑ Ⓒ Ⓓ   5 Ⓐ Ⓑ Ⓒ Ⓓ   8 Ⓐ Ⓑ Ⓒ Ⓓ
2 Ⓐ Ⓑ Ⓒ Ⓓ   6 Ⓐ Ⓑ Ⓒ Ⓓ   9 Ⓐ Ⓑ Ⓒ Ⓓ
3 Ⓐ Ⓑ Ⓒ Ⓓ   7 Ⓐ Ⓑ Ⓒ Ⓓ   10 Ⓐ Ⓑ Ⓒ Ⓓ
4 Ⓐ Ⓑ Ⓒ Ⓓ

Test 7

1 Ⓐ Ⓑ Ⓒ Ⓓ   5 Ⓐ Ⓑ Ⓒ Ⓓ   8 Ⓐ Ⓑ Ⓒ Ⓓ
2 Ⓐ Ⓑ Ⓒ Ⓓ   6 Ⓐ Ⓑ Ⓒ Ⓓ   9 Ⓐ Ⓑ Ⓒ Ⓓ
3 Ⓐ Ⓑ Ⓒ Ⓓ   7 Ⓐ Ⓑ Ⓒ Ⓓ   10 Ⓐ Ⓑ Ⓒ Ⓓ
4 Ⓐ Ⓑ Ⓒ Ⓓ

Test 8

1 Ⓐ Ⓑ Ⓒ Ⓓ   5 Ⓐ Ⓑ Ⓒ Ⓓ   8 Ⓐ Ⓑ Ⓒ Ⓓ
2 Ⓐ Ⓑ Ⓒ Ⓓ   6 Ⓐ Ⓑ Ⓒ Ⓓ   9 Ⓐ Ⓑ Ⓒ Ⓓ
3 Ⓐ Ⓑ Ⓒ Ⓓ   7 Ⓐ Ⓑ Ⓒ Ⓓ   10 Ⓐ Ⓑ Ⓒ Ⓓ
4 Ⓐ Ⓑ Ⓒ Ⓓ

Matching Letters and Numbers
Practice Tests

DIRECTIONS: In these tests of clerical ability, Column I consists of sets of numbered questions that you are to answer one at a time. Column II consists of possible answers to the set of questions in Column I. Select from Column II the one answer that contains only the numbers and letters, regardless of their order, that appear in the question in Column I. If none of the four possible answers is correct, blacken "E" on your answer sheet.

A Sample Question Explained

COLUMN I: **Set of Questions**	**COLUMN II:** **Possible Answers**
1. 2-Q-P-5-T-G-4-7	(A) 5-G-8-P-4-Q (B) P-R-7-Q-4-2 (C) Q-5-P-9-G-2 (D) 4-2-5-P-7-Q (E) None of these.

The Correct Answer to the Sample Question is (D). How did we arrive at that solution? First, remember that the instructions tell you to select as your answer the choice that contains only the numbers and letters, regardless of their order, that appear in the question. The answer choice in Column II does not have to contain *all* of the letters and numbers that appear in the question. But the answer cannot contain a number or letter that does not appear in the question. Thus, begin by checking the numbers and letters that appear in Answer (A). You will note that while 5-G-P-4-Q all appear in the Sample Question, the number 8, which is included in Answer (A), does *not* appear in the question. Answer (A) is thus incorrect. Likewise, Answer (B) is incorrect as the letter R does not appear in the Sample Question; Answer (C) is incorrect, as the number 9 does not appear in the question. In checking Answer (D), however, one notes that 4-2-5-P-7-Q all appear in the Sample Question. (D) is therefore the correct choice. Answer (E) is obviously eliminated.

Now proceed to answer the following test questions on the basis of the instructions given above.

Test 1

Time: 20 minutes. 20 questions.

The following are representative examination-type questions. They should be carefully studied and completely understood.

DIRECTIONS: In this test of clerical ability, Column 1 consists of sets of numbered questions that you are to answer one at a time. Column II consists of possible answers to the set of questions in Column I. Select from Column II the one answer that contains only the numbers and letters, regardless of their order, that appear in the question in Column I. If none of the four possible answers is correct, blacken "E" on your answer sheet.

COLUMN I: Set of Questions	COLUMN II: Possible Answers
1. 6-4-T-G-9-K-N-8	(A) Z-8-K-G-9-7
2. K-3-L-6-Z-7-9-T	(B) 7-N-Z-T-9-8
3. N-8-9-3-K-G-7-Z	(C) L-3-Z-K-7-6
4. L-Z-G-6-4-9-K-3	(D) 4-K-T-G-8-6
5. 9-T-K-8-3-7-N-Z	(E) None of these

Set of Questions	Possible Answers
6. 2-3-P-6-V-Z-4-L	(A) 3-6-G-P-7-N
7. T-7-4-3-P-Z-9-G	(B) 3-7-P-V-4-T
8. 6-N-G-Z-3-9-P-7	(C) 4-6-V-Z-2-L
9. 9-6-P-4-N-G-Z-2	(D) 4-7-G-Z-T-3
10. 4-9-7-T-L-P-3-V	(E) None of these

COLUMN I: Set of Questions	COLUMN II: Possible Answers
11. Q-1-6-R-L-9-7-V	(A) F-3-N-K-J-4
12. 8-W-2-Z-P-4-H-0	(B) Q-H-4-0-5-M
13. N-J-3-T-K-5-F-M	(C) O-W-2-Z-4-8
14. 5-T-H-M-0-4-Q-J	(D) R-9-V-1-Q-6
15. 4-Z-X-8-W-0-2-L	(E) None of these

Set of Questions	Possible Answers
16. S-2-L-8-U-Q-7-P	(A) 9-Q-T-K-2-7
17. 4-M-0-6-T-F-W-1	(B) F-0-1-4-W-M
18. J-M-4-X-W-Z-5-8	(C) U-2-8-P-Q-S
19. H-Q-2-9-T-I-K-7	(D) Z-M-4-5-8-Q
20. 8-M-Z-V-4-P-5-Q	(E) None of these

Test 2

Time: 20 minutes. 20 questions.

The following are representative examination-type questions. They should be carefully studied and completely understood.

DIRECTIONS: In this test of clerical ability, Column 1 consists of sets of numbered questions, which you are to answer one at a time. Column II consists of possible answers to the set of questions in Column I. Select from Column II the one answer that contains only the numbers and letters, regardless of their order, that appear in the question in Column I. If none of the four possible answers is correct, blacken "E" on your answer sheet.

COLUMN I: Set of Questions	COLUMN II: Possible Answers
1. Z-5-3-L-7-K-4-G	(A) T-4-K-5-G-2
2. K-V-6-T-2-7-4-L	(B) 7-K-4-G-Z-5
3. G-T-V-9-L-4-5-3	(C) L-5-2-G-K-7
4. G-T-5-N-9-2-K-4	(D) T-2-7-L-6-V
5. K-4-5-T-G-2-6-P	(E) None of these

Set of Questions	Possible Answers
6. V-K-Z-5-2-L-8-9	(A) N-K-8-3-5-7
7. N-Z-2-L-V-3-5-8	(B) V-N-5-8-2-L
8. N-P-3-9-V-5-6-Z	(C) 9-Z-3-V-P-6
9. Z-3-K-T-7-4-5-N	(D) K-5-Z-9-V-8
10. V-L-K-9-N-5-2-7	(E) None of these

COLUMN I: Set of Questions	COLUMN II: Possible Answers
11. 7-8-L-5-Z-9-P-V	(A) 9-V-4-L-N-3
12. N-6-4-L-3-Z-G-9	(B) N-4-5-Z-3-9
13. V-9-3-4-K-N-5-L	(C) 8-5-Z-L-9-P
14. L-V-9-2-N-8-T-5	(D) N-9-8-V-L-T
15. 5-Z-L-9-P-V-2-8	(E) None of these

Set of Questions	Possible Answers
16. L-2-4-8-V-P-7-N	(A) N-2-7-L-8-V
17. V-4-7-8-N-T-Z-6	(B) 2-V-T-8-G-7
18. T-L-5-N-6-8-7-V	(C) 8-6-T-L-N-4
19. L-6-N-T-2-G-8-4	(D) V-7-6-N-T-8
20. T-L-V-3-4-G-8-7	(E) None of these

Test 3

Time: 15 minutes. 13 questions.

The following are representative examination-type questions. They should be carefully studied and completely understood.

DIRECTIONS: *The codes given in Column I below begin and end with a capital letter and have an eight-digit number in between. You are to arrange the codes in Column I according to the following rules.*
1. *Arrange the codes in alphabetical order, according to the first letter.*
2. *When two or more codes have the same first letter, arrange the codes in alphabetical order according to the last letter.*
3. *When two or more of the codes have the same first and last letters, arrange the codes in numerical order, beginning with the lowest number.*
The codes in Column I are numbered (1) through (5). Column II gives you a selection of four possible answers. You are to choose from Column II the lettered choice that gives the correct listing of the codes in Column I arranged according to the above rules.

COLUMN I: Set of Codes	COLUMN II: Possible Answers
1. (1) S55126179E (2) R55136177Q (3) P55126177R (4) S55126178R (5) R55126180P	(A) 1, 5, 2, 3, 4 (B) 3, 4, 1, 5, 2 (C) 3, 5, 2, 1, 4 (D) 4, 3, 1, 5, 2
2. (1) T64217813Q (2) I642178170 (3) T642178180 (4) I64217811Q (5) T64217816Q	(A) 4, 1, 3, 2, 5 (B) 2, 4, 3, 1, 5 (C) 4, 1, 5, 2, 3 (D) 2, 3, 4, 1, 5
3. (1) C83261824G (2) C78361833C (3) G83261732G (4) C88261823C (5) G83261743C	(A) 2, 4, 1, 5, 3 (B) 4, 2, 1, 3, 5 (C) 3, 1, 5, 2, 4 (D) 2, 3, 5, 1, 4
4. (1) A11710107H (2) H17110017A (3) A11170707A (4) H17170171H (5) A11710177A	(A) 2, 1, 4, 3, 5 (B) 3, 1, 5, 2, 4 (C) 3, 4, 1, 5, 2 (D) 3, 5, 1, 2, 4
5. (1) R26794821S (2) O26794821T (3) M26794827Z (4) Q26794821R (5) S26794821P	(A) 3, 2, 4, 1, 5 (B) 3, 4, 2, 1, 5 (C) 4, 2, 1, 3, 5 (D) 5, 4, 1, 2, 3

COLUMN I: Set of Codes	COLUMN II: Possible Answers
6. (1) D89143888P (2) D98143838B (3) D89113883B (4) D89148338P (5) D89148388B	(A) 3, 5, 2, 1, 4 (B) 3, 1, 4, 5, 2 (C) 4, 2, 3, 1, 5 (D) 4, 1, 3, 5, 2
7. (1) W62455599E (2) W62455090F (3) W62405099E (4) V62455097F (5) V62405979E	(A) 2, 4, 3, 1, 5 (B) 3, 1, 5, 2, 4 (C) 5, 3, 1, 4, 2 (D) 5, 4, 3, 1, 2
8. (1) N74663826M (2) M74633286M (3) N76633228N (4) M76483686N (5) M74636688M	(A) 2, 4, 5, 3, 1 (B) 2, 5, 4, 1, 3 (C) 1, 2, 5, 3, 4 (D) 2, 5, 1, 4, 3
9. (1) P97560324B (2) R97663024B (3) P97503024E (4) R97563240E (5) P97652304B	(A) 1, 5, 2, 3, 4 (B) 3, 1, 4, 5, 2 (C) 1, 5, 3, 2, 4 (D) 1, 5, 2, 3, 4
10. (1) H92411165G (2) A92141465G (3) H92141165C (4) H92444165C (5) A92411465G	(A) 2, 5, 3, 4, 1 (B) 3, 4, 2, 5, 1 (C) 3, 2, 1, 5, 4 (D) 3, 1, 2, 5, 4
11. (1) X90637799S (2) N90037696S (3) Y90677369B (4) X09677693B (5) M09673699S	(A) 4, 3, 5, 2, 1 (B) 5, 4, 2, 1, 3 (C) 5, 2, 4, 1, 3 (D) 5, 2, 3, 4, 1
12. (1) K78425174L (2) K78452714C (3) K78547214N (4) K78442774C (5) K78547724M	(A) 4, 2, 1, 3, 5 (B) 2, 3, 5, 4, 1 (C) 1, 4, 2, 3, 5 (D) 4, 2, 1, 5, 3
13. (1) P18736652U (2) P18766352V (3) T17686532U (4) T17865523U (5) P18675332V	(A) 1, 3, 4, 5, 2 (B) 1, 5, 2, 3, 4 (C) 3, 4, 5, 1, 2 (D) 5, 2, 1, 3, 4

Test 4

Time: 15 minutes. 13 questions.

The following are representative examination-type questions. They should be carefully studied and completely understood.

DIRECTIONS: The codes given in Column I below begin and end with a capital letter and have an eight-digit number in between. You are to arrange the codes in Column I according to the following rules.
1. *Arrange the codes in alphabetical order, according to the first letter.*
2. *When two or more codes have the same first letter, arrange the codes in alphabetical order according to the last letter.*
3. *When two or more of the codes have the same first and last letters, arrange the codes in numerical order, beginning with the lowest number.*

The codes in Column I are numbered (1) through (5). Column II gives you a selection of four possible answers. You are to choose from Column II the lettered choice that gives the correct listing of the codes in Column I arranged according to the above rules.

COLUMN I: Set of Codes	COLUMN II: Possible Answers
1. (1) L51138101K (2) S51138001R (3) S51188111K (4) S51183110R (5) L51188100R	(A) 1, 5, 3, 2, 4 (B) 1, 3, 5, 2, 4 (C) 1, 5, 2, 4, 3 (D) 2, 5, 1, 4, 3
2. (1) J28475336D (2) T28775363D (3) J27843566P (4) T27834563P (5) J28435536D	(A) 5, 1, 2, 3, 4 (B) 4, 3, 5, 1, 2 (C) 1, 5, 2, 4, 3 (D) 5, 1, 3, 2, 4
3. (1) G42786441J (2) H45665413J (3) G43117690J (4) G43546698I (5) G41679942I	(A) 2, 5, 4, 3, 1 (B) 5, 4, 1, 3, 2 (C) 4, 5, 1, 3, 2 (D) 1, 3, 5, 4, 2
4. (1) S44556178T (2) T43457169T (3) S53321176T (4) T53317998S (5) S67673942S	(A) 1, 3, 5, 2, 4 (B) 4, 3, 5, 2, 1 (C) 5, 3, 1, 2, 4 (D) 5, 1, 3, 4, 2
5. (1) R63394217D (2) R63931247D (3) R53931247D (4) R66874239D (5) R46799366D	(A) 5, 4, 2, 3, 1 (B) 1, 5, 3, 2, 4 (C) 5, 3, 1, 2, 4 (D) 5, 1, 2, 3, 4

COLUMN I: Set of Codes	COLUMN II: Possible Answers
6. (1) A35671968B (2) A35421794C (3) A35466987B (4) C10435779A (5) C00634779B	(A) 3, 2, 1, 4, 5 (B) 2, 3, 1, 5, 4 (C) 1, 3, 2, 4, 5 (D) 3, 1, 2, 4, 5
7. (1) I99736426Q (2) I10445311Q (3) J63749877P (4) J03421739Q (5) J00765311Q	(A) 2, 1, 3, 5, 4 (B) 5, 4, 2, 1, 3 (C) 4, 5, 3, 2, 1 (D) 2, 1, 4, 5, 3
8. (1) M33964217N (2) N33942770N (3) N06155881M (4) M00433669M (5) M79034577N	(A) 4, 1, 5, 2, 3 (B) 5, 1, 4, 3, 2 (C) 4, 1, 5, 3, 2 (D) 1, 4, 5, 2, 3
9. (1) D77643905C (2) D44106788C (3) D13976022F (4) D97655430E (5) D00439776F	(A) 1, 2, 5, 3, 4 (B) 5, 3, 2, 1, 4 (C) 2, 1, 5, 3, 4 (D) 2, 1, 4, 5, 3
10. (1) W22746920A (2) W22743720A (3) W32987655A (4) W43298765A (5) W30987433A	(A) 2, 1, 3, 4, 5 (B) 2, 1, 5, 3, 4 (C) 1, 2, 3, 4, 5 (D) 1, 2, 5, 3, 4
11. (1) P44343314Y (2) P44141341S (3) P44141431L (4) P41143413W (5) P44313433H	(A) 2, 3, 1, 4, 5 (B) 1, 5, 3, 2, 4 (C) 4, 2, 3, 5, 1 (D) 5, 3, 2, 4, 1
12. (1) D89077275M (2) D98073724N (3) D90877274N (4) D98877275M (5) D98873725N	(A) 3, 2, 5, 4, 1 (B) 1, 4, 3, 2, 5 (C) 4, 1, 5, 2, 3 (D) 1, 3, 2, 5, 4
13. (1) H32548137E (2) H35243178A (3) H35284378F (4) H35288337A (5) H32883173B	(A) 2, 4, 5, 1, 3 (B) 1, 5, 2, 3, 4 (C) 1, 5, 2, 4, 3 (D) 2, 1, 5, 3, 4

Test 5

Time: 11 minutes. 10 questions.

DIRECTIONS: *The codes given in Column I below begin and end with a capital letter and have an eight-digit number in between. You are to arrange the codes in Column I according to the following rules.*
1. *Arrange the codes in alphabetical order, according to the first letter.*
2. *When two or more codes have the same first letter, arrange the codes in alphabetical order according to the last letter.*
3. *When two or more of the codes have the same first and last letters, arrange the codes in numerical order, beginning with the lowest number.*

The codes in Column I are numbered (1) through (5). Column II gives you a selection of four possible answers. You are to choose from Column II the lettered choice that gives the correct listing of the codes in Column I arranged according to the above rules.

COLUMN I: Set of Codes	COLUMN II: Possible Answers
1. (1) L42615798B (2) L52734869A (3) J42715698A (4) L42715698B (5) J42713968A	(A) 5, 2, 3, 1, 4 (B) 5, 3, 2, 1, 4 (C) 3, 5, 1, 2, 4 (D) 3, 5, 2, 4, 1
2. (1) R62145987M (2) Q62145893M (3) Q62145983M (4) O62147398N (5) R51279638N	(A) 4, 2, 3, 1, 5 (B) 4, 3, 2, 1, 5 (C) 2, 3, 4, 1, 5 (D) 4, 2, 3, 5, 1
3. (1) W17543629O (2) W17543692P (3) W17543629P (4) W16543792Q (5) W17546329O	(A) 5, 1, 3, 2, 4 (B) 1, 5, 2, 3, 4 (C) 1, 5, 3, 2, 4 (D) 5, 1, 4, 3, 2
4. (1) K73652498V (2) K73654928V (3) H736452892X (4) H73945862V (5) K63754928X	(A) 4, 3, 2, 1, 5 (B) 3, 4, 1, 2, 5 (C) 4, 3, 1, 2, 5 (D) 3, 4, 5, 2, 1
5. (1) S26471835M (2) S26471385M (3) V26147853M (4) S26417835N (5) U26418753N	(A) 1, 2, 4, 5, 3 (B) 2, 1, 4, 3, 5 (C) 1, 2, 4, 3, 5 (D) 2, 1, 4, 5, 3

COLUMN I: Set of Codes	**COLUMN II:** Possible Answers

COLUMN I:
Set of Codes

COLUMN II:
Possible Answers

6. (1) D75924631A
   (2) B79542316C
   (3) D75923461A
   (4) B79543261C
   (5) D57924316C

(A) 4, 2, 1, 3, 5
(B) 2, 4, 3, 1, 5
(C) 2, 4, 1, 3, 5
(D) 4, 2, 3, 1, 5

7. (1) M95724163P
   (2) M85724163Q
   (3) N85741236P
   (4) M85721436Q
   (5) N85714263P

(A) 1, 2, 4, 3, 5
(B) 2, 4, 1, 5, 3
(C) 1, 4, 2, 5, 3
(D) 4, 2, 1, 5, 3

8. (1) A42875369O
   (2) A42875693O
   (3) A42869753O
   (4) A24875369Q
   (5) A42786975O

(A) 5, 3, 1, 2, 4
(B) 3, 5, 2, 1, 4
(C) 5, 3, 2, 1, 4
(D) 3, 5, 4, 1, 2

9. (1) E61598732C
   (2) F16359247C
   (3) E61593742C
   (4) E16359742G
   (5) F16395742C

(A) 1, 3, 4, 5, 2
(B) 4, 3, 1, 2, 5
(C) 1, 3, 4, 2, 5
(D) 3, 1, 4, 2, 5

10. (1) T37942518I
    (2) X37492185J
    (3) U73491258J
    (4) T37941258I
    (5) X73492185I

(A) 1, 4, 3, 2, 5
(B) 4, 1, 3, 5, 2
(C) 4, 1, 3, 2, 5
(D) 1, 4, 5, 2, 3

Test 6

Time: 12 minutes. 10 questions.

Code Table

Code letters:	Y	E	N	C	H	I	O	L	J	A
Corresponding numbers:	1	2	3	4	5	6	7	8	9	0

DIRECTIONS: The Table above provides a corresponding number for each of the 10 letters used as codes in the questions. On the first line there are 10 selected letters. On the second line there are the 10 numerals, including zero. Directly under each letter on the first line there is a corresponding number on the second line. Every question consists of three pairs of letter and number codes. Each pair of codes is on a separate line. Referring to the Code Table above, determine whether each pair of letter and number codes is made up of corresponding letters and numbers. In answering each question, compare all three pairs of letter and number codes. Then mark your answers as follows:

A. *if in* none *of the three pairs of codes do* all *letters and numbers correspond*
B. *if in only* one *pair of codes do* all *letters and numbers correspond*
C. *if in only* two *pairs of codes do* all *letters and numbers correspond*
D. *if in* all three *pairs of codes do* all *letters and numbers correspond*

1. JOHALI   975486
   YECOHN   124753
   ACJYLO   049187

2. NJYHEL   391528
   IOCEAY   674201
   CLYNHJ   481359

3. HOLIJA   578690
   ECILAY   246801
   LYJEAN   819203

4. ONHYAI   735106
   JILCHE   978452
   IYOAEC   617924

5. HOLYNC   578934
   JOYNHE   970352
   LECAOJ   824179

6. NYEILA   312680
   LHONJY   857391
   ENIACO   236045

7. JENOYI   923016
   LIACEH   830425
   NJLHCO   398547

8. ECILAJ   346809
   YNHOJC   136794
   OLYNCH   781340

9. LYNOEJ   813729
   IYACOL   610478
   CALNHE   408352

10. JONYAL   973108
    NELCIY   328461
    OLHAJE   785092

Test 7

Time: 12 minutes. 10 questions.

Code Table

Code letters: T E L U S Q N I X C

Corresponding numbers: 8 1 5 3 7 6 2 0 4 9

DIRECTIONS: The Table above provides a corresponding number for each of the 10 letters used as codes in the questions. On the first line there are 10 selected letters. On the second line there are the 10 numerals, including zero. Directly under each letter on the first line there is a corresponding number on the second line. Every question consists of three pairs of letter and number codes. Each pair of codes is on a separate line. Referring to the Code Table above, determine whether each pair of letter and number codes is made up of corresponding letters and numbers. In answering each question, compare all three pairs of letter and number codes. Then mark your answers as follows:

A. *if in* none *of the three pairs of codes do* all *letters and numbers correspond*
B. *if in only* one *pair of codes do* all *letters and numbers correspond*
C. *if in only* two *pairs of codes do* all *letters and numbers correspond*
D. *if in* all three *pairs of codes do* all *letters and numbers correspond*

1. LUXQIT   534608
   XUTLSN   468572
   EXUTIC   143809

2. ELTUNX   156324
   QUELTS   631587
   USISQT   370768

3. ITENXQ   081236
   TNXQIL   924601
   NUISET   230748

4. CUSTEL   937815
   ECQUIX   196304
   UQENTS   361287

5. LQITES   460817
   TIXLUC   804539
   STINEQ   780216

6. IQXTUL   064835
   CUTESI   938170
   LEXQIT   514608

7. UQESTX   361782
   TINCLS   802957
   NESTIL   217805

8. QINTEX   602814
   CEUSIT   923708
   SUNEQL   732165

9. XIEQTL   601685
   TSUNCE   873091
   EUNIXT   182048

10. LITENS   508127
    NLQXCU   256493
    IQENTC   061289

Test 8

Time: 12 minutes. 10 questions.

Code Table

Code letters:	N	E	Z	S	O	R	L	H	A	T
Corresponding numbers:	0	1	2	3	4	5	6	7	8	9

DIRECTIONS: *The Table above provides a corresponding number for each of the 10 letters used as codes in the questions. On the first line there are 10 selected letters. On the second line there are the 10 numerals, including zero. Directly under each letter on the first line there is a corresponding number on the second line. Every question consists of three pairs of letter and number codes. Each pair of codes is on a separate line. Referring to the Code Table above, determine whether each pair of letter and number codes is made up of corresponding letters and numbers. In answering each question, compare all three pairs of letter and number codes. Then mark your answers as follows:*

A. *if in* none *of the three pairs of codes do* all *letters and numbers correspond*
B. *if in only* one *pair of codes do* all *letters and numbers correspond*
C. *if in only* two *pairs of codes do* all *letters and numbers correspond*
D. *if in* all three *pairs of codes do* all *letters and numbers correspond*

1. TNZAHL   902856
    ROSELN   543160
    LANSZE   680321

2. SZENLA   321068
    ROTAHL   549876
    ZTOLRS   294653

3. HTORZS   894523
    ENLART   106857
    OSZTRA   432968

4. THESOR   971345
    OSAZRE   438251
    ALHOEZ   867412

5. TALHRO   986754
    ZSRNTH   235097
    NLAHSE   068731

6. ORTELZ   459163
    ELRSAH   165387
    SEZONT   312408

7. AHLTON   875940
    RENTSZ   510932
    SANTOZ   380942

8. SNATZE 308921
 THOLRA 974652
 ZONEAR 240185

9. SONATE 340891
 AERNLS 815063
 NEATRO 018954

10. HORTEA 745908
 OZSRTN 423591
 LOTHER 649815

Answer Key for Matching Letters And Numbers Practice Tests

Test 1

1. D	6. C	11. D	16. C
2. C	7. D	12. C	17. B
3. A	8. A	13. E	18. E
4. E	9. E	14. B	19. A
5. B	10. B	15. C	20. D

Test 2

1. B	6. D	11. C	16. A
2. D	7. B	12. E	17. D
3. E	8. C	13. A	18. D
4. A	9. E	14. D	19. C
5. A	10. E	15. C	20. E

Test 3

1. C	5. A	9. C	13. B
2. B	6. A	10. A	
3. A	7. D	11. C	
4. D	8. B	12. D	

Test 4

1. A	3. B	5. C	7. A	9. D	11. D	13. A
2. D	4. D	6. D	8. C	10. B	12. B	

Test 5

1. B	3. C	5. D	7. C	9. D
2. A	4. C	6. B	8. A	10. B

Test 6

1. C	3. D	5. A	7. B	9. D
2. D	4. B	6. C	8. A	10. D

Test 7

1. C
2. C
3. A
4. D
5. C
6. D
7. C
8. C
9. A
10. D

Test 8

1. C
2. D
3. A
4. D
5. D
6. B
7. C
8. C
9. D
10. A